A SONG F

A Song for Europe
Popular Music and Politics in the Eurovision Song Contest

Edited by

IVAN RAYKOFF
The New School, USA

and

ROBERT DEAM TOBIN
Whitman College, USA

ASHGATE

Published by
Ashgate Publishing Limited
Gower House
Croft Road
Aldershot
Hampshire GU11 3HR
England

Ashgate Publishing Company
Suite 420
101 Cherry Street
Burlington, VT 05401-4405
USA

Ashgate website: http://www.ashgate.com

British Library Cataloguing in Publication Data
A song for Europe: popular music and politics in the
   Eurovision Song Contest. – (Ashgate popular and folk music series)
   1. Eurovision Song Contest 2. Song festivals – Social aspects – Europe
   3. Song festivals – Political aspects – Europe
   I. Raykoff, Ivan II. Tobin, Robert Deam
   306.4'8424'0794

Library of Congress Cataloging-in-Publication Data
A song for Europe: popular music and politics in the Eurovision song contest / Edited by Ivan Raykoff and Robert Deam Tobin.
      p. cm. – (Ashgate popular and folk music series)
   Includes bibliographical references.
   ISBN-13: 978-0-7546-5878-8 (hardback: alk. paper)
   ISBN-13: 978-0-7546-5879-5 (pbk.: alk. paper) 1. Eurovision Song Contest. 2. Popular music–Competitions–Europe. 3. Popular music–Political aspects–Europe. I. Raykoff, Ivan. II. Tobin, Robert Deam.

   ML76.E87S66 2007
   782.42164'0794–dc22

                                                            2006030251

ISBN 978-0-7546-5878-8 (Hbk)
ISBN 978-0-7546-5879-5 (Pbk)

Printed and bound in Great Britain by MPG Books Ltd, Bodmin, Cornwall.

Contents

List of tables

List of contributors

Ivan Raykoff, co-editor, is an assistant professor in the Arts Concentration at Eugene Lang College, The New School, in New York. He studied piano at the Eastman School of Music and the Liszt Academy in Budapest, and received his PhD in Critical Studies and Experimental Practices from the University of California–San Diego in 2002. He is completing a book on the image of the concert pianist in popular culture titled *Dreams of Love: Representing the "Romantic" Pianist*, and his chapter on piano transcriptions and gay identity appears in *Queer Episodes in Music and Modern Identity* (2002).

Robert Deam Tobin, co-editor, is a professor of German and chair of the humanities at Whitman College in Walla Walla, Washington. He received his PhD in German from Princeton University in 1990. The author of two books—*Warm Brothers: Queer Theory and the Age of Goethe* (2000) and *Doctor's Orders: Goethe and Enlightenment Thought* (2001)—he works in gay and lesbian studies and in German studies. He has also published extensively in contemporary popular culture, with essays on the TV series *Six Feet Under* and *Queer as Folk*, and contemporary German movies and literature.

Michael Baumgartner studied composition at California State University–Northridge, and received his MA in musicology and film studies from the University of Zürich and his PhD in musicology from the University of Salzburg. His dissertation examines representations of female statues in operas by Othmar Schoeck, Kurt Weill, and Thea Musgrave. From 1990 to 2006 he was senior editor of the research project on the complete works of Swiss composer Othmar Schoeck. Currently he is a Killam postdoctoral fellow at the University of British Columbia, writing on Jean-Luc Godard's use of sound in his films.

Alf Björnberg is Professor of Musicology at Göteborg University, Sweden, in the Department of Culture, Aesthetics, and Media. He received his PhD from Göteborg University in 1987 with a dissertation analyzing songs in the Swedish preliminaries of the Eurovision Song Contest. From 1987 to 1994 he was Lecturer and Research Fellow in the Department of Music at Aalborg University, Denmark. His research interests include popular music, music and the media, and music analysis. He has published work on music video, music broadcasting, and Swedish mainstream popular music.

Shelley D. Brunt received her PhD in ethnomusicology from the Elder Conservatorium of Music, The University of Adelaide, Australia. An interest in Japanese popular music, television and culture led her to Tōkyō where she has conducted field research on the annual *Kōhaku utagassen* (Red and White Song

Contest). Her dissertation and subsequent publications have focussed on the 50th edition of this event, examining constructions of gender, identity, community and the nation as conveyed through mediated song performance.

Matthew Gumpert is an Associate Professor in the Department of American Culture and Literature at Kadir Has University in Istanbul. He received his PhD in Comparative Literature from Harvard University in 1992, specializing in ancient Greek and Latin literature and classical influences on modern culture. Gumpert previously taught at the University of Colorado, University of Wisconsin, and Bilkent University. His publications include *Grafting Helen: The Abduction of the Classical Past* (University of Wisconsin Press) as well as articles in *Criticism*, *French Forum*, and the *Journal of Modern Greek Studies*.

Dana Heller is Professor of English and Director of the Humanities Institute and Graduate Program at Old Dominion University in Norfolk, Virginia. Her research interests include popular culture, gender studies, and gay and lesbian studies. She is the author of *The Feminization of Quest Romance: Radical Departures* (1990), *Family Plots: The De-Oedipalization of Popular Culture* (1995), and the editor of *Cross Purposes: Lesbians, Feminists, and the Limits of Alliance* (1997), *The Selling of 9/11: How a National Tragedy Became a Commodity* (2005), *The Great American Makeover: Television, History, Nation* (2006) and *Makeover Television: Realities Remodeled* (2007).

Thorsten Hindrichs is a faculty member in the Department of Musicology at Johannes Gutenberg University in Mainz, Germany. He also lectures on music history at the Wissenschaftliche Hochschule für Unternehmensführung in Vallendar. Hindrichs received his MA in musicology in 2001. His research interests include music of the Italian Renaissance, guitar music, and rock and popular music. Having published several articles on these topics as well as a monograph on composer Philipp de Monte (1521–1603), he is currently completing his PhD dissertation on guitar music in Germany around 1800.

Bjorn Ingvoldstad, an assistant professor at Bridgewater State College, received his PhD from the Department of Communication and Culture at Indiana University. His dissertation on media in Lithuania addresses the volatile relationship between local cultures and the forces of westernization and globalization after the fall of socialism. Bjorn first stumbled across a Eurovision broadcast in 1998, transfixed by the gender-bending triumph of Dana International. He subsequently covered Skamp's victory in Lithuania's 2001 national Eurovision preliminaries as a reporter for Lithuanian Radio's English-language program "Radio Vilnius."

Dafna Lemish is Associate Professor in the Department of Communication at Tel Aviv University. Lemish received her PhD from Ohio State University in 1982. Her research interests include the role of media in children's lives and in the construction of gender identities. Editor of the new *Journal of Children and Media*,

Lemish is the author of *Children and Television: A Global Perspective* (forthcoming), co-author of *Media and the Make-believe Worlds of Children* (2005), and co-editor of *Global Trends in Media Education* (2003) and *Children and Media at Times of Conflict and War* (2007).

Katherine Meizel is a PhD candidate in ethnomusicology at the University of California–Santa Barbara, currently completing her dissertation on the mediation of identity politics in *American Idol*. Her research interests include popular music, Sephardic song, and the cross-cultural study of vocal practices and pedagogies. A graduate of the Oberlin College Conservatory of Music and the San Francisco Conservatory of Music, she also holds undergraduate and advanced degrees in vocal performance.

Lutgard Mutsaers is a lecturer and researcher in Popular Music Studies at Utrecht University in the Netherlands. She received her MA in musicology and her PhD in cultural history with a dissertation on the Dutch impact of international popular dance crazes. Her publications include several books and articles on the history of popular music in the Netherlands. Mutsaers has been an active member of the International Association for the Study of Popular Music (IASPM) since its early days, and also claims the rare distinction of having watched every live broadcast of the Eurovision Song Contest.

Mari Pajala received her MA in Cinema and Television Studies and her PhD in Media Studies, both from the University of Turku, Finland. Her PhD dissertation examines the Eurovision Song Contest and nationality in the context of Finnish television history. She has also published articles on romance fiction in film and popular music fandom. She is currently working as a post-doctoral research fellow at the University of Turku and studies contemporary popular television as a technology of memory.

Thomas Solomon is Associate Professor in the Grieg Academy-Institute for Music at the University of Bergen, Norway. He received his MM in ethnomusicology and his PhD in cultural anthropology from the University of Texas–Austin. He has taught ethnomusicology and popular music studies at New York University, The University of Minnesota, and Istanbul Technical University. He has done field research in highland Bolivia on music, ecology, and identity, and in Istanbul on Turkish rap music and hip-hop youth culture in local and global perspectives. His publications include articles in *Ethnomusicology* and *Popular Music*.

Dean Vuletic is a PhD candidate in East Central European history at Columbia University, and his dissertation is on politics and popular music in socialist Yugoslavia. He received his undergraduate degree in European Studies from the Australian National University, where he first began to explore the political dimensions of the Eurovision Song Contest. After pursuing a Master's degree in East European studies at Yale University as a Fulbright scholar, he worked for the international service of Czech Radio in Prague. He has published a number of articles on Croatian history and politics.

General Editor's preface

The upheaval that occurred in musicology during the last two decades of the twentieth century has created a new urgency for the study of popular music alongside the development of new critical and theoretical models. A relativistic outlook has replaced the universal perspective of modernism (the international ambitions of the 12-note style); the grand narrative of the evolution and dissolution of tonality has been challenged, and emphasis has shifted to cultural context, reception and subject position. Together, these have conspired to eat away at the status of canonical composers and categories of high and low in music. A need has arisen, also, to recognize and address the emergence of crossovers, mixed and new genres, to engage in debates concerning the vexed problem of what constitutes authenticity in music and to offer a critique of musical practice as the product of free, individual expression.

Popular musicology is now a vital and exciting area of scholarship, and the *Ashgate Popular and Folk Music Series* aims to present the best research in the field. Authors will be concerned with locating musical practices, values and meanings in cultural context, and may draw upon methodologies and theories developed in cultural studies, semiotics, poststructuralism, psychology and sociology. The series will focus on popular musics of the twentieth and twenty-first centuries. It is designed to embrace the world's popular musics from Acid Jazz to Zydeco, whether high tech or low tech, commercial or non-commercial, contemporary or traditional.

Professor Derek B. Scott
Chair of Music
University of Salford

Additional reading and resources

For readers interested in a thorough and entertaining chronological survey of the Eurovision Song Contest including voting results, we recommend *The Eurovision Song Contest, 50 Years: The Official History* by John Kennedy O'Connor (London: Carlton Books, 2005). An earlier compendium that covers the contest up to 1997 is *The Complete Eurovision Song Contest Companion 1999* by Paul Gambaccini, Jonathan Rice and Tony Brown (London: Pavilion, 1999).

A necessary resource for any Eurovision fan is the *Congratulations* anniversary packet that includes songs by "all the winners and favourites" from 1956 to 2005 on four DVDs or four CDs—available from the ESC's official website www. eurovision.tv, which also provides extensive current news and information, photos and video clips, and a live-streaming Internet broadcast of the competition each May. Other exceptional resources include the Eurosong fansite www.eurosong.net, the independent Eurovision news website www.esctoday.com, and the Internet radio station http://escradio.net for live-streaming Eurovision songs.

For this volume we have relied on "The Diggiloo Thrush" website at www. diggiloo.net for detailed information on contest rankings, names of performers and composers, and song lyrics in the original language as well as English translations.

Introduction

"Even intelligent people with good taste in music have taken to pronouncing Eurovision in respectful tones, but it is really the 'Euro' bit of the word that they revere."

Andrei Kurkov[1]

Celebrating its 50th anniversary in 2005, the Eurovision Song Contest is the largest and most-watched international festival of popular music, as well as one of the world's longest-running annual television programs. Established in 1956 by the European Broadcasting Union as a live televised spectacle to unify post-war western Europe through music, the contest features singers who represent a participating nation with a new original pop song. Viewers vote for their favorite song (but not for their own country's song), and the winning country hosts the event the following year. The 2005 contest, held in Kiev, featured contestants representing over three dozen European nations and attracted hundreds of millions of viewers across the continent and abroad.[2]

Eurovision is probably best known for catapulting ABBA to international fame when the Swedish pop group took first place with "Waterloo" in 1974. Now-famous names such as Céline Dion, Olivia Newton-John and Julio Iglesias performed in the contest early in their careers. A few Eurovision songs have gained international airplay over the years: "Nel blu, dipinto di blu" (more famous as "Volare") is probably the contest's most familiar song, though it placed only third in 1958; "L'amour est bleu" ("Love is Blue," 1967), "Eres tu" ("Touch the Wind," 1973) and Gina G.'s "Just a Little Bit" (1996) have also hit the American charts. The Irish step-dancing show *Riverdance* became a major international theatrical sensation soon after it premiered as the interval act of the 1994 contest held in Dublin.

The Eurovision Song Contest was originally modeled after the San Remo Festival, an annual popular music competition held in Italy since 1951.[3] During the Cold War, Eurovision's success in western Europe prompted Eastern Bloc countries to organize their own short-lived Intervision Song Contest (1977–80), actually a continuation

---

1   Andrei Kurkov, "A Song for Europe in the Wake of Revolution," *The Observer* (15 May 2005).

2   According to the Museum of Broadcast Communication's *Encyclopedia of Television*, "the contest has developed into a spring ritual now viewed by 600 million people in 35 countries." Matthew Murray, "Eurovision Song Contest," <www.museum.tv/archives/etv/E/htmlE/eurovisionso/eurovisionso.htm> Accessed 24 February 2006. In 2005 there was also a spectacular Eurovision 50th anniversary show, *Congratulations*, broadcast from Copenhagen on October 22.

3   See Dario Salvatori, *Sanremo 50: La vicenda e i protagonisti di mezzo secolo di Festival della canzone* (Rome: Edizioni RAI Radiotelevisione italiana, 2000).

of the Sopot International Song Festival held in Poland since 1961.[4] Other similar events include the Benidorm International Song Festival (in Spain, since 1959) and the Yamaha Music Festival (or World Popular Song Festival) in Japan (1970–89). Many television viewers today are familiar with the *Pop Idol* phenomenon, which started in the United Kingdom and has become enormously successful in the United States as *American Idol*. While this show has many similarities to Eurovision, it does not require exclusively original songs and does not have the same element of international competition. Eurovision has never been broadcast by a major television network in the United States, but NBC has announced plans to develop an American version of the show with contestants representing individual states.[5]

This collection of essays is the first interdisciplinary study of the social, cultural and political significance of the Eurovision Song Contest. Fifteen essays by an international group of scholars examine the event through various academic approaches, including musicology, communications and media studies, history, politics, aesthetics, race and ethnicity, and gender and sexuality studies. With chapters on Switzerland, Germany, the Netherlands, Finland, Lithuania, Russia, the former Yugoslavia, Turkey and Israel, this collection offers a wide-ranging view of the contest's participating countries. Furthermore, it intentionally broadens the scope of inquiry beyond the European realm to examine comparable televised international song competitions in the Middle East and Japan.

With the fall of the Berlin Wall in 1989 and the European Union's eastward expansion in 2004, as well as the recent challenges to ratifying a new EU constitution, the perennial question of a shared European cultural identity arises again. Eurovision, founded as Europe was similarly refashioning itself in the aftermath of World War II, provides one context for re-examining the definition of "Europe" and notions of European identity in the new century. Modernity characterizes the ideal of post-war Europe to which the Eurovision Song Contest provides literal and figurative access: a society that is democratic, capitalist, peace-loving, multicultural, sexually liberated and technologically advanced. Each of the chapters in this collection examines the challenges of this ideal—and the negotiation of such access—through particular theoretical, analytical and historical perspectives.

For many contributors, the song contest is an arena in which participating nations stage their relationship to this vision of Europe. Ivan Raykoff considers how Eurovision's reception as "camp" maps onto political factors surrounding membership in the European Union, depending on whether countries see themselves as central or peripheral to the project of European identity. In the case of Finland, Mari Pajala argues, long-time political and geographic marginality contributes to typically defeatist attitudes about Eurovision participation, while Dean Vuletic suggests that

---

4   The Sopot Festival was initiated by Władysław Szpilman, the hero of Roman Polanski's 2002 film *The Pianist*. For a historical overview see Marcin Mierzejewski, "Teaching the World to Sing," *The Warsaw Voice Online* (31 July 2003), <www.warsawvoice.pl/view/3105> Accessed 24 February 2006.

5   Josef Adalian, "NBC turning on 'Eurovision,'" *Variety.com* (9 February 2006), <www.variety.com/article/VR1117937807?categoryid=1071&cs=1&s=h&p=0> Accessed 24 February 2006.

the former Yugoslavia—the only Communist country to take part in the contest—demonstrated other kinds of ambivalence about its relationship to western Europe. Some "peripheral" participants reveal the complexities of an evolving national identity still caught somewhere between East and West, as Bjorn Ingvoldstad shows in the case of Lithuania. Matthew Gumpert interprets Turkey's winning entry of 2003 as a case of "auto-Orientalism," an intricate play of stereotypes through which "the East watches the West watch the East" (p. 154).

Other contributors consider marginality in terms of the social politics surrounding Eurovision. Addressing western Europe's post-colonial situation, Lutgard Mutsaers relates how non-white singers represented the Netherlands in the contest long before any other country. Sexual identity has often been an implicit theme around Eurovision, perhaps most spectacularly when the transsexual Dana International won for Israel in 1998.[6] Robert Deam Tobin asserts that the queer community finds in Eurovision a means toward European citizenship, while Dafna Lemish demonstrates the social and personal investments many Israeli gay men have with the contest. According to Dana Heller's analysis of the "faux lesbianism" of Russia's 2003 entry, the contest's inevitable cultural misunderstandings call into question certain liberal assumptions about sexuality.

The paradigm of center and periphery can also apply to musical aspects, as when Eurovision's dominant musical conventions contrast with more distinctive "local" sounds and styles. According to one study, the "perfect" conventional Eurovision song conforms to a seven-part compositional formula: 1) fast pace and catchy rhythms, 2) memorable and repetitive lyrics, 3) a harmonically or dynamically contrasting chorus, 4) a key change leading to 5) a clearly defined finish, plus 6) an appealing dance routine and 7) costumes.[7] Analyzing some of these classic Eurovision songs, Thorsten Hindrichs offers a case study of the contest's most prolific composer, who has held a near-monopoly on Germany's participation in the show, and Michael Baumgartner presents Switzerland's frequent dilemma in deciding which of its three dominant cultural traditions (French, German or Italian) would best represent the country musically in the contest. On the other hand, as Alf Björnberg explains, some countries have chosen to assert a local ethnic identity through their performances in recent years, moving away from the pan-European Europop ideal that had generally characterized contest entries up until the 1990s.

Eurovision's elaborate voting ritual constitutes the second half of each year's show, as a representative from each participating country reports the scores assigned by an expert jury or, since 1998, by viewers' telephone voting. Songs are awarded from 0 to 8, 10 or 12 points; excitement grows as the votes are tallied and the winning

---

6   On Dana International's pre-Eurovision career and cultural significance, see Ted Swedenburg, "Saida Sultan/Danna International: Transgender Pop and the Polysemiotics of Sex, Nation, and Ethnicity on the Israeli-Egyptian Border," *The Musical Quarterly* 81/1 (Spring 1997): 81–108. On the singer's play with language and gender, see Liora Moriel, "Diva in the Promised Land: A Blueprint for Newspeak?" *World Englishes* 17/2 (1998): 225–37.

7   "Boom Bang-a-Bang and Ding-a-Dong: Pop Science Reveals 'Waterloo' as the Perfect Eurovision Song" (2005), analysis by Harry Witchel in collaboration with the Music Choice company, <partners.musicchoice.co.uk/content_files/Eurovision20050505.doc> Accessed 24 February 2006.

song/country is eventually determined. This procedure generates a substantial amount of data each year, and charts of scores and rankings provide an endless trove for statistical analyses by fans and scholars.[8] Artistic value is supposed to determine song rankings, but there are many extra-musical variables that can influence the outcome too.[9] In his chapter, Thomas Solomon makes a case for political and cultural context influencing the vote as he frames certain events and factors surrounding Turkey's 2003 victory.

The final two chapters of the collection take the focus on popular music and politics in international song contests beyond the European realm to envision, as Katherine Meizel writes, "a multinational set of studio stages wherein the politics of national, regional, ethnic and even religious identity are continuously being performed" (p. 159). Meizel describes the *Idol* franchise's "pan-Arab" song contest and how its contestants fared in the context of the regional as well as the subsequent "global" competition. Shelley Brunt relates the history of Japan's popular and long-running Red and White Song Contest, which predates Eurovision by five years and demonstrates a similarly complex interplay of gender, national and global identifications.

Many people deserve recognition for helping to make this book possible, but we would like to extend special thanks to Heidi May, our commissioning editor at Ashgate, and series editor Derek Scott for their support of this project. Mark Prentice, our student assistant supported by the Abshire Fund at Whitman College, provided exceptionally keen assistance with editing and proof-reading. Arun Bharali has our eternal gratitude for the encouragement and research help he provided to two Eurovision-deprived Americans during early stages of this project. Six contributors to this collection (Björnberg, Brunt, Pajala, Raykoff, Solomon and Tobin) presented their papers at the 13th biennial conference of the International Association for

---

8   One article analyzes ESC voting patterns from 1975 to 1992, before the participation of new East European nations, to reveal three main blocs (Western, Northern and Mediterranean) based on political, cultural, linguistic and/or geographic connections: Gad Yair, "Unite, Unite, Europe: The Political and Cultural Structures of Europe as Reflected in the Eurovision Song Contest," *Social Networks* 17/2 (1995): 147–61. A follow-up article expands on this premise to consider reciprocal voting between blocs as an explanation for Western dominance: Gad Yair and Daniel Maman, "The Persistent Structure of Hegemony in the Eurovision Song Contest," *Acta sociologica: Journal of the Scandinavian Sociological Association* 39/3 (September 1996): 309–25.

9   On the significance of the jury voting system, see Marco Haan, S. Gerhard Dijkstra and Peter Dijkstra, "Expert Judgment versus Public Opinion: Evidence from the Eurovision Song Contest," *Journal of Cultural Economics* 29/1 (February 2005): 59–78. On the significance of performance order, see Wändi Bruine de Bruin, "Save the Last Dance for Me: Unwanted Serial Position Effects in Jury Evaluations," *Acta psychologica* 118/3 (March 2005): 245–60. On favoritism among Eurovision voting cliques, see Bertjan Doosje and S. Alexander Haslam, "What Have They Done for Us Lately? The Dynamics of Reciprocity in Intergroup Contexts," *Journal of Applied Social Psychology* 35/3 (March 2005): 508–535. On vote exchanges as a factor of linguistic and cultural proximity, see Victor Ginsburgh and Abdul Noury, "Cultural Voting: The Eurovision Song Contest" (2004), <www.core.ucl.ac.be/services/psfiles/dp05/dp2005_6.pdf> Accessed 26 February 2006.

the Study of Popular Music, held in Rome in July 2005; two other contributors (Gumpert and Heller) presented their papers at the 2004 meeting of the Modern Language Association, held in Philadelphia, on a panel titled "Performing Gender on the Margins of Europe." Our thanks also to the conference organizers for giving Eurovision studies a place on these programs. We hope that the present volume will inspire further reflection on this unique cultural institution from scholars, critics and fans alike.

Ivan Raykoff and Robert Deam Tobin
April 2007

Chapter 1

Camping on the borders of Europe

Ivan Raykoff

The Eurovision Song Contest, the annual music competition Europeans love to hate, is a study in contradictions, widely celebrated by its fans and just as widely disparaged by its critics. In 1982 a French minister of culture called it "a monument to drivel," while Norway's contestant in 1966 later became her own country's minister of culture and even hosted the broadcast in 1986. From its inception, Eurovision has seemed to reflect the political zeitgeist of Europe, even to anticipate certain political developments; the first contest, with seven participating West European countries, took place a year before the signing of the Treaty of Rome, which established the Common Market.[1] On the other hand, the show always seems to be somewhat behind the times in terms of popular music tastes and trends; there is little that is innovative about Eurovision songs, and much that qualifies as retro and camp. Indeed, the notion of camp provides a key to understanding the complex relationship between politics and aesthetics evidenced throughout the history of the Eurovision Song Contest (ESC).

Aesthetic contradictions are certainly the most prevalent and persistent aspect of Eurovision's reception. While composers and performers strive for the most appealing original pop song and performance spectacle to win votes from the widest range of viewers, critics endlessly lament the music's derivative stylings, banal lyrics, gaudy productions, and lowest-common-denominator approach. "The pleasure of Eurovision music has always been its absolute incompetence," one British reviewer asserts, "undiluted by style, flair, intelligence, wit or even the sniff of a good tune."[2] This analysis hardly explains the Europop perfection of ABBA's "Waterloo," probably the contest's most famous winning song, and many other catchy tunes and memorable performers over the decades, but it does articulate the "so-bad-it's-good" quality that many consider characteristic of Eurovision.

These aesthetic debates owe something to language issues, too. English has become the *lingua franca* of Eurovision songs, with the greatest number of winning songs overall (including ABBA's "Waterloo"), even though it is the national language of only two participating countries.[3] France has always sung in French (except for

---

1   Switzerland, Luxembourg, The Netherlands, Belgium, West Germany, Italy, and France took part in the inaugural contest, which was also broadcast by Britain, Denmark, and Austria. Except for Switzerland, the same countries that participated in the first ESC were also charter members of the European Economic Community established by the Treaty of Rome.

2   Marcus Berkmann, "Pop Music: Trying to Get With It," *The Spectator* (8 April 1995): 42.

3   Aside from Britain and Ireland, 26 nations have presented English-language songs as of 2005. By comparison, French-language songs, the second most frequent winners, have been presented only by Francophone nations: France, Monaco, Belgium, Luxembourg, and Switzerland. In 2005, almost all entries were sung in English (Turkey, Switzerland, and France

Breton once in 1996), and still maintains the policy of announcing its voting results in French. Not surprisingly, a writer for *Le Figaro* laments the ESC's lack of linguistic diversity and its imitation of American pop styles, suggesting that Europeans are acting like "members of a subjugated province through music that could not possibly have been more undifferentiated in its variety, speaking a poorly mastered language as if they were 300 million slaves, stringing together only the language's most rudimentary expressions."[4] Spain's contestant in 1968 insisted on singing in Catalan, prohibited under Franco's regime, so the government replaced him with another performer who sang in Spanish. Ironically, that song is titled "La, la, la," and its refrain consists entirely of those innocuous syllables. Eurovision songs have often featured meaningless vocables and nonsense words as a way to circumvent language barriers among participating nations and potential voters. Monaco entered "Boum-badaboum" in 1967, Britain won with "Boom Bang-a-Bang" in 1969, Holland won in 1975 with "Ding Dinge Dong," and Sweden won in 1984 with "Diggi-Loo, Diggi-Ley." For many critics, this infantile approach to linguistic diversity also detracts from Eurovision's artistic dignity.

Geography further complicates the ESC, especially since 1973 when Israel began participating in the contest even though it is not usually considered part of Europe. In fact, any member of the European Broadcasting Union (EBU) is eligible to compete, including Mediterranean nations such as Lebanon, Egypt, Libya, Tunisia, Algeria, and Morocco.[5] This wide geographic scope is partly a legacy of French colonialism in North Africa and British involvement in the Middle East, geopolitical factors still influential during the EBU's formative years.[6] Of these non-European countries only Morocco has participated in the contest (once in 1980). Lebanon's first foray into Eurovision would have been in 2005, but it was forced to withdraw because of laws requiring the national television network to censor any Israeli participation.[7]

Eurovision's most tormented contradiction is the highly political nature of an event supposedly devoted to the neutral and nonpartisan goals of unity and cooperation

---

were the exceptions) and all the national announcers (except France) presented their country's vote tallies in English.

    4   Benoit Duteurtre, 'Anti-US Go Home,' *World Press Review* 49/9 (September 2002) <www.worldpress.org/Europe/667/cfm> Accessed 10 June 2005.

    5   The EBU, founded in 1950 and unrelated to the European Union, is the world's largest professional association of national public-service broadcasters. Its Eurovision programming network carries news and sports events as well as the eponymous annual song contest. The International Radio and Television Organization (OIRT), a parallel association of broadcasters of the former East Bloc, merged with the EBU in 1993.

    6   "The Pioneering Years: EBU and Eurovision from 1950 to 1970," special issue of *Diffusion EBU: 100th Meeting of the EBU Administrative Council* (Geneva: Gilliéron, 1997), p. 9.

    7   "Lebanon Withdraws from Eurovision," *BBC News Online* (18 March 2005), see also <www.eurovision.tv/english/982.htm> Accessed 10 June 2005. This problem also arose in 1978, when many Arab television stations cut to a commercial break during Israel's performance, and stopped the broadcast when it became evident that Israel would win the contest.

through shared musical culture.[8] "The Eurovision Song Contest is not a political event," organizers of the 2005 competition insisted, "it is like the Olympic Games: we come in peace, and we hold the contest in peace. We have to be above politics!"[9] Nevertheless, both blatant and subtle political aspects have been evident throughout the contest's history.[10] Greece withdrew from the 1975 contest because Turkey was making its Eurovision debut; the following year Greece presented "Panaghia mou" (My homeland), a song protesting the Turkish invasion of Cyprus.[11] In 1969 the contest was held in Madrid, but Austria refused to participate in protest of Franco's regime. In 1982, during the Falklands War in Argentina, Britain hosted the contest and Spain contributed a tango. "Eurovision is legendary as an arena for settling diplomatic scores, venting ethnic grievance, baiting national rivals and undermining governments," writes another British commentator, following his country's tendency to regard the contest as largely an exercise in Continental intrigues.[12]

The early history of the EBU itself highlights this contradiction between political factors and apolitical ideals. On the one hand, membership and voting rights in the EBU were accorded only to national broadcasting organizations (such as the BBC in Britain, or Italy's RAI), not to national governments. According to an official history of the EBU, this distinction "was supposed to prevent the kind of political interference by individual countries which had poisoned the atmosphere in the last years of the IBU [International Broadcasting Union, founded in 1929 as a kind of 'League of Nations' of radio broadcasters, but compromised by Nazi control during World War II] and the OIR [Organization Internationale de Radiodiffusion, which became the broadcasting union for Communist East European nations]. The EBU did not want politicians, but pragmatic experts." On the other hand, ideology was still a significant motivation during the 1950s, EBU's formative years: "The breakneck speed with which television soon started to develop gave everyone the feeling of belonging to an avant-garde—not only technologically, but also politically—tackling European

---

8   Philip Bohlman discusses the significance of nationalism and national identifications in the ESC even beyond Europe's borders, considering the case of Céline Dion's 1988 winning song as "a symbol for the national aspirations of French Canadians in Quebec," or the music of Ofra Haza (a contestant in 1983) and Dana International (1998) as negotiating "the multiple histories of Israel's past and the multiple identities of its present." Philip V. Bohlman, *World Music: A Very Short Introduction* (New York: Oxford University Press, 2002), pp. 88–98.

9   Svante Stockselius, Executive Supervisor of the 2005 ESC, quoted on the official Ukrainian ESC website (27 April 2005) <www.eurovision.ua/en/news/000141/> Accessed 10 June 2005. While contest regulations posted on the official ESC website do not specifically prohibit songs with political content, Rule 12 seems to come closest to addressing this concern: "The lyrics and/or performance of the songs shall not bring the Contest Final or the Eurovision Song Contest as such into disrepute." For complete ESC rules see <www.ebu.ch>.

10   Jose Miguel Galvan Deniz, "Eurovision Shows Political Side," *BBC News Online* (14 March 2005) <http://news.bbc.co.uk/1/hi/entertainment/music/4337783.stm> Accessed 10 June 2005.

11   This antagonism has declined in recent years with improved relations between Greece and Turkey. In 2003 Greece voted for Turkey's song, and in 2005 Turkey awarded its highest score of 12 points to Greece, which won the contest that year.

12   Andrew Mueller, "The Politics of Pop," *The Guardian* (26 March 2005).

cooperation in a friendly atmosphere and getting results at a time when politicians still hardly dared dream of an effective European Union."[13] The development of Eurovision illustrates media technology's relationship to modernity and democracy, and how it can serve as a catalyst for political transformation.

Eurovision's political associations have only intensified in recent decades. The democratic revolutions of 1989 in eastern Europe inspired new enthusiasm for the ideal of European unity and integration, and, not surprisingly, many participants in the 1990 contest exploited the political moment with songs about the fall of the Berlin Wall: "Brandenburger Tor" (Brandenburg Gate) from Finland, "Keine Maurern mehr" (No more walls) from Austria, and Germany's own song "Frei zu leben" (Free to live). The winning entry that year was Italy's "Insieme: 1992" (All together: 1992), a song looking forward to the Maastricht Treaty and the new European Union. "Europe is not far away," the lyrics promise, "it's no longer a dream and we're no longer alone." Ironically, the 1990 contest was held in Zagreb, where the show's hostess proclaimed that "Yugoslavia is very much like an orchestra, the string section and the wood section all sit together,"[14] but by 1992 that ensemble of nationalities had disintegrated into a protracted civil war. Another case of civil strife may have resulted in Ireland's unprecedented string of Eurovision victories in 1992, 1993, 1994, and 1996. Many fans considered this winning streak to be Europe's rebuke to Britain and a sign that Ireland's future would come through its ties to the continent beyond the British Isles.

Recent Eurovision victories by Estonia (2001), Latvia (2002), Turkey (2003), and Ukraine (2004) demonstrate the arrival of a "new Europe" on the cultural and political stage. Indeed, the 50th ESC, held in Kiev in May 2005, was a significant event for Ukraine. Just a few months earlier, a popular uprising had overturned the country's disputed presidential election. The Orange Revolution rejected the apparent victory of Moscow's favored candidate, claiming widespread fraud and voter intimidation in a rigged election facilitated by the state-controlled media. Supporters of the pro-western opposition candidate, Viktor Yushchenko, camped out in Kiev's Independence Square by the hundreds of thousands. Six days later the Parliament and Supreme Court invalidated the poll results and ordered a new election, which was won by Yushchenko.

The Orange Revolution highlighted the significant geopolitical challenges Ukraine faces as it evolves away from its eastward ties to Russia and its Soviet past towards western-style political, economic, and social reforms, perhaps eventually membership in the European Union as well.[15] Thus the plan to host Eurovision in Kiev six months after the revolution was a highly symbolic opportunity, especially because a song associated with the protest was chosen to represent the country. "Razom nas bahato" (Together we are many) had become the unofficial anthem

---

13 "The Pioneering Years," p. 9.

14 Mark Steyn, "Eurovision Harmony Dies a Death," *The Daily Telegraph* (24 May 2005): 20.

15 Paul Quinn-Judge and Yuri Zarakhovich, "The Orange Revolution: Why Russia, the U.S. and Europe Care So Much About Ukraine's Disputed Presidential Election," *Time* (6 December 2004).

of the Orange Revolution. Its lyrics include protest chants referring to the rigged election: "Falsifications, no! Machinations, no! ... Yushchenko is our president, yes, yes, yes!" Another line says no to *ponyatiyam*, Russian mobster slang for a "gentlemen's agreement," referring to Russia's unfair influence over Ukrainian politics. "We aren't cattle, we aren't goats, we are sons and daughters of Ukraine!" refers to an offhand insult by the prime minister about the throngs of protesters in Kiev.[16]

A few weeks before the contest, however, Eurovision executives decreed the song to be "too political" and demanded revisions.[17] The band complied, rewriting the song's specific revolutionary references; the line about cattle and goats became "What you wanna say to your daughters and sons." An added verse in English declares, "We won't stand this, revolution is on, 'cause lies be the weapon of mass destruction!" (apparently a reference to American foreign policy and the war in Iraq, which would seem to contradict efforts at being apolitical). The new version concludes with the refrain "Together we are many, we can't be defeated!" echoed in Russian, Polish, Czech, German, Spanish, and French too. With "Razom nas bahato" Eurovision achieved depoliticization and globalization in the same stroke, transforming a street song of local protest shouts into a multilingual and non-referential slogan for just causes anywhere—but it placed only 19th out of 24 in the competition.

While Eurovision seemed to mark the end of a revolution in 2005, it indirectly started one in 1974. The same year "Waterloo" won for Sweden, Portugal took last place with the song "E depois do adeus" (After the goodbye). Military generals who were plotting to overthrow the country's authoritarian dictatorship decided that the song's debut broadcast on national radio would be the signal for the beginning of the coup, which led to the famous Carnation Revolution. While there was no literal connection between the uprising and the song itself, its lyrics seem to reflect the social and political situation in poetic terms. The song begins, "I wanted to know who I was, what I'm doing here, who has abandoned me, whom I forgot." It continues with typical love song sentiments and an enigmatic lesson: "Leaving is dying, like loving is winning and losing." The following year Portugal's song "Madrugada" (Dawn) expressed the optimism born of the country's revolution:

I'm singing about the people who have just discovered themselves
And raise their voices to celebrate,
I'm singing the praises of the land that is reborn,
There can't be enough songs like this.

Of course, countless popular songs describe love and desire, or breakup and heartache, but the Eurovision context can lend a political connotation to familiar amorous sentiments. During Franco's regime, some Spanish entries employed romantic references as subtle metaphors for freedom and reform. "En un mundo

---

16 Vera Rich, "Song for Ukraine Doesn't Cut It as a Song for Europe," *Index on Censorship* (23 May 2005).

17 Sophia Kishkovsky, "Ukrainian Song Rewritten for Eurovision Contest," *New York Times* (15 March 2005): E2.

nuevo" (In a new world, 1971) promises "At the end of the road all the dreams that you have inside will come true ... if you fill your life with love and peace in a new happy world." Jan Feddersen wonders, "Didn't 'En un mundo nuevo' thus anticipate, or promote, or even subversively call forth the new democratic era in Spain?"[18] The following year, "Amanace" (It's dawning) proposes, "Let's try to start over again today, why not? If you want to, friendship and love will be our flag. ... Let's search for new blue colors in the sky, let's win the battle against incomprehension."

Even more specifically, some Eurovision songs present an analogy between romantic union and European Union. In 1963, Britain was denied membership in the Common Market because of objections from France. Two years later, Britain took second place with "I Belong," which reflects an attitude of optimistic anticipation: "But now my heart has recovered from past affairs that turned wrong, all my dreams are uncovered, I belong! I belong!" In 1973, the year Britain, Ireland, and Denmark became full members of the European Community, the British entry was "Power to All Our Friends," a song celebrating the virtues of community and camaraderie: "Power to all our friends, to the music that never ends, to the people we want to be, baby, power to you and me!" Though Sweden did not join the EU until 1995, that country's most famous song, "Waterloo" (1974), seems to speak to a similar integration and the inevitability of that relationship: "Promise to love you for ever more, couldn't escape if I wanted to, knowing my fate is to be with you!"

Placing Eurovision alongside the history of the European Union clarifies some of the aesthetic contradictions of its reception – that is, why certain countries regard the contest with indifference or disdain while others take the enterprise more seriously, even if they also have some fun with it. For many West European nations the long process of political and economic integration, although once slow and cumbersome, has been largely accomplished—and for these players Eurovision seems a tired concept. The six countries that participated in the first ESC and signed the Treaty of Rome tend to be among Eurovision's main skeptics; indeed, Italy and Luxembourg abandoned the contest already in the early 1990s. Perhaps French and Dutch voters rejected the new European Constitution in 2005 not only over worries about "the Polish plumber and the Latvian mason" taking their jobs, but because East Europeans had been stealing the ESC in recent years as well.[19] It was probably humiliating for Belgium and the Netherlands to be eliminated from the 2005 contest because of poor

---

18   Jan Feddersen, *Ein Lied kann eine Brücke sein: die deutsche und internationale Geschichte des Grand Prix Eurovision* (Hamburg: Hoffmann und Campe, 2002), p. 119.

19   Anthony Browne, "How Song Contest Defeat Clouds Dutch Euro-Vision," *The Times* (24 May 2005). Elaine Sciolino, "Unlikely Hero in Europe's Spat: The Beckoning 'Polish Plumber,'" *New York Times* (26 June 2005): 1. Another columnist writes, "The French have not won since 1977, and the country seems increasingly disillusioned by a contest it can no longer dominate. A week from now, millions of Frenchmen and women will vote against the EU constitution, for rather similar reasons." Ben MacIntyre, "Oj, oj, oj! It's Europe in Harmony," *The Times* (21 May 2005). "It has suddenly dawned on the French that, as a result of the expansion to the east, there's no way they can carve up the European Union in a way they succeeded in doing for almost 50 years. Just like Eurovision, it has now slipped outside their control." Peter Osborne, "We Can All Be Winners with a New Eurovision," *The Evening Standard* (23 May 2005): 15.

scores in the semi-finals (topped by Romania, Moldova, Croatia, and Hungary, for example), or for Britain, France, and Germany to end up at the very bottom of the rankings that year.[20]

Countries that joined the EU in the 1980s (Greece, Spain, and Portugal) and 1990s (Austria, Sweden, and Finland) still show a fair amount of enthusiasm for the ESC,[21] but they are often outdone by East European countries emerging from a half-century of political, economic, and social isolation. A Romanian delegate visiting the 1993 contest explained, "We have always wanted to belong to Europe and the Song Contest is the only part of Europe that functions without political union. For this reason, we want to be a part of this world."[22] Poland, Hungary, Slovakia, Slovenia, Estonia, and Lithuania joined the ESC a decade before they were allowed to join the EU, predicting Europe's gradual expansion towards the East.[23] When Estonia won the competition in 2001, the prime minister declared, "We are no longer knocking at Europe's door. We are walking through it singing."[24] Serbia and Montenegro made its first post-Yugoslav appearance in Eurovision in 2004, finishing in second place (the highest ranking for a debut nation in the contest's history), and the following year the EU indicated its willingness to negotiate closer ties with the country as a first step towards possible membership.[25]

In 2003, a year before it became a member of the EU, Poland's song was "Zadnych granic/Keine Grenzen" (No borders), with lyrics in Polish, German, and Russian describing a world with "no stupid quarrels, no different races, no wars, no states," and "unlimited peace without flags." As one columnist explains,

> Many of the countries of the old Soviet bloc have a particular affection for Eurovision, as it was the only such televised entertainment permitted in the old Soviet Union. Belarus, for example, sees Eurovision as a way out of its international isolation, and the entire country was caught up when they decided to enter for the first time last year. A Ministry of Culture spokesman said: "Participation in Eurovision is an excellent opportunity for a young state to establish a positive image and tell the world about itself."

---

20   One explanation is that Eurovision's "Big Four" of Britain, France, Germany, and Spain—the countries that contribute most to the EBU budget—automatically qualify to participate in the ESC each year, bypassing the semi-final round and relegation rules that apply to other participants. This may lead to songs and productions of lesser quality, or less recognition from voters who get to hear those songs only during the finals.

21   By comparison, the geographical reach of the ESC first expanded in the early 1960s to include Norway, Finland, Spain, Portugal, and Ireland. In the 1970s the contest added the Mediterranean contingent: Malta, Greece, Turkey, and Israel. Cyprus and Iceland were included in the 1980s.

22   Feddersen, *Ein Lied*, p. 274.

23   "Euro Visions," *The Economist* (12 May 2005). James Button, "Finetuning the Politics of Modern Europe," *The Age* (23 May 2005).

24   Peter Culshaw, "Eurovision Sceptic? Nein, non, ni," *The Telegraph* (19 May 2005).

25   Nicholas Wood, "Serbia Moves a Step Closer to the European Union," *New York Times* (13 April 2005).

Conversely, the same writer notes, the British tend to view Eurovision as "an anachronistic joke. ... For a country whose language is dominant, and whose pop culture gets global coverage, it's easy for us to sneer."[26]

Here the notion of camp provides a useful theoretical perspective on the interplay of politics and aesthetics in Eurovision's reception. In his 1983 essay on the origins and definitions of the term, Mark Booth argues that "camp is primarily a matter of self-presentation rather than of sensibility," a performative practice invested in the rearrangement of power structures and values: "To be camp is to present oneself as being committed to the marginal with a commitment greater than the marginal merits."[27] This definition invites a number of questions in relation to Eurovision: Who considers the ESC an exercise in camp? Who constitutes the marginal? Who determines the value of the marginal? And how can such self-presentation provoke a rearrangement of power structures and values? By considering voting tendencies and reception history in four long-time Eurovision contenders—Britain, Norway, Germany, and Israel—we might come closer to understanding how the notion of marginality informs camp attitudes in the context of Eurovision and European identity.

Britain, to begin with, is famously Euro-skeptical. Expressing anxiety over the Maastricht Treaty in 1992, one columnist wrote, "We should be cutting ourselves off from Europe in every way possible. We should even withdraw from the Eurovision Song Contest—or else enter it, with 'One World Cup and Two World Wars.'"[28] Actually, the country has enjoyed a long and successful participation in the ESC since 1957, and a recent study of voting patterns suggests that despite assumptions to the contrary, "the UK has been consistently 'in tune' with the rest of Europe since the early 1990s"—meaning that it demonstrates "some deeper understanding of what the rest of Europe appreciates."[29] This claim might not apply to the dreaded *nul points*, or zero score, of 2003, when the UK entry did not receive any votes at all—an embarrassment credited to European opposition to Britain's involvement in the Iraq war even more than to an inferior song and poor performance in the show.[30]

British audiences tend to view Eurovision as an entertaining farce rife with Continental quirkiness. One columnist asserts that "the competition has never required much deep thought. Instead, it's about pointing and laughing at the outlandish costumes, the off-key notes and the often questionable choreography of our European

---

26   Culshaw, "Eurovision Sceptic?"

27   Mark Booth, "*Campe-toi!* On the Origins and Definitions of Camp," in *Camp* (London: Quartet, 1983). Reprinted in *Camp—Queer Aesthetics and the Performing Subject: A Reader*, ed. Fabio Cleto (Ann Arbor: University of Michigan Press, 1999), p. 69.

28   Mat Coward, "Backchat," *New Statesman & Society* (2 October 1992): 55.

29   Daniel Fenn, Omer Suleman, Janet Efstathiou and Neil F. Johnson, "How Does Europe Make Its Mind Up? Connections, Cliques, and Compatibility Between Countries in the Eurovision Song Contest" (2005): 2, 9. <http://arxiv.org/abs/physics/0505071> Accessed 15 November 2005.

30   Gerald Mizejewski, "Britain Strikes Out at '03 Eurovision," *The Washington Times* (28 May 2003): A15.

neighbours."[31] This attitude is evidenced in famous spoofs such as Monty Python's "Europolice Song Contest" (1970), in which the contest hostess announces, "And that's the final entry, la dernière entrée, das final Entry. And now, Guten Abend! Das scores, the scores, les scores, dei scores, oh! scores, ha! scores"—and Monaco wins with "Bing Tiddle Tiddle Bong."[32] Two British mockumentaries from 1998 are *A Song for Eurotrash* and Graham Norton's *Eurovision Masterclass* (both by Rapido Television), while *Europigeon* (BBC, 1998) has Graham Fellows endeavoring to submit his song "Pigeons in Flight" for consideration as the British ESC entry—and when that fails, as the Norwegian entry. Anglo dismissal of the contest is personified by Terry Wogan, the BBC's Eurovision host since 1972. Wogan's commentary is sardonic and flippant, "his lugubrious dryness encompassing what comes across as a form of casual xenophobia."[33] As Wogan once quipped, "The camp aspect of this contest is fascinating. You go to somewhere like Estonia and you've never seen so many transvestites in your life!"[34] One commentator sums up Wogan's style by noting that "irony is truth with teeth and Terry has left toothmarks all over Europe."[35]

In terms of Booth's definition of camp, Anglo attitudes towards the ESC demonstrate a tongue-in-cheek commitment to this pan-European enterprise tempered by frustrations that the marginal—that is, ESC's newer players far across the continent—exercise an influence greater than they really merit. This attitude is evident in Wogan's frequent irritation over the apparent predominance of political voting. He has railed against the "Balkan conspiracy" when former Yugoslav republics give high votes to each other, and dismissed the former Soviet republics for "keeping on terms with the Big Bear" when they favor Russia's contestant.[36] Australian author Tom Gleisner carries camp dismissal of the marginal East even further in his guidebook spoof, *Molvania: A Land Untouched by Modern Dentistry* (2003), and the book's website features two of the imaginary nation's recent Eurovision entries ("Elektronik-Supersonik," from 2004, is "a melodic fusion combining hot disco rhythms with Cold War rhetoric").[37]

Norway provides another example of camp attitudes from a geographically peripheral country self-consciously aware of its own marginality (or perhaps superiority). Unlike the UK, however, Norway mocks itself. The country, which voted against EU membership in 1995, has both a long involvement in the ESC and the dubious distinction of placing last in score rankings more than any other country

---

31 Sarah Freeman, "Help Me Make It Through the Night," *The Yorkshire Post* (20 May 2005) <www.yorkshiretoday.co.uk> Accessed 6 August 2005.

32 From "How to Recognize Different Parts of the Body," *Monty Python's Flying Circus* (season 2, episode 22). See also "Song for Europe" (series 2, episode 5, 1996) of the television series *Father Ted*, which features the intentionally losing song "My Lovely Horse."

33 Tim Luscombe, "Terry-land: Nul point," *The New Statesman* (23 May 2005).

34 *Adrian Motte*, "National Anthems," *The Sun* (21 May 2005): 27.

35 *Nancy Banks-Smith*, "Privates on Parade," *The Guardian* [Manchester] (27 May 2003): 22.

36 In the 2004 competition, for example, Ukraine received high votes from its regional neighbors: 12 points each from Russia, Poland, Lithuania, Latvia, and Estonia, and 10 points each from Belarus and Serbia.

37 See <www.molvania.com.au/molvania/eurovision.html> Accessed 15 August 2005.

in the contest's history. Of its ten years at the bottom of the list, four occasions (1963, 1978, 1981 and 1997) were with *nul points*, making Norway the focus of some good-natured ridicule. A front-page article in *The Wall Street Journal* was titled "Songs of Norway No Longer Belong in Grieg's League," noting that "a sure way to lose [Eurovision] is to present a Laplander, clad in reindeer skins, singing a children's song." Norway responds with a commitment to its own marginality greater than it may merit: "Norway gets a laugh out of the contest, but it also has a maverick's pride in losing" and "a national sense of honor" about its zeroes. [38] This attitude occasionally encourages somewhat over-the-top entries, such as the glam-metal camp of Wig Wam's "In My Dreams" in 2005. Norway exemplifies another of Booth's definitions of camp as "a self-mocking abdication of any pretensions to power."[39]

Germany is somewhere in the middle—in the middle of Europe, historically bridging East and West, a central player in EU politics and economics, and contradictory on Eurovision's camp spectrum—so it lately has to decide whether to be serious or silly about its contest participation. For such a central player, Germany has only won Eurovision once—in 1982, with "Ein bißchen Frieden" (A little peace), a pacifist song performed by a teenage girl strumming a white guitar. Her song communicated both sentimentality and *Weltuntergang* anxiety during the time of Ronald Reagan's sanctions against the Soviet Union, the deployment of Pershing nuclear missiles in Germany, the British invasion of the Falklands, and the assassination of Anwar Sadat plus attempts on the lives of Ronald Reagan and Pope John Paul II. At the same time, a popular peace movement was underfoot in Germany, the American hostages had just been released in Iran, and Solidarity was forming in Poland. As she sang:

> I know my songs won't help very much,
> I'm just a girl who says what she feels,
> Alone I'm helpless, a bird in the wind
> That feels that the storm begins.

On the apolitical side of the camp spectrum, Germany tried eccentricity in 1998 with Guildo Horn and his band The Orthopedic Stockings. An older and not particularly attractive singer known for outlandish costumes and onstage pranks, Horn sang "Guildo hat euch lieb" (Guildo loves you), claiming "If the stars weren't so far away … from there I'd send you proof of my love: nut biscuits and raspberry ice cream." He rang cowbells and leapt maniacally across the stage during his Eurovision performance. Two years later Stefan Raab represented his country with a nonsense rap song titled "Wadde Hadde Dudde Da?" (Now whaddya got there?), a phrase

---

38   L. Erik Calonius, "Songs of Norway No Longer Belong in Grieg's League," *The Wall Street Journal* (2 January 1985): 1. Jahn Teigen, the singer who had scored that distinction in 1978, became a national hero and continued his singing career with a best-selling song titled "This Year's Loser." Ironically, four months after this article appeared, Norway won the 1985 contest, and won again in 1995.

39   *Camp*, p. 74.

he overheard a woman in the park asking her dog, which was carrying something in its mouth. These examples privilege banality, another case for camp's undue commitment to the marginal, and they also fared quite well with ESC voters.

Israel presents the most celebrated and complicated case for marginality and camp in Eurovision. In 1979, the contest was held for the first time outside of Europe, in Jerusalem; two decades later an Israeli transsexual's victory crossed the borders of gender identity as well. Dana International's 1998 triumph with the song "Diva" represents a campy overvaluation of the marginal in keeping with Booth's definition. One way this occurs is by emphasizing constructs of femininity, the "second sex," through the performer's transgender persona, flamboyant performance and the message of the song itself:

> There is a woman who is greater than life,
> With senses she only owns.
> There is magic, and there are rough days,
> And a stage, which is all hers. ...
> Viva la diva, viva Victoria, Aphrodite.
> Viva la diva, viva Victoria, Cleopatra.

Dana International represented her country over strong resistance from Israel's Orthodox minority, which considered her peripheral to their ideal of national identity. A sound bite that gained international coverage came from the deputy minister of health, who worried that "Everybody abroad will say: 'Look at those Jews and what they are sending to perform, some kind of crossbreed.'"[40] Another conservative politician stated that the ESC should "stay in the land of the gentiles."[41]

But the Israeli Broadcasting Authority defended their Eurovision choice in terms of an expedient political image: "We should be seen as a liberal, free country that chooses songs on their merits, not on the basis of the body of the man or woman."[42] In this way Dana International's victory represented geographically peripheral Israel as "international" too, and served to rally liberal West European values towards the image of a secular and progressive nation. A similar approach caused another uproar two years later, when the Israeli group Ping Pong sang "Sameyakh" (Be happy), about a woman on a kibbutz longing for her Syrian boyfriend, in the 2000 ESC; the singers then waved Israeli and Syrian flags at the end of their performance. "We represent a new kind of Israeli who wants to be normal and have peace," the band's artistic director explained. "We want to have fun and not go to war, but the right wing is not happy about that message."[43]

---

40 Allison Kaplan Sommer, "The Divine Miss Dana," *The Jerusalem Post* (10 May 1998).

41 "Facing the Music, Transsexual Diva Returns to Storm of Controversy," Associated Press (12 May 1998).

42 Sommer, "The Divine Miss Dana."

43 Cited in Suzanne Goldenberg, "Outraged Israel Disowns Daring Eurovision Entry," *Guardian Unlimited* (12 May 2000) <www.guardian.co.uk/international/story/0,3604,219846,00.html> Accessed 20 February 2006.

These four cases studies show the utility as well as the complexity of camp as a key to the interplay of aesthetics and politics in Eurovision. They also demonstrate that this theoretical concept can travel beyond the Anglo-American domain—where it has been most cultivated, discussed, and analyzed—to work productively in other cultural contexts as well. Eurovision, on the other hand, seems peculiar to the European context, where it serves as a popular-culture mirror to the unique political experiment of the European Union. The ESC's many contradictions reflect the many types of marginality that still define national and cultural identities across the continent today. Terry Wogan puts it well when he describes Eurovision's "grand illusion that it brings together the diverse peoples and cultures of Europe on one great wing of song, when all it makes manifest is how far apart everybody is."[44]

44   Paul Gambaccini, Tim Rice, Jonathan Rice, and Tony Brown, *The Complete Eurovision Song Contest Companion* (London: Pavilion Books, 1998), p. 7.

Chapter 2

Return to ethnicity:
The cultural significance of musical
change in the Eurovision Song Contest

Alf Björnberg

At the 1989 IASPM conference in Paris I presented a paper discussing the Eurovision Song Contest (ESC) and its musical and cultural import.[1] Re-reading this published article today, it strikes me as embarrassingly evident, but also stimulatingly thought-provoking, that practically all the predictions I made for future developments of the ESC—largely extrapolations of tendencies prevalent up to that point in time—have since proven inaccurate. This applies not least to matters of musical style: despite the importance constantly ascribed in the media discourse surrounding the event to the notion of nationally representative musical styles, it appeared relevant at that time to argue that "the music presented in the ESC may be characterized as a somewhat artificial 'ultra-mainstream,' stylistically situated right in the centre of the mainstream of European popular music."[2]

Since the beginning of the 1990s, however, the range of musical styles represented in the ESC has widened considerably. This musical-stylistic development, together with other changes affecting the event in recent years, indicate the necessity of rethinking the ESC and the particular configuration of popular music styles, national cultures, European politics, transnational media, and audience participation constituted by the contest. The purpose of this chapter is to analyze these changes and to discuss how these, and the contest as such, may be interpreted in cultural and political terms within a contemporary European context.

Theorizing the Eurovision Song Contest

One of the first problems encountered when dealing with the ESC is the unique nature of the event as a regularly recurring, transnationally broadcast, live musical entertainment spectacle and an important item in the regular program exchange between member organizations of the European Broadcasting Union (EBU). The contest might also be construed as a display of a pan-European popular music culture, which, however, raises the crucial issue of whether this musical culture may be taken

---

1   Alf Björnberg, "Musical Spectacle as Ritual: The Eurovision Song Contest," in *1789–1989: Musique, Histoire, Démocratie*, vol. II, ed. Antoine Hennion (Paris: Editions de la Maison des Sciences de l'Homme, 1992), pp. 373–82. IASPM is the International Association for the Study of Popular Music.

2   Ibid., p. 376.

to exist as a distinct entity or whether it just consists of a heterogeneous conglomerate of nationally or regionally specific musical cultures. Before proceeding to an analysis of the developments within the ESC, it thus appears necessary to discuss what the event actually is and how it may be theorized and contextualized.

In my previous article, I argued that one of the main functions of the ESC is to serve as an arena for the display of the professionalism of public-service media organizations, and also, as the only major joint program production carried out by the EBU, to serve as a means to the promotion and development of cooperation within the union.[3] Historically, this has no doubt been true for a large part of the contest's period of existence. The creation of the ESC was enabled by the establishment in the 1950s of the first West European network of TV relay stations, for the first time rendering possible international live audiovisual transmission across parts of the continent. The early years of ESC history coincide with the realization of instant global communication by way of the first communication satellites, a technological development celebrated in popular culture manifestations such as the Tornados' 1962 hit "Telstar," or The Beatles' "All You Need Is Love," featured as the British contribution to the first "global" live television broadcast, *Our World*, in June 1967.

Throughout the 1950s, 1960s and 1970s, this gradually expanding global mediascape offered fascinating, previously unimaginable opportunities to attend live events anywhere on the globe, opportunities primarily used for international sports but also for the rare entertainment event. Due to the significant part historically played by public-service broadcasting in European mediascapes, from a European perspective this development was closely tied to the development of public-service television. This connection also served to define the ESC as a normal and regular programming item, that is, to posit the event and the music presented therein as strictly mainstream, insofar as the latter concept may be defined by criteria based on the practices of production and distribution rather than musical-stylistic criteria.[4] However, the significance which the contest has held for the organizing public-service broadcasting companies does not appear sufficient as the sole explanation of the attraction which the event has held for European television audiences.

One obvious way in which the ESC differs from ordinary, nationally aimed public-service programming is its distinctly international outlook. In this respect, the contest may be regarded as an example of an international event culture which otherwise is primarily the arena of international sports, such as the Olympic Games or the World Cup. Like these sports events, the ESC fills the function of focusing issues of national identity and prestige in an international setting. The parallel between the ESC and televised sports can be carried further: according to Garry Whannel, there are "three principal sets of practices in television—those related to journalism, to entertainment and to drama," and if the forms and genres of television are plotted in a triangle with these three at the corners, television sports "can be seen as sited at the intersection of these three practices and is therefore placed at the centre of

3   Ibid., pp. 380–81.
4   See Alison Huber, "Learning to Love the Mainstream," in *Looking Back, Looking Ahead: Popular Music Studies 20 Years Later*, ed. Kimi Kärki, Rebecca Leydon, and Henri Terho (Turku: IASPM-Norden, 2002), pp. 428–31.

the triangle." Although the ESC is situated closer to the "entertainment" corner of Whannel's triangle, it is similar to sports in its combination of entertainment with the drama of competition: both the ESC and sports events are "coherent and autonomous sets of rule-governed activity," and "these structures are narrative structures in that they pose an initial enigma—'Who will win?'—which will be resolved by the end of the event."[5] Even "the increasing cross-penetration of the sport and show business star system" referred to by Whannel has been noticeable in the ESC, as in the career move of Real Madrid goalkeeper Julio Iglesias into the 1970 ESC final. As for the "journalism" corner of Whannel's triangle, in recent years there has been a distinct tendency, at least in Sweden, for the ESC to be increasingly considered a relevant source for news items in the press as well as the broadcast media.

A crucial difference in relation to sports, however—at least in degree if not in kind—is that, in the ESC, the competing performances carry potentially dense cultural meanings associated with issues of national, regional, and European identity and their musical representations. Inherent in the particular reception conditions of transnational broadcasting there is ample scope for misinterpretation of the cultural significance which any particular contest entry representing a "foreign" country may possess in its original context. This appears to be a pertinent illustration of the role of communication and information technology, pointed out by Zygmunt Bauman, as means which "[allow] information to travel independently from … the objects of which the information informed," and thus as "means which set the 'signifiers' free from the hold of the 'signifieds.'"[6] Speaking of ESC contest entries as totally free-floating signifiers would surely be an exaggeration, but the particular communication situation implies that these signifiers may be regarded as highly unstable and not very well culturally anchored (as in the Swedish press comments on "foreign" styles in the ESC cited below). On the other hand, I would argue that this is not particular to the ESC: throughout the history of popular music, national popular-music styles have been functioning as free-floating signifiers, liable to extensive appropriation and re-interpretation in contexts alien to those of their origins.

In terms of the categories of popular music culture, characterizations of ESC music as a distinct example of commercial popular music are not uncommon. To the extent that this is taken as a statement on economic realities, I would argue, however, that notions of commercialism are largely irrelevant in the context of the ESC. In view of the media exposure and coverage of the event, the number of big international hits or major international careers to come out of the ESC is surprisingly small. The Swedish pop group ABBA, whose international career was launched by their victory in the 1974 ESC, appears to be the single major exception to prove the rule.[7] It would

---

5   Garry Whannel, *Fields in Vision: Television Sport and Cultural Transformation* (London: Routledge, 1992), pp. 60–63.

6   Zygmunt Bauman, *Globalization: The Human Consequences* (Cambridge: Polity Press, 1998), p. 14.

7   Other instances of artists whose international careers were launched, or at least furthered, by the ESC include the Italian Domenico Modugno, whose contest entries in 1958 and 1959 became major international hits, and the Québécoise Céline Dion, who won the contest representing Switzerland in 1988; however, in the latter case, the significance of the ESC victory for her North American career seems doubtful.

seem that such use of the term *commercial* generally serves as expression of an aesthetic judgment, in a not uncommon conflation of economics and aesthetics. At least as viewed from a Swedish perspective, the commercial interest in the contest is largely limited to a local (that is, national) scale; although not insignificant on this level, the commercial import of the ESC does not appear very relevant as an explanation either of the impetus behind the event or of its audience impact.

With the spread of the Internet in the course of the last decade the ESC has also emerged as a peculiar conflation of mainstream media "superculture" and fan-based "affinity interculture," to borrow useful terms coined by Mark Slobin.[8] The number of hits provided by Web search engines for the search string "Eurovision Song Contest" runs to some 500,000–600,000. It seems, though, that the grass-roots fan culture reflected in these figures, although having been made more visible via the Internet, has existed for considerably longer. At least since the early 1980s, the ESC has constituted a favored field for the attention of fans and collectors, and in some senses it constitutes the ideal collectors' fad: it comprises a large and heterogeneous but finite and collectible field of audiovisual material, supplemented annually by a well-defined increment, and offers plenty of quantitative data for those inclined to focus on such matters.[9]

To summarize the preceding discussion: depending on the focus of the observer, the ESC can be perceived as representing several kinds of phenomena. Apart from the nominal purpose of the event—to select annually, by way of a contest, "the best" of a number of popular songs of European origin—it is also a lavish entertainment show intended for prime-time television; a display of public-service broadcasting professionalism; a thrilling dramatized narrative of success and failure; a display of musical representations of national identities; a marketing device for perhaps not-very-commercial "commercial music"; and the focal point for a widely dispersed fan/collector culture. All these aspects of the ESC may affect the ways in which it also functions as a scene for the enactment of culture-specific patterns of meaning in popular music.

Center and periphery

Throughout the history of the ESC, it appears that the attention raised by the event has been considerably greater in nations which in geographical and/or cultural terms belong to the "periphery" of Europe than in its geographically/culturally "central" nations. This is certainly true of Sweden and of the neighboring Nordic countries

8   Mark Slobin, *Subcultural Sounds: Micromusics of the West* (Hanover, NH: Wesleyan University Press, 1993).

9   Swedish ESC fans and collectors were very helpful when I was acquiring material for my PhD dissertation in the mid-1980s. The dissertation was published in 1987 in Swedish; for an English-language summary of some of the main points see Alf Björnberg, "Sounding the Mainstream: An Analysis of the Songs Performed in the Swedish Eurovision Song Contest Semi-Finals 1959–1983," in *Popular Music Research: An Anthology from NORDICOM-Sweden*, ed. Keith Roe and Ulla Carlsson (Göteborg: University of Göteborg, 1990), pp. 121–31.

(Denmark, Finland, Iceland, and Norway), which together form a culturally fairly homogeneous region on the northern outskirts of the continent. An exhaustive analysis of the reasons for this differential interest in the ESC would have to reach far back in European political and cultural history, but one contributing contemporary factor is arguably the often high degree of monopoly which has until recently—prior to the deregulation of broadcasting media in the late 1980s and the 1990s—been accorded to public-service media organizations in many nations on the European periphery. Again, the Nordic countries offer distinct examples of this.

Contest results such as the victories of Danish entries in 1963 and 2000, of Swedish entries in 1974, 1984, 1991, and 1999, and of Norwegian entries in 1985 and 1995, indicate that one of the functions of the ESC may be to offer a space for a symbolic "revenge of the margins," an opportunity for culturally peripheral nations to come out on top of those nations normally playing the principal parts in the dissemination of popular culture. This was illustrated quite clearly at the press conference arranged on the night of Norway's first ESC win in 1985: judging from the artists' mixed reactions of immense pride and bewildered incredulity, this "success at last" seemed to constitute an intensely longed-for release from the decades-old national trauma of repeated losses. The qualification procedures necessitated by the post-1989 increase of the number of countries willing to participate, and used in the contest in various forms since 1993, offer yet another demonstration of the inversion of roles, an opportunity for a popular-cultural division of Europe into major- and minor-league nations not necessarily coinciding with political-economic hierarchies.[10]

The particular voting system used in the ESC also offers a means for the manifestation of allegiances within the periphery, as votes can be used to demonstrate feelings of regional community by being cast for neighbouring countries to which a perceived kinship exists (in Swedish press comments, this phenomenon is often referred to with the slightly contemptuous phrase "buddy voting"). In my earlier article I analyzed some examples of this phenomenon in the early ESC history, subsequently concluding that the significance of these "regional clusters" appeared to be gradually decreasing.[11] However, post-1989 developments have shown this conclusion to be highly premature, as new participant countries have shown little hesitation towards using this tactic.

The patterns of buddy voting in the ESC have acquired particular significance with the replacement of expert juries by televoting, as the results of votes cast by hundreds of thousands of television viewers may be taken to indicate more widespread cultural concerns than the votes of a few hundred "expert" jurors. Televoting was first introduced in 1997 and became compulsory in 1999,[12] and, as might be expected, the

---

10 In 1999, a change of rules guaranteed Eurovision's "Big Five" (England, Germany, France, Spain, and Italy) a place at the contest regardless of their position in the preceding year's finals. Expressed in the terms used here, this could be characterized as an instance of "the center striking back" at the periphery.

11 Björnberg, "Musical Spectacle as Ritual," p. 379.

12 Countries with a weak telephone infrastructure were allowed to use a back-up jury in case the televoting procedure malfunctioned. The 2004 ESC was the first time all participating countries used televoting.

1999 ESC provided several examples of buddy voting in regional clusters. One of these consisted of the Nordic countries (with the exception of Finland, which did not participate that year), another of the former Yugoslav republics Bosnia-Herzegovina, Croatia and Slovenia, while Belgium and the Netherlands formed a third mini-cluster. Perhaps the most interesting instance of buddy voting, however, was the mutual exchange of 12 points between Germany and Turkey, a phenomenon apparently due to the large group of Turkish immigrants in Germany and to the German choice of contest entry: the multilingual world-beat song "Reise nach Jerusalem/Kudüs'e seyahat" (Journey to Jerusalem) performed by the ethnically mixed group Sürpriz. This example gives an indication of how the effects of European migration are reflected in new musical-cultural mixtures within the ESC.

As already hinted at, reactions in the Swedish media coverage of the contest to the practice of buddy voting have been mainly critical. Commentators seem to regard the phenomenon as a manifestation of the inability of unsophisticated citizens of the new European nations to comply with the alleged nominal purpose of the contest: to select the best popular song on the basis of inadequately specified musical-aesthetic criteria.[13] Such patronizing invocation of the autonomy of "the music itself" appears particularly inappropriate in the context of the ESC, with its manifestly dense and multilayered texture of cultural meanings.

An arguably more productive reading of the phenomenon of buddy voting in the televoting age may take as its point of departure Bauman's discussion of "mobility" in the processes of globalization. Bauman argues that "with time of communication imploding and shrinking to the no-size of the instant, space and spatial markers cease to matter, at least to those whose actions can move with the speed of the electronic message," and that within the framework of the power structure of global media the "locals"—those who lack this kind of mobility—"watch the globals."[14] Viewed in this context, the practice of buddy voting may be seen as the creative response of the immobile television audience to the increasing mobility of pop artists, and of musical-stylistic markers, within global communication networks. It could also be argued that the interactive mechanisms of the ESC allow for significant representations of the "locals" in other ways: arguably the hitherto most highly charged moment in the history of the ESC came in 1993, the first year Bosnia-Herzegovina participated, when the country's votes were presented in a hardly decipherable sound-only transmission from war-torn Sarajevo.[15]

---

13   For instance, in a 2003 news item, Swedish record company manager Bert Karlsson—during the last few decades a principal operator on the domestic mainstream pop market—joined forces with Ivan Shapovalov, manager of the Russian duo t.A.T.u., in criticizing the alleged political motivations underlying eastern European voting patterns. *Aftonbladet* (25 May 2003).

14   Baumann, *Globalization*, pp. 13, 53.

15   According to the official ESC *Media Guide*, "although the Balkan war had virtually destroyed the Bosnian national broadcaster, a military satellite dish ensured Sarajevo could deliver its votes without problems." Eurovision Song Contest *Media Guide 2005*, p. 50 <www. eurovision.tv/english/1272.htm>. As far as I remember, however, the transmission was far from problem-free, and it was precisely the audible fragility of the connection which gave the moment its significance.

One obvious way in which the distinction between center and periphery also figures in the ESC is through differences in musical style. As already noted, throughout the history of the contest, the notion of nationally specific popular music styles has played an important part in the media discourse surrounding the event. Although the aim that each participating country should be represented by a popular music style indigenous to that country has never been officially prescribed in the contest rules, it has often been implied or regarded as desirable. In my earlier article, however, I claimed that at least since the beginning of the 1980s, "examples of specifically national styles have been few and mostly limited to entries from nations previously unrepresented in the contest," the main tendency instead being an increased standardization in the direction of the "artificial 'ultra-mainstream'" referred to above.[16] Seen from an ethnocentric West European point of view, such examples of nationally specific styles might be regarded as failures created by those not quite sophisticated enough to master the musical language of the West European mainstream.

In the early days of the ESC, such a view—that domestic popular music in general was rather unsophisticated and homely—also formed a clearly discernible part of the self-image expressed by Swedish broadcasting officials and music industry representatives. However, in the wake of the successes of ABBA and other Swedish ESC winners, and the increasing professionalization and commercial competence of the Swedish music industry, the tenor of Swedish ESC criticism gradually changed from the late 1970s onwards. Critics, including music industry spokesmen, aligned themselves with a "modern" West European viewpoint, from which audibly "strange" and "ethnic" contest entries were regarded with a rather derogatory incomprehension. In the 1980s, such reactions were evoked by ESC entries such as the Turkish "Pet'r Oil" in 1980, or the Spanish "¿Quien maneja mi barca?" (Who sails my boat) in 1983; a Swedish tabloid commented that the latter song sounded "like the theme song of an Arabic B movie," although there was no indication that the critic in question had any degree of familiarity with that particular cinematic genre.[17] Similar attitudes have prevailed into the 21st century: after the Ukrainian win in the 2004 ESC, a Swedish newspaper critic wrote, "Ruslana is evidently already a star back home in the Ukraine ... but it is doubtful whether she has talent enough for a career outside the Eastern bloc."[18] Comments like this appear increasingly problematic as post-1989 ESC music in general has taken a turn in a perceptibly "ethnic" direction.

Popular music, modernity and ethnicity

The particular conflation of international popular music and issues of national musical culture in the context of the ESC has resulted in an inherent tension between homogenizing tendencies (that is, adaptation to the West European mainstream) and attempts at cultural/stylistic specificity. The notion of national (or otherwise

---

16 Björnberg, "Musical Spectacle as Ritual," p. 376.

17 *Göteborgs-Tidningen* (24 April 1983).

18 *Göteborgs-Posten* (16 May 2004).

geographically or culturally defined) popular styles is in itself at least as old as popular music as such, but it is also partly an ideological construct connected to the rise of nationalism in the 19th and early 20th centuries, as popular music has always been characterized by musical mixtures across stylistic and cultural boundaries.

Although the term "world music" was not coined until the late 1980s, the musical-cultural processes of stylistic change, acculturation and exploitation described by the term have been around much longer.[19] As Simon Frith has pointed out, "there is no such thing as a culturally 'pure' sound."[20] This does not contradict the fact that most national popular music cultures are imbued with dense layers of specific cultural significance which may take very long for an outsider to learn, whence it would be more appropriate to speak of national popular-music genres rather than national popular-music styles. Such cultural meanings, however, are not very efficiently communicable in the transnational television context of the ESC, and as I've argued above, in that respect musical-stylistic markers of national specificity may function as free-floating signifiers. Regardless of the origin of these musical styles, any European nation may well be represented in the contest by a tango, reggae song, flamenco or rap number, as, for instance, in the Swedish entry "Augustin" (1959), the Finnish "Reggae O.K." (1981), the Danish "Shame on You" (2004) and the Ukrainian "Razom nas bahato" (Together we are many, 2005), respectively.

As already stated, modern media of global communication have arguably precipitated the decline of the notion of national popular music styles. Discussing developments within Québécois mainstream pop, Line Grenier writes of the increasing irrelevance of "the conflation of political, geographical and cultural boundaries which constituted one of the backbones of popular music," and which used to be "epitomised by the modern Western nation-state."[21] One possible consequence of this process is the development of "international" popular music cultures, such as the European "ultra-mainstream" referred to above. In an article discussing 1980s Europop, Simon Frith writes that ABBA

> took clean white pop to an intensity (or rather, superficiality) of cleanliness and whiteness that rendered them abstract. ... It was because not a single element of their sound was "naturally" Swedish that they could be heard, in the mid-1970s, as a profoundly Swedish (read European) band. No popular American (or then British) musicians could have been so rootless.[22]

It should be observed that Frith, when characterizing ABBA as "rootless," is not describing the psychological or cultural conditions under which the group created their music, but rather suggesting how that music was construed by international

---

19   For a useful historical overview see Pedro van der Lee, "Sitars and Bossas: World Music Influences," *Popular Music* 17/1 (1998): 45–70; also Timothy D. Taylor, *Strange Sounds: Music, Technology & Culture* (New York: Routledge, 2001), pp. 117–20.

20   Simon Frith, "Introduction," in *World Music, Politics and Social Change*, ed. Simon Frith (Manchester: Manchester University Press, 1989), p. 3.

21   Line Grenier, "The Aftermath of a Crisis: Quebec Music Industries in the 1980s," *Popular Music* 12/3 (1993): 225.

22   Simon Frith, "Euro Pop," *Cultural Studies* 3/2 (1989): 168.

audiences: as containing nothing which from an outsider's perspective could be identified as recognizably Swedish.[23] Rather than being experienced as a lack, however, this very absence of cultural specificity in ABBA's music meant that it could function as an affirmative musical signifier denoting modernity and global mobility to listeners across the world.

However, an alternative response to the problematic status of national popular music styles, a response which appears to have become increasingly relevant in the context of the ESC in recent years, is to attempt a creative (re)construction of national or ethnic identity in music. Here I am referring to the emergence since 1989 of contest entries in a folkloristic musical style. Several entries from the new ESC participants of eastern and south-eastern Europe in the 1990s and early 2000s have featured a distinctly ethnic sound, at least to the ears of West European audiences. For the latter, these countries seem to represent a somehow more authentic or explicit ethnicity than the more modernized and "disethnified" West European societies, as witnessed by the success of the Turkish "Every Way That I Can" in 2003 and the Ukrainan "Dikiye tantsy" (Wild dances) in 2004. In addition to this, however, at least since the mid-1990s, several West European contest entries with a distinctly ethnic sound have appeared. An illustrative example is the Norwegian 1995 ESC winner "Nocturne," an almost completely instrumental number featuring a minor-key modal melody and ethnic instrumentation including violin, keyed-fiddle and tin whistle. The following year the Swedish entry "Den vilda" (The wild one) continued the trend with a repetitive modal melody, a percussion-based arrangement and archaizingly alliterating lyrics. The same year's winner, the Irish entry "The Voice," was a fairly straightforward Celtic song in a neo-ethnic arrangement.

Seen in retrospect, this kind of music appearing in the ESC at this time is not very surprising. The mid-1990s was the time of the introduction of the genre label "ethnotechno," created to describe the use of "identifiably 'ethnic' music samples in popular musics, dance musics in particular."[24] As described in detail by Timothy Taylor, the genre was largely launched by the commercial success of Enigma's international hit "Return to Innocence" in 1993, with the characteristically Celtic New Age sound of Irish songstress Enya as another significant source. Although not predominant in quantitative terms, this kind of West European neo-ethnic music has continued as a perceivable trend within the ESC into the 21st century; a recent example is the comeback performance of Swedish folk-rock group Nordman in the Swedish 2005 ESC preliminaries. In a sense, the function of this genre as the expression of the construction of ethnicity *per se* was taken to its logical conclusion in the Belgian 2003 entry "Sanomi," where the Celtic-inspired modality and percussion-dominated arrangement was combined with lyrics in an incomprehensible made-up language. This, as well as the band's name, Urban Trad, seemed apt indications of the nature of the project: a free construction of ethnicity from the vantage point of modernity.

---

23 However, in the early 1980s, a group of Georgian music scholars visiting Gothenburg, when exposed to traditional Swedish keyed-fiddle music, could immediately recognize the resemblance of this to ABBA's music—a similarity that none of the Swedish scholars present could perceive. (Personal communication, Professor Emeritus Jan Ling.)

24 Taylor, *Strange Sounds: Music, Technology & Culture*, p. 131.

Philip Bohlman theorizes two kinds of "other" in relation to Western (European) culture: an "external" and an "internal" other.[25] In consequence of the preceding discussion, the internal other represented in the context of the ESC could be differentiated further into two different types: 1) that represented by music from "ethnic" countries (the nations of south-western, south-eastern and eastern Europe) embodying for West European audiences values of authenticity, and 2) that represented by "ethnic" music—as we have seen, often grounded in notions of historical, pre-modern ethnicity—from "non-ethnic" countries (the nations of western and north-western Europe). In line with predominant Western attitudes, both of these "others" can be approached with an exoticist fascination for the unfamiliar. It could perhaps be argued, however, that there are tendencies within the ESC towards a blurring of this distinction, as indicated by the previously mentioned 1999 German entry "Reise nach Jerusalem/Kudüs'e seyahat"—should this be characterized as German or Turkish music?

The last example also serves as an indication of the increasing significance of ethnicity with regard to the artists performing in the ESC. Since the early days of the contest, it has been a common practice for European artists to represent another country than their own country of origin; a particularly lively exchange of artists has taken place, on the one hand, among the Nordic countries and Germany, and on the other, among the Francophone countries. What is new in the post-1989 ESC is the increasing presence of artists of non-European origin. A pioneering country in this respect was France, which was represented by black Caribbean artists in 1990 (Joëlle Ursull) and 1992 (Kali).[26] As new patterns of migration change the make-up of European populations, even nations wont to think of themselves as ethnically homogeneous have been increasingly represented by artists of a "foreign" ethnic background. Caribbean-born Dave Benton, who represented Estonia in 2001, was the first black artist ever to win the contest. Another case in point is Sweden: in 2002 the country was represented by three female black singers under the punning name Afro-Dite, and in the Swedish national preliminaries of recent years there has been a perceivably high representation of artists who are either first- or second-generation immigrants or of ethnically mixed origin (this was the case for 9 of the 32 songs featured in the 2005 preliminaries). There have also been instances of immigrant artists performing both in their "new" and their "old" country: for example, the Greek-Swedish duo Antique, after their breakthrough on the Swedish pop market in 1999 with a Greek-tinged brand of Europop, went on to represent Greece in the 2001 ESC, and one half of the duo, songstress Elena Paparizou, reappeared in 2005 performing the winning Greek entry, "My Number One."

---

25   Philip V. Bohlman, "Composing the Cantorate: Westernizing Europe's Other Within," in *Western Music and Its Others: Difference, Representation, and Appropriation in Music*, ed. Georgina Born and David Hesmondhalgh (Berkeley: University of California, 2000), pp. 187–212.

26   According to Line Grenier and Jocelyne Guilbault, this is one of several indications of an on-going change in cultural relationships between France and Francophone countries in other continents. Line Grenier and Jocelyne Guilbault, "Créolité and Francophonie in Music: Socio-musical Repositioning Where It Matters," *Cultural Studies* 11/2 (1997): 229.

Conclusion

From a West European point of view, the post-1989 changes within the ESC might be regarded as a result of a continuing expansion of the market for world music and the gradual incorporation of this music into mainstream culture. In cultural terms, it could be argued that this development involves, both as its precondition and its consequence, the gradual emancipation of culture-specific musical-stylistic traits from signifying roots in a particular cultural context, whereby they come to function as free-floating signifiers representing an unspecified cultural anchorage in general. In this respect, the ESC's "ethnic turn" ties in with other prominent trends in contemporary West European culture, characterized by key phrases such as folk culture, historicism, and cultural roots, and manifested in phenomena such as computer games, live role-play games, medieval fairs, and so on. In these contexts, the attainment of a sense of historical cultural roots is sought by means of an active construction of the past rather than historical accuracy. By a similar token, the ethnic diversity displayed in the contest could be seen as the result of a deliberate attempt at a sort of representational multiculturalism on behalf of the organizers within public-service television.

As I have argued above, however, the dense cultural meanings manifested within the context of the ESC renders an unequivocal evaluation of the event impossible. The meanings crystallized in the ESC, in its old West European heartland as well as in the new East European nations, indicate that what 15 years ago seemed to have sedimented into a rigidly regulated and predictable mainstream ritual, emptied of cultural significance, has proven able to represent a wide range of cultural and political issues. Adopting a formulation from Timothy Rice, the neo-ethnic musical constructions of national identity displayed in the ESC, combining musical expressions of "rootless" modernity with a revised conception of "roots music," may prove capable of signifying "a progressive, attenuated nationalism ... that recognises and even celebrates cultural diversity and cultural connections to others."[27]

---

27 Timothy Rice, "Bulgaria or Chalgaria: The Attenuation of Bulgarian Nationalism in a Mass-mediated Popular Music," *Yearbook for Traditional Music* 34 (2002): 43.

Chapter 3

Eurovision at 50:
Post-Wall and Post-Stonewall

Robert Deam Tobin

Why have gays, lesbians, bisexuals, transvestites, transsexuals and other queer people played an increasingly open role in the Eurovision Song Contest (ESC)? A queer British website, RainbowNetwork.Com, proffers ten light-hearted explanations for the purported gayness of the event, including "the sheer pleasure of lightweight pop music." The authors claim that "gay culture at its best embraces tinny pop music, rubbish lyrics, flashy stage shows and one-hit wonder stars. Eurovision also embodies these stellar qualities."[1] According to the site, gays also enjoy "the drama and the tragedy" of the show. Similar arguments return in the writings of a number of Eurovision fans. Asked why there were so many homosexuals in the Grand Prix scene, Ivor Lyttle, the editor of *Eurosong News*, answers: "In any case the Grand-Prix fans like decorations. They respond to the gestures of the female singers, to the tragedies and the triumphs."[2] Jan Feddersen, author of an exhaustive compendium on Eurovision history, echoes these sentiments when he reports that homosexuals find in the Grand Prix "the stuff of dreams: triumphs, the fall of favorites … jewelry, clothes and strange sounding languages … [and] queens of the night who demand our love."[3]

The campy outrageousness of Eurovision does have a queer appeal, but beyond these aesthetic and cultural considerations there are real political reasons why queers might find in the ESC what Lyttle calls "an important counterpoint to heterosexual culture."[4] Eurovision, especially as it has developed since the 1990s after the fall of the Berlin Wall, offers a model of European citizenship that is particularly amenable to needs that are present in queer populations and communities—a model of citizenship that ultimately relies on the possibility of camp performances of identity.

Whatever the explanation, it is certainly true that there is a strong queer presence in the ESC today. Some of the more obvious examples of this include performers such as

- Iceland's openly gay contestant in 1997, Paul Oskar;
- the beautiful male-to-female transsexual Dana International, who dedicated

---

1   Charlotte Cooper, "What's So Gay about Eurovision" (16 May 2005) <http://RainbowNetwork.com> Accessed 15 August 2005.

2   Cited in Jan Feddersen, *Ein Lied kann eine Brücke sein: die deutsche und internationale Geschichte des Grand Prix Eurovision* (Hamburg: Hoffmann und Campe, 2002), p. 213.

3   Ibid., p. 416.

4   Ibid., p. 213.

her sensational 1998 victory to Israel for its 50th birthday and to gays and lesbians everywhere;[5]

- the transvestites who comprised Slovenia's 2002 group "Sestre" (Sister), one of whom had been second runner-up at the European Miss Transvestite Pageant of 1997;[6]
- and, in 2003, the singers of the Russian girl-group t.A.T.u., who staged themselves as lesbians.

If anything, queer fans are even more noticeable than queer performers. Each spring, European gay and lesbian periodicals are full of announcements of Eurovision parties, gossip about contestants, and chatter about the chances of various songs. Many European queer subcultures feature celebrations and parodies of the contest, such as the "Eurosong Travestival" put on by the Dutch drag queens Coco Coquette, Jet Lag, Eileen Wayback, and Desiree della Stiletto, who comprise the group "Chicks with Dicks." The cabaret show, which features competitors from such countries as Wonderland and Wasteland, has been running annually in the Netherlands since 2003.[7] Paul Oskar and Dana International have starred in gay pride parades throughout Europe.

The term "queer" is used here in the weak sense of the word, that is, as an umbrella term for gays, lesbians, bisexuals, transsexuals, transvestites, and other people who defy sexual norms. The openly gay Paul Oskar, the transsexual Dana International, the transvestites in Sestre, and the faux lesbians in t.A.T.u. give a sense of the variety of non-heteronormative sexualities increasingly associated with the competition. But the ESC also allows for a notion of citizenship that is "queer" in a more rigorous sense—that is, a kind of citizenship that deconstructs identity claims. For many queer participants and fans, the contest makes it possible to challenge and subvert the conventional standards of cultural belonging. The sense of citizenship that Eurovision offers is of course distinct and different from the legal status of a citizen of a particular state that is a member of the European Broadcasting Union (EBU), which runs the show. Instead, this understanding of citizenship relates more to a sense of belonging to a community, having a say in that community, having equal rights in that community, and feeling represented by that community.[8] Queers and many other disenfranchised minorities find in the ESC a chance to experience this broader kind of citizenship.

---

5   Ibid., p. 324.

6   Her name was "Emperatrizz," a.k.a. Damjan Levec. William Dean, "Sestre," *Night Lights* (29 May 2002) <www.cleansheets.com/articles/dean_05.29.02.shtml> Accessed 15 August 2005.

7   For an image of the EuroSong Travestival, see <www.chickswithdicks.nl/images/eurovisie2005.jpg> Accessed 24 February 2006.

8   Amy L. Brandzel offers a useful summary of discussions of citizenship with leads to other sources in "Queering Citizenship? Same-Sex Marriage and the State," *GLQ* 11/2 (2005): 174.

European citizenship post-Wall

Just what it means to be a "citizen of Europe" is a vexing question that touches upon acute sensibilities and sociopolitical debates in the early 21st century. On the level of culture, Eurovision offers its own vision of European citizenship. Although the website of the EBU makes clear that the broadcasting organization is distinct from and unrelated to the European Union and that its reach extends throughout the Mediterranean region to countries more usually considered to be parts of Africa and Asia, its Eurovision programming has nevertheless always stood for Europe. Established in 1956 by Marcel Bezençon—a friend and admirer of Jean Monnet, the founder of the European Economic Union—the ESC was one such program intended from the outset to unite Europe through televised cultural events.[9] If anything, it does so now more than ever. The former London correspondent for *The Washington Post* T.J. Reid argues that "Eurovision has become a celebration of Europeanness, a great annual coming-together that strengthens the growing sense among 500 million people that they all belong to a single place on the world map."[10] The British journalist Ben MacIntyre concurs, asserting that "the Eurovision Song Contest is a cultural monument to what most Europeans think it means to be European." He concludes: "In the end, Eurovision is less a contest than an idea, a vision of Europe, a long-running exercise in hopeful internationalism that is simultaneously naff, hilarious and oddly touching."[11]

With the fall of the Berlin Wall, a new model of citizenship emerged in Europe out of the rubble of the Cold War. Much of this new sense of identity was bound up in the European Union (EU), which had evolved substantially from the economic union created by the 1957 Treaty of Rome. In 1985, the Treaty of Schengen began the process of eliminating border controls between European nations, harmonizing procedures related to entry into Europe, unifying policies on asylum, and facilitating cross-border police activities. Although not initially negotiated within the framework of the European Union, the Schengen protocols have been taken over by the EU (though not every member of the EU is a signatory to the Treaty of Schengen, and some signatories are not members of the EU). In 1993, the Treaty of Maastricht set the agenda for unifying Europe politically, increasing the power of the European Parliament, strengthening the European Central Bank, and taking steps toward the introduction of the single currency, the Euro.[12] The resulting political system is a unique patchwork of overlapping jurisdictions and rights, sparking occasional

---

9 Complaining about the bureaucratic hindrances to the establishment of the ESC, Marcel Bezençon writes that "Eurovision was made for Europe, in spite of Europe." "Eurovision—A Simple Idea that Worked," *Eurovision: 5th Anniversary* (Geneva: Gilléron, 1959), p. 3.

10 T.J. Reid, *The United States of Europe: The New Superpower and the End of American Supremacy* (New York: Penguin, 2004), p. 198.

11 Ben MacIntyre, "Oj, oj, oj! It's Europe in harmony," *Times Online* (21 May 2005) <www.timesonline.co.uk/article/O,,1068-1621005,00.html> Accessed 15 August 2005.

12 Andreas Eckhardt, "Die Musik- und Kulturförderung der Europäischen Union: Grundlagen, Zielsetzung und Förderprojekte," *Musik und Politik: Dimensionen einer undefinierbaren Beziehung*, ed. Berhard Frevel (Regensburg: ConBrio, 1997), p. 203.

comparisons to such historical entities as the Habsburg Empire and the Holy Roman Empire.[13]

As if this weren't complicated enough, there are other frameworks of European citizenship besides the European Union. Most notable among these is the Council of Europe, established in 1950. Like the EBU, it is a more inclusive body than the EU. There are now 46 members of the Council, including all members of the EU. The map of member countries includes all of western Europe and—with the exception of Belarus—every country on the continent of Europe up to and including Turkey, Russia, Armenia, Azerbaijan, and Georgia. Unlike the EBU, the Council of Europe does not include North African or Middle Eastern states, although some have proposed that it grow in those directions. A primary focus of the Council is the protection of human rights. In order to join, all members of the Council must sign the European Convention for the Protection of Human Rights and Fundamental Freedoms, the world's first international treaty defending human rights. I will return momentarily to the role of the European Convention for the Protection of Human Rights in protecting the rights of gays and lesbians, but for now the important point is that—even on the relatively straightforward level of politics and government—multiple and overlapping organizations define "European citizenship."

When the much less clearly defined cultural notions of citizenship are factored in, it becomes evident that being "a citizen of Europe" is a status signified by a complex network of sometimes contradictory signifiers. In this context, the ESC is perhaps the largest and best-organized institution promoting a cultural kind of pan-European identity. As Feddersen points out in his weblog report on the 2005 competition, Eurovision is "the only Europeanizing project going on beneath the political preambles."[14]

This complex concept of European cultural citizenship has required a rethinking of national identity. It is not the case that national identities have dissipated, as Mark Leonard, director of foreign policy at the Center for European Reform in London, argues: "National identities haven't waned at all. If anything, they've become stronger. But the EU has changed the nature of nationalism within Europe, so it's no longer about fighting wars with each other, but managing diversity peacefully."[15] The ESC offers a remarkable laboratory in which to manage the diversity among European countries while also negotiating the boundaries of national and supranational European identity. Even critics of the contest recognize its new approach to nationality, as one contributor to an Internet discussion on the subject notes: "the various nation states

---

13   On the Habsburg Empire, see Ian Reifowitz, *Imagining an Austrian Nation: Joseph Samuel Bloch and the Search for a Multiethnic Austrian Identity, 1846–1919* (New York: Columbia University Press, 2003), p. 2. On the Holy Roman Empire, see Niall Fergusson, "Europeans vs. Europe: Federalist Style," *The New Republic* (20 June 2005), p. 14.

14   Feddersens Kommentar 12: "Europe trudelt in Kiew ein," *NDRTV.de* (16 May 2005) <www.ndrtv.de/grandprix/news/20050516_kommentar_feddersen_12html> Accessed 15 August 2005.

15   Richard Bernstein, "Europe is Still Europe," *New York Times* (7 June 2005): A10.

express national difference within the context of European unity—a symbolic form of nationalism as aesthetics."[16]

The constituencies most anxious to demonstrate their European identity in the laboratory of Eurovision are those whose European identity is most contested. Historically, popular music has been an especially welcoming field to those on the margins of society—as Feddersen notes, "popular music is always the domain of new-comers, not of those who already have everything."[17] It is for this reason, perhaps, that a sense of shame and embarrassment so often accompanies the embrace of Eurovision in more powerful West European countries—as though one were admitting one's vulnerability by acknowledging an enjoyment of the ESC.[18] Two types of marginalization come to mind. One besets those governments and countries at the margins of Europe who are attempting to prove that they belong to Europe. In the case of these countries, it is often parties within the political and cultural elites who are intensely interested in the ESC. The other type of marginalization affects those disenfranchised groups throughout Europe who feel excluded from full acceptance as "Europeans." In this second case, it is a matter not of elites, but rather of members of ethnic and sexual minorities. I will focus primarily on this second type of marginalization.

While the governments and elites of countries on the periphery of Europe have found in the ESC an opportunity to express their desire to be part of European power structures, more marginal populations, especially within "Old Europe," discover in Eurovision a chance to participate in the ideal of Europe. For example, it is frequently claimed that Turkish "guest workers" in Germany are such a powerful bloc in ESC televoting that Germany typically gives the maximal 12 points to Turkey. Feddersen points out that other immigrant groups sway the German vote toward Bosnia-Herzegovina, Poland, Croatia, and Russia, as well as Turkey.[19] Immigrant groups in other countries, such as the Portuguese in France, are alleged to have a similar influence on voting. In 2004, many Bosnians thought that their country's Serbian minority had overwhelmed the phone lines and given Serbia 12 points, while many in Macedonia believed that its Albanian minority had caused its 12 points to go to Albania.[20]

Some Internet bloggers have suggested that people should vote by nationality, rather than by location—Turkish citizens in Germany would thus vote as Turks and

---

16   Rebecca, "The Eurovision Song Contest," *pen-l* (11 May 1998) <www.mail-archive. com/pen-l@galaxy.csuchico.edu/msg27098.html> Accessed 15 August 2005.

17   Feddersens Kommentar (18): "Osteuropa," *NDRTV.de* (19 May 2005) <www.ndrtv. de/grandprix/news/20050519_kommentar_feddersen_18.html> Accessed 15 August 2005.

18   For more on the embarrassment provoked by *Schlager*, the kind of music most frequently associated with Eurovision in Germany, see Sunka Simon, "Identity Formation in German Schlager-Hits," *Glossen* 15 (2002) <www.dickinson.edu/glossen/heft15/simon. html> Accessed 15 August 2005.

19   Feddersen, *Ein Lied*, p. 361.

20   Ana Petruseva, "Old Foes Serenade Serbia in Istanbul," *Institute for War and Peace Reporting* (22 May 2004) <www.iwpr.net/index.pl?archive/bcr3/bcr3_200405_499_2eng. txt> Accessed 18 August 2005.

not as Germans, which would mean that they couldn't vote for Turkey.[21] Of course, it would be virtually impossible for the EBU to enforce such a requirement. More to the point, in the interests of creating a pan-European television community, the EBU has no inclination to reinforce the legal standing of citizenship in this way. Neither at the level of the performer nor at the level of the televoting fan has the EBU ever been concerned with ascertaining legal citizenship. Many people, for instance, are surprised to learn that Céline Dion, a Canadian citizen, performed for Switzerland in 1988. But her performance is entirely in accordance with the rules. Many performers are not legal citizens of the country they represent, and certain countries, such as Luxembourg, are known for generally hiring foreigners to sing for them. Since the contest rules were changed in 1999 to allow songs to be in any language, linguistic ability is also no longer a criterion for citizenship either. Many have decried this change of rules as a cultural loss because it has in practice meant that more songs are sung in English, but for Feddersen the elimination of language requirements means "that Europe, and not the nation state, takes center stage at the contest."[22]

Similarly, there are no restrictions concerning the legal citizenship of televoters. Asked about the concern that Turkish migrant workers in Germany would vote reflexively and uncritically for Turkey, Jürgen Meier-Beer, a television executive responsible for producing Germany's ESC broadcast, responds with the fighting words that "the solution to the problem would be German citizenship for the Turks in Germany."[23] Ralph Siegel, the composer who has written a vast number of German ESC entries, has consciously played with support for dual citizenship, baldly asserting in this context that "a little support from the Turkish community couldn't hurt."[24] Admittedly, one has to ask whether these populations are really large enough to affect the vote in any significant way. Meier-Beer, for instance, points out that in 2000 twice as many Germans voted for Denmark as voted for Turkey, which shows not that the tiny Danish minority in Schleswig-Holstein was throwing the German vote to Denmark, but rather that the voting process "cannot be dominated by minorities if the majority takes part in the vote."[25] Nonetheless, Eurovision has in essence offered all residents of all competing countries voting rights, something that progressives have only haltingly been able to achieve at the local level in some communities within Europe. It therefore offers a kind of democracy to significant subgroups in Europe who are otherwise disenfranchised. By the standards of the ESC, membership in Europe is available without regard to race, national origin, ethnicity, linguistic ability, religion, sexual orientation, or gender status.

---

21   See "Dirks Grandprix Tagebuch 2004" Internet weblog <www.seidu.de/about/tagebuch/grandprix/archives/2004_5.jsp> Accessed 15 August 2005.

22   Ralf Lehnert, "Eurovision Goes English," *Deutsche Welle* (13 May 2004) <www.dw-world.de/dw/article/0,1564,1201637,00.html> Accessed 16 August 2005.

23   Cited in Feddersen, *Ein Lied*, p. 419.

24   Ibid., p. 283.

25   Cited in ibid., p. 422.

Eurovision post-Stonewall

In recent years, one of the minorities that has taken to the ESC with particular gusto is the gay, lesbian, and transsexual population. It is important to remember that for several decades after the founding of Eurovision, consensual homosexual activities were illegal in many European states. England and Wales, for example, only began to decriminalize homosexuality in 1967, with Scotland following in 1980 and Northern Ireland in 1982. West Germany started decriminalizing homosexuality in 1969, and Austria in 1971. In his memoir *Midlife Queer*, Martin Duberman reminds his readers that police fired bullets into a gay pride march in Barcelona in 1977 and that in the same year the British editor of *Gay News* was convicted on charges of blasphemy.[26] Even in 2005, gay pride parades were denounced and attacked in Jerusalem, banned in Warsaw, harassed in Latvia, and generally poorly treated in many parts of eastern Europe.[27] In all these European countries, decriminalization has taken place slowly and penalties have often remained for certain aspects of same-sex relationships that were not in place for male-female relationships. Frequently, for instance, the age of consent was higher for homosexual activities than for heterosexual ones. In many parts of Europe, certain rights remain in the preserve of heterosexuality even today, including the right to marry and the right to found a family, either through adoption or artificial insemination. Thus in many ways, homosexuals, transsexuals, intersexuals, and other people who defy gender norms did not have access to full citizenship in the nation states of Europe when the ESC was founded, and even to this day queers are not fully enfranchised.

While gays, lesbians, bisexuals, and transsexuals may have earned the right to distrust the nation state, they have increasingly found an ally in the new supranational structures of Europe. Various pan-European political institutions have been a driving force in whatever progress has been made in this situation of queer people in Europe. In 1998, the European Parliament made clear that it would not admit any nation that failed to respect the rights of gays and lesbians.[28] In 2005, EU officials continued this tradition when they warned that Poland could lose its EU voting rights if its newly elected president, Lech Kaczynski, continued to oppose gay rights.[29] Particularly, the Council of Europe's European Convention for the Protection of Human Rights and

---

26 Martin Duberman, *Midlife Queer: Autobiography of a Decade, 1971–1981* (Madison, WI: University of Wisconsin Press, 1996), p. 86.

27 "Gay Marches Ignore Ban in Warsaw," BBC News (11 June 2005) <http://news.bbc.co.uk/2/hi/europe/4084324.stm> Accessed 15 August 2005.
"Protests Disrupt Latvia Gay March," BBC News (23 July 2005) <http://news.bbc.co.uk/2/hi/europe/4711261.stm> Accessed 15 August 2005.

28 The resolution was passed on 17 September 1998. At the time, the countries specifically concerned were Cyprus, Romania, Bulgaria, Estonia, Hungary, and Lithuania. "European Parliament Adopts Urgency Resolution on Equal Rights for Gays and Lesbans in the EU," *Lithuanian Gay League* (10 October 1998) <www.gay.lt/article_en.asp?ID=6#back> Accessed 18 August 2005.

29 Nicholas Watt, "Polish leader's anti-gay stance threatens EU voting rights," *The Guardian* (25 October 2005) <www.guardian.co.uk/eu/story/0,7369,1599957,00.html> Accessed 24 February 2006.

Fundamental Freedoms has been interpreted to protect many of the rights of gays and lesbians. In 1981, the European Commission on Human Rights found that Northern Ireland's ban on homosexuality was a violation of human rights, forcing that part of the United Kingdom to decriminalize sexual activities between members of the same sex. In 1988, it ruled against Ireland's sodomy laws. In 1997, the Commission determined that Great Britain was in violation of the Convention because it had separate ages of consent for homosexual and heterosexual activities, setting off a wave of equalization of age-of-consent laws throughout Europe. The European Court of Human Rights, which replaced the Commission in 1998, has continued to be gay-friendly, most notably striking down in 1999 the ban on gays in the military in Britain.[30] In 1999, it decided that a Portuguese law denying parental rights to a gay father was also in violation of the Convention.[31]

The ESC itself has been directly touched by the European concern for the rights of queer people. When the transvestite trio Sestre appeared to have been chosen to represent Slovenia in 2002, various conservative forces in that country agitated to exclude them from further participation in the competition. Hearing about the controversy, the European Parliament expressed its concern that "the rights of sexual minorities might be violated in Slovenia," pointing out that "the rights of sexual minorities are an unalienable part of human rights, the respect for which is prerequisite for entry into the EU." Slovenian objections to the group Sestre were dropped.[32]

The support on the part of European institutions for the rights of sexual minorities has been so high that it has become a part of European identity. On the one hand, Europe's support for gay and lesbian rights allows it to position itself in contrast to the United States, which is seen as overly influenced by conservative religious forces that remain relatively unimportant in the European political scene. Along with opposition to capital punishment, liberal laws on sex became touchstones of the European supranational consensus in the 1990s. On the other hand, a contrast is asserted between a liberal Europe's current tolerance of sexual identities and the repression of sexual minorities in certain conservative parts of the Islamic world, for example. Pim Fortuyn, the openly gay and adamantly pro-Western Dutch politician who was assassinated in 2002, embodied the new claim that the secular West's acceptance of diverse sexual lifestyles lent it legitimacy in comparison with the theocratic Islamic world. Sandip Ray, an editor for the Pacific News Service, argues provocatively that, "though nobody will explicitly make the link, legalizing same-sex marriage may be less about gay rights and more about codifying an ideal of European values—another brick in the wall of Fortress Europa before it's too late,

---

30   Sameera Dalvi, "Homosexuality and the European Court of Human Rights: Recent Judgments against the United Kingdom and their Impact on Other Signatories to the Convention on Human Rights," *University of Florida Journal of Law and Public Policy* 15 (2004), pp. 467–513.

31   See <www.ilga.info/Information/Legal_survey/europesupporting%20files/Historic %20judgment_denial%20of%20parental%20rights%20to%20gay%20father%20.htm> Accessed 18 August 2005.

32   Dean, "Sestre."

before multiculturalism becomes all about tolerating the intolerant."[33] According to this analysis, guaranteeing the rights of sexual minorities has become a marker of European identity. Alisa Solomon, for example, argues that Israel's entries to Eurovision—most obviously Dana International's participation—assert Israel's membership in the sexually liberal West rather than the orthodox theocracies of the Middle East.[34] Europe came to position itself as the champion of gays, lesbians, and transsexuals. By the same token, hostility within Europe to the idea of a unified Europe often surfaces in homophobic ways. Thus the 2005 victory of Lech and Jaroslav Kaczynski's Law and Justice Party in Poland was built on a nationalist backlash to EU membership that relied on aggressive anti-gay rhetoric.[35]

One set of rights that became particularly relevant to gay and lesbian couples in the 1990s concerns bi-national pairs. Mainstream gay movements in Europe have tried to insure that civil unions allow for residency of non-national partners, making it easier for a foreign partner to obtain legal citizenship. The primary political demand of the 1997 Christopher Street Day parade in Berlin was the rights of bi-national pairs. For that event, Berlin's gay and lesbian magazine *Siegessäule* featured a multiracial pair on the cover and was devoted to issues of multiculturalism in the queer community.[36] This focus on issues of bi-national gay and lesbian couples is one concrete reason that queers would participate in the spirit of internationalism that embodied Europe in the 1990s.

In addition to these political reasons for connecting Europe—and, by extension, the ESC—to gay-friendly policies, there seems to be an overlap between the aesthetic sensibilities that flourish in Eurovision and those that are cultivated in queer European subcultures. Nowadays, descriptions of the ESC typically consider it "the campest competition around."[37] One reporter writes that the competition is "a huge high-camp joke in much of Europe."[38] Deutsche Welle refers to it as "Europe's campy Eurovision Song Contest."[39] Even in the United States, reporters know what's at stake in "the ultracampy Eurovision Song Contest."[40] Needless to say, at least

33 Sandip Roy, "Can Gay Marriage Protect Europe from Subway Bombers?" *Pacific News Service* (13 July 2005) <http://news.pacificnews.org/news/view_article.html?article_id =a517da0536e361e88382124f9dd53bb3> Accessed 22 March 2007.

34 Alisa Solomon, "Viva la Diva Citizenship: Post-Zionism and Gay Rights," *Queer Theory and the Jewish Question*, ed. Daniel Boyarin, Daniel Itzkovitz, and Ann Pellegrini (New York: Columbia, 2003), pp. 149–65.

35 Tomek Kitzlinski and Pavel Lescowicz, "New Anti-Gay Regime in Poland," *The Gully* (10 November 2005) <www.thegully.com/essays/gaymondo/051110_poland_election. html> Accessed 25 February 2006.

36 *Siegessäule* (July 1997).

37 Sarah Freeman, "Help Me Make It Through the Night," *Yorkshire Post Today* (20 May 2005).

38 Ana Petruseva, "Old Foes Serenade Serbia in Istanbul," *Institute for War and Peace Reporting* (22 May 2004) <http://www.iwpr.net/index.pl?archive/bcr3/bcr3_200405_499_ 2eng.txt> Accessed 18 August 2005.

39 Lehnert, "Eurovision Goes English."

40 Gerald Mizejewski, "Britain Strikes Out at '03 Eurovision: Snub Seen as Rebuke for War in Iraq," *The Washington Times* (28 May 2003): A15.

since Christopher Isherwood and Susan Sontag first popularized the term, camp has been regarded as queer. Indeed, it is probable that the campiness—or the perceived campiness—of the *concours* has grown as gays, lesbians, and transsexuals have become a more visible part of the ESC and as Europe has become more closely associated with the rights of sexual minorities.

The underlying ambiguity of camp and irony—of loving something while sending it up—makes these rhetorical structures an important tool in any critique of identity that doesn't merely reject identity bluntly. In both putting forth and parodying local music traditions and international Europop, the campiness of the ESC allows performers and fans alike simultaneously to claim and disavow regional, national, and continental identities. By the late 1980s and early 1990s queer politics, in the more rigorous sense of a critique of identities, had begun to develop in Europe.[41] A cornerstone of queer thinking was the critical deconstruction not only of sexual identities but also of national and racial identities. In an important essay from 1992, Lisa Duggan expresses concern that the queer movement was relying on liberal and nationalist tropes that posited sexuality and nationality as "unitary" and an "unproblematic given." Implicit in her argument is the need for a critique of nationality that is concurrent with the critique of sexuality.[42] In "Sexuality and Nationality" Eve Kosofsky Sedgwick emphasizes that "nationality" is just as recent a conceptualization as "sexuality" and certainly has no claim to essential truth.[43] Eurovision seems to offer many queer viewers a space for experimenting with alternative forms of national, cultural, and European identity.

In the realm of sexuality, camp humor has proven to be one of the best tools to maintain a sense of cultural identity while critiquing essentialism. Camp can similarly assist in the project of queering the nation. One sees the role of camp in an event such as the Alternative Miss Ireland contest, in which drag queens compete to offer a different image of Ireland. In 2005, a German transvestite named Heidi Konnt, dressed up in the trappings of Alpine and Germanic civilization, won the title of Alternative Miss Ireland, showing just how different the campy image of Ireland could be. Insightfully, one commentator in an Irish gay magazine compared the Alternative Miss Ireland contest to "Eurovision on speed," underscoring the ESC's usefulness as a model for the playful reconstruction of sexual and cultural identity.[44] The fluidity of nationality, sexuality, and gender found in the Alternative Miss Ireland contest echoes the complex national and sexual semiotics performed by Dana International in the 1998 ESC. As Solomon observes, Dana International took fuller advantage than anyone else to date of the opportunities available within the Eurovision framework to claim "diva citizenship," Lauren Berlant's term for

---

41   See, for instance, *Grenzen lesbischer Identitäten*, ed. Sabine Hark (Berlin: Querverlag, 1996).

42   Lisa Duggan, "Making It Perfectly Queer," *Socialist Review* (January–March 1992): 11–31.

43   Eve Kosofsky Sedgwick, *Tendencies* (Durham, NC: Duke University Press, 1993).

44   Ciaran O'Neill, "First Impressions," *Free! Magazine for the Irish Gay Scene* 31 (April 2005): 11.

a "dramatic coup in a public sphere" by an otherwise disenfranchised person.[45] Waving the Israeli flag as she acknowledged her victory, Dana International both asserted her membership in Israel and Israel's membership in the arena of European popular culture, while also queering, critiquing, and subverting the image of Israel and Europe.

To conclude, the ESC's popularity among queer communities has to do with the alternative sense of citizenship that it offers. The contest and its parent organization, the EBU, are part of a group of institutions—including the European Union; the European Central Bank, with its currency, the Euro; and the Council of Europe with its Court of Human Rights—that have forged a new sense of European citizenship that is polyvalent and indicated by multiple overlapping, but not always congruent, signifiers. All of these governmental and capitalist institutions exert their own forms of power on the structure of sexuality. But in the slippage that occurs between these institutions, a variety of otherwise disenfranchised Europeans (such as the "New Europeans" of former socialist countries of the East, guest workers and migrant groups within much of Europe, as well as gays and lesbians) can stake a claim to European identity. Gays and lesbians would be particularly interested in staking such a claim because of the increasing association between Europe and liberal attitudes about sexual minorities. The campy aesthetic of the show does not hurt its standing among queer audiences either, because it perfectly reflects the postmodern sense of citizenship in Europe that appeals to many queer people.

The referenda in France and Holland in 2005 that rejected a proposed constitution for the European Union have put a sobering pause on excessive hopes for experimentation with political structures and concepts in Europe. Many commentators predict a return of the nation-state, a decline in the influence of Europe, perhaps even the abandonment of the Euro. In any case, the sexually liberal agenda associated with Europe may be on hold for a while, or in danger of being hijacked by xenophobic forces. But the artists who compose and perform for Eurovision—as well as the fans who celebrate the show—can continue to use the ESC as a space to experiment with alternative, perhaps utopian, forms of citizenship.

---

45   Solomon, "Viva la Diva Citizenship," p. 150.

Chapter 4

Chanson, canzone, Schlager, and song: Switzerland's identity struggle in the Eurovision Song Contest

Michael Baumgartner

Swiss identity is a fragile thing. This claim may seem paradoxical, since it's easy to think of identifiably "Swiss" scenes and the country's most famous products: snow-capped Alps, rustic chalets, chocolate, clocks and watches, Swiss Army knives, Swiss guards, and Swiss cheese. As the world's oldest surviving republic, Switzerland has long been associated with political neutrality, humanitarianism, banking and finance as well.[1] But when Switzerland represents itself to the outside world, as it does in the Eurovision Song Contest, the fluidity and complexities of its national identity come to the fore.

The Eurovision Song Contest (ESC) is an event in which the cultural differences of many European countries (plus Israel and Turkey) are celebrated and renewed every year in a major televised media spectacle. Few participating countries comprise more than one distinct cultural identity. Switzerland, with its four official languages (German, French, Italian, and Rhaeto-Romanic or "Romansch") and respective regional traditions, offers the most prominent example of multicultural national identity in the ESC. This chapter examines how Switzerland has projected a national identity through its contributions over the years, most importantly through its choice of language and its use of national symbols.

If all the points of all ESC finals from 1956 through 2005 are added up, Switzerland has scored 2,079 points and holds sixth place overall.[2] This is a surprisingly impressive result for a relatively small country with a sporadic music industry and limited market for domestic artists. Swiss popular musicians, who tried to define Swiss commercial music starting in the early 1960s, could only orient themselves abroad—most obviously to neighboring France, Italy, and Germany, which each have their own thriving popular music traditions and commercial markets.

---

1   The Federal Charter that unified three Swiss cantons against the Habsburgs in 1291 may have been a later forgery, but this date is often claimed as the beginning of the early confederacy's independence, which was secured in 1315 with the Battle of Morgarten. In 1648 the Treaty of Westphalia conclusively recognized Switzerland's independence from the Holy Roman Empire.

2   This statistic is somewhat deceiving, as Switzerland has participated in the ESC since 1956 while other countries started entering songs much later. Israel, for example, first participated in 1973, and now has a total of 1,832 points.

Next to the globally dominant Anglo-American music industry, France was able to build up the second most influential one in Europe thanks to its large domestic audience and the wide international success of the *chanson*. Switzerland has been most successful in the ESC with *chansons*, beginning with the first contest in 1956 (when Lys Assia won with "Refrain") and culminating in Céline Dion's victory in 1988. Italy, with its *canzone* tradition, has had its own song contest since 1951, the San Remo Festival, which has complicated Switzerland's ESC participation in interesting ways. From 1969 to 2000 Germany had a regular televised song contest, the *ZDF-Hitparade*, featuring the specifically German genre of *Schlager* (literally, "hit" songs). Despite the popularity of *Schlager* in Germany and Austria, however, Switzerland has been less likely to represent itself in this musical direction.

Most recently, with the addition of many new countries to the ESC in the 1990s, a change of musical taste connected with this enlargement (the rise of so-called "ethnic pop") and much younger audiences than in earlier years meant that Switzerland— continuing with French *chanson*, German *Schlager*, and Italian *canzoni*—performed poorly in the competition. Only after adapting to the trend in 2005 (with the Estonian girl-group Vanilla Ninja singing in English) did the country begin to be successful again.

The "Swiss-made" myth

Despite its multicultural disposition, Switzerland has not generally represented itself in the ESC through national or regionally specific cultural codes. Up through the 1990s, only songs composed in an undistinguished European pop jargon (showing more French and Italian influence than Anglo-American) had much chance to win the contest. As a result, Swiss folkloric elements were used only sporadically in ESC songs with moderate success.

Of the 47 Swiss contributions between 1956 and 2006, only three songs contain references to Swiss national symbols or folkloric elements: "Giorgio" (1958), "Swiss Lady" (1977), and "Moitié moitié" (Half and half, 1987). In the last song only the title alludes to something Swiss—*moitié moitié* is a fondue mixture of two different cheeses, and serves here as a metaphor for love, since in a relationship one "shares happiness, but hides unhappiness."

"Giorgio" tells the story of a Swiss-German woman who spends her weekend with an Italian gigolo in Ascona on the Lago Maggiore in Ticino, the Swiss-Italian region.[3] The German lyrics, sung with a fake Italian accent, are interspersed with

---

3   The Swiss-Italian region of Ticino is a vacation and retirement area for many German Swiss. Though most of the Swiss entertainment industry is located in the German and French regions of the country, Switzerland exports what is exotic to itself, the warmth and openness of the "Mediterranean" part of the country. In the 1956 Swiss national preliminary Anita Traversi (born in Ticino) sang "Bandella Ticinese" (Ticino band), and at the 1960 Swiss national preliminary she tried again to launch a Swiss-Italian topic with the song "Malcantonesina" (The girl from the Malcantone valley). In 1964 Georges Pilloud presented his love affair with Ticino in the *canzone* "Amore in Ticino" (Love in Ticino). A further song with a reference to Ticino was "San Gottardo" (St Gotthard, the famous mountain pass), which finished second in the 1981 national preliminary behind Peter, Sue & Marc's "Io senza te" (Me without you).

Italian words such as "Chianti," "risotto," and "polenta," stereotypically Italian rather than Swiss symbols. The music also magnifies the Italian cliché: its tarantella rhythm is more Neapolitan than Swiss-Italian, and a short interlude played by a mandolin recalls the first motif played by the solo mandolin in the Allegro of Antonio Vivaldi's D major mandolin concerto (RV 93). "Giorgio" made a favorable impression, finishing in second place in 1958, while the "real" Italian *canzone* of the year, Domenico Modugno's worldwide hit "Nel blu dipinto di blu" (Volare), ranked third with almost half as many points.

Swiss symbols were integrated more clearly into "Swiss Lady," sung in German despite the English title. The song tells the story of the "man from the mountains" who tours the world with his "Swiss lady," an alphorn, and enchants the people with her "voice." In fact, a Persian jazz trumpeter named Mostafa Kafa'i Azimi played the alphorn in the Pepe Lienhard Band. The song opens with a typical folk alphorn motif, and the alphorn returns in the second half of the chorus, which begins with a stylized yodel—another Swiss musical symbol. A second solo instrument in the song is a piccolo flute, a reference to the hit single "Piccolo Man" that the Pepe Lienhard Band released the same year. The piercing piccolo sets an effective contrast to the hollow, eerie sound of the alphorn.

"Swiss Lady" illustrates how fragile national symbols can seem in the Swiss context. The somber alphorn, the Swiss instrument *par excellence*, is contradicted by the agile piccolo flute, which cannot be attributed to any particular country. Furthermore, national distinctions are blurred by the fact that a Persian musician plays the alphorn. The driving rock accompaniment sets a clear counterpoint to the traditional yodel and alphorn sound, and provides distance from the aural Swiss symbols as an ironic comment.

A cultural chameleon

From the first ESC competition in 1956 to the 2005 contest, Switzerland has submitted 22 songs in French, 11 in German, 9 in Italian, 3 in English, and 1 in Romansch. This tally is surprising, since (Swiss) German is by far the most widely spoken language in the country. Between 1956 and 1970 only three Swiss entries were sung in German: "Giorgio" (1958), "Irgendwoher" (From somewhere, 1959), and "Bonjour, bonjour" (1969). Switzerland's apparent reluctance to send performers into the contest singing in German could be attributed to the fact that in postwar Europe Switzerland did not want to be too closely identified with Germany, or that German-language songs did not usually market well internationally. On the other hand, each of these three songs achieved relatively high rankings in the contest (second, fourth, and fifth place, respectively). Between 1970 and 1990 Switzerland sent seven German-language songs, but none of these entries did particularly well.

In a few cases, a German-language song was disguised by choosing a more recognizable foreign-language title, such as "Giorgio" (1958), "Bonjour, bonjour"

(1969), "Mikado" (1975), "Swiss Lady" (1977), and "Piano, piano" (1985).[4] Accents could also confuse national identifications: Paola del Medico performed "Bonjour, bonjour" with an affected French accent. Singing German *Schlager* with a French accent was very popular in Germany from the 1950s to the 1970s. One of the key figures who sang in this manner, the venerated French chanteuse Mireille Mathieu, did extremely well with her German songs. Actually, "Bonjour, bonjour" sounds more like a French *chanson* than a German *Schlager*, and its rhythm, downward sequenced melody and solo trumpet recall the extremely popular title song from the film *Un homme et une femme* (1966) composed by Francis Lai.

It is surprising that Switzerland never sent a song to the ESC in *Schwiizertütsch*, or Swiss-German, the unique dialect of German that is the country's number-one spoken language, with over four million speakers. Sending a Swiss-German song to the ESC would be a perfect representation of the country's national identity and multicultural make-up, and would also contribute to European language diversity. Several attempts were made at various Swiss national preliminaries, but without any success. In 1983 "D'äenglischübig" (The English lesson) performed by Christian Hunziker finished sixth out of nine, four years later "Verschänk doch dini Liebi" (Give away your love) performed by Nöggi finished last, and in 2000 "Glückstränä" (Tears of joy) performed by the group Autseid ("outside") finished fifth of six. One should not forget that in 1969 the folk tune "Grüezi wohl Frau Stirnimaa" (Hello, Mrs Stirnimaa) performed by the group Minstrels sold 1.5 million singles in 27 countries, and the song has persisted into this millennium (in 2001 Carlos Peron produced a popular remix version). Despite the popularity of Swiss rock groups singing in *Schwiizertütsch* for Swiss-German audiences, this is the only case of a song in that language having been somewhat successful abroad.[5]

After winning the ESC in 1988, Switzerland hosted the following year's contest in Lausanne, and finally had the courage to submit a song in Romansch, the fourth language of the country (spoken only by a very small population in the canton of Graubünden). "Viver senza tei" (To live without you), performed by the group Furbaz, finished 13th. The group's two earlier attempts to enter the ESC failed at the national preliminaries: in 1987 "Da cumpignia" (Together) finished third, and in

---

4   Austria too would occasionally disguise a German-language song with an "international" title: Udo Jürgens sang "Merci chérie" (Thank you, darling) for his country in 1966, Schmetterlinge called their 1977 entry "Boom Boom Boomerang," and Wilfried sang "Lisa, Mona Lisa" in 1988. Even Germany entered a number of songs with non-German titles during the first 25 years of the ESC, including "Bonne nuit, ma chérie" (Good night, my darling, 1960), "Prima Ballerina" (1969), and "Johnny Blue" (1981).

5   The center of the *Schwiizertütsch* rock scene is Berne. The folk singer Mani Matter (1936–72) is considered the first influential musician to perform in Swiss German. After a fatal car accident he became somewhat of a legend for future generations, notably the singer Polo Hofer with his group Rumpelstilz in the 1970s. From the 1980s onwards Züri West became the most popular group singing in Swiss-German until the 1990s, when Patent Ochsner (also from Berne) and performers such as Gölä (Berne) and Sina (from the Canton Valais) were able to capture a wide, predominantly young audience with fresh and contemporary songs. None of these singers was ever involved in the ESC.

1988 "Sentiments" (Feelings) finished second behind Céline Dion's winning song. Interestingly, no one has tried to compete with a song in Romansch before or after.[6]

Even though Switzerland has so far entered ten Italian-language songs in the ESC, hardly any of these were successful. Oddly enough, the only ones which were relatively well received were performed by Swiss-German artists: "Io senza te" (Me without you, 1981) by Peter, Sue & Marc came in fourth place, and ten years later "Canzone per te" (A song for you) by Sandra Simó came in fifth.[7] Only two Swiss-Italian singers have represented Switzerland at the ESC, Anita Traversi and Barbara Bertà. Traversi participated in the Swiss national preliminaries seven times between 1956 and 1976, and made it into the ESC twice, singing "Cielo e terra" (Heaven and earth) in 1960 and "I miei pensieri" (My thoughts) in 1964. However, neither *canzone* was very successful: "Cielo e terra" ranked eighth, and "I miei pensieri" came in 13th place with zero points. Berta's "Dentro di me" (Inside of me) in 1997 fared no better, coming in 22nd place. Why did the Swiss-Italians not succeed?

The answer may have to do with Swiss *canzone* singers seeking inspiration from Italy, and Italy's complicated relationship with the ESC. The ESC is clearly secondary for the Italian record industry, RAI (Italian state television network), and consequently Italian audiences; the San Remo Festival, founded in 1951, represents for the Italian music business and fans a far more important song contest. The only link between the ESC and San Remo is that the winner of San Remo is given the opportunity to represent Italy at the ESC. If the winner declines the offer, RAI turns to the artist who finished in second place, and if this performer turns down the opportunity, then they ask the third-place contestant.

Accordingly, San Remo winners represented Italy in the ESC from 1956 to 1966 and again in 1972 and 1997, but Italy only won the contest twice: in 1964 with Gigliola Cinquetti singing "Non ho l'età" (I'm not of age), and in 1990 with Totò Cotugno singing "Insieme: 1992" (All together: 1992). Despite a respectable fourth-place finish with "Fiumi di parole" (Rivers of words) in 1997, Italy ceased to participate thereafter when RAI decided it was not viable to broadcast the ESC. Indeed, the average television audience for the San Remo festival is around fifteen million viewers, while in 1991, the year Eurovision was held in Italy, only three million people watched the ESC (perhaps because it was not broadcast live, but at two or three o'clock in the morning). Today the ESC is virtually unknown in Italy, and the San Remo Festival remains the only annual contest for young artists.[8]

Not surprisingly, Swiss-Italian singers consider the San Remo Festival a role model, but they cannot participate since the rules require Italian citizenship. Gianni

6   In other countries performers who sang in marginal languages were similarly unsuccessful. The 1999 French national preliminary included a song in Breton ("Les droits de l'âme," The rights of the soul, by Alex), one in French and Hebrew ("Go Ahead," by Anath), one in Basque ("Irradaka," Resentment, by Kukumiku), and one in Arabic ("Ihtidael," Equinox, by Israhn). None of these songs did particularly well, though "Les droits de l'âme" finished fourth.

7   Another Swiss-German singer performing in Italian, Jane Bogaert, finished in 20th place with "La vita cos'è" (What is life?) in 2000.

8   Information about the ESC and San Remo festival was kindly provided by Matteo Aldrovandi, president of the Italian OGAE-Fan Club.

Mascolo, who represented Switzerland at the ESC in 1968 with "Guardando il sole" (Looking into the sun), was an Italian citizen and therefore able to participate at San Remo in 1965 together with Dusty Springfield. Their song "Di fronte all'amore" (In front of love) was among the finalists but did not win.[9] Paolo Meneguzzi, who was born in Lugano, Switzerland, but also has an Italian passport, participated three times at San Remo. His 2004 entry "Guardami negli occhi" (Look into my eyes) was the best-selling CD single in Italy in that year. Since his success in Italy is so high, he is unlikely to represent Switzerland in the ESC.[10]

Most of all, Switzerland's multicultural make-up, its "fragile identity," manifests itself in the ESC contributions by the popular trio Peter, Sue & Marc. Their four entries were in four different languages: "Les illusions de nos vingt ans" (The illusions of our youth, 1971) in French, "Djambo, Djambo" (1976) in English, "Trödler & Co." (Junk dealer & Co., 1979) in German, and "Io senza te" (1981) in Italian. Peter, Sue & Marc embody the Swiss dilemma, the integration of three distinct European cultural regions—German, French, and Italian—in one country, and they also serve as a metaphor for the representation of Switzerland at the ESC: a cultural chameleon.[11]

The French connection

French, the second most widely spoken language in Switzerland, is the preferred language of Swiss ESC entries; with songs in French Switzerland won the contest twice, came in second twice, third three times and fourth twice. The French *chanson* is an internationally recognized and beloved genre, and France, Monaco, Luxembourg, and Belgium have been regularly performing in French at the ESC, so juries and audiences have had frequent exposure to French *chansons*. No wonder Swiss artists have looked to the thriving French music industry for inspiration.

For the first ten years Switzerland's French-language ESC entries were modeled after the postwar *chanson* in the style of Edith Piaf and other French singers. "Refrain," the winning song of the very first contest in 1956 (held in Lugano, providing something of a "home-team advantage" for Switzerland), was written by composer Géo Voumard and lyricist Emile Gardaz; it was not performed by a native French speaker, but by the Swiss-German Lys Assia.[12] After their initial success

---

9   Another Swiss-Italian singer with an Italian passport, Marisa Frigerio, also participated at San Remo (in 1975) with the song "Dolce abitudine" (Sweet habits). However, her four attempts between 1974 and 1978 to represent Switzerland in the ESC did not succeed.

10   It has happened that famous San Remo stars would participate in the Swiss national preliminary for a chance to sing in the ESC: Mina competed in 1969 with "Dai, dai, domain" (Come on, tomorrow) and "Non crederei" (I would not believe it), and Rita Pavone in 1979 with "Dieci cuori" (Ten hearts).

11   Consider as well the interlocking identities evident in some contestants' names: Véronique Müller and Jean-Jacques Egli have a French first name and German surname.

12   Lys Assia participated with four songs in three consecutive contests: in 1956 with "Refrain" and "Das alte Karussel" (The old carousel), in 1957 with "L'enfant que j'étais" (The child that I was), and in 1958 with "Giorgio." At that time Assia (her real name is

Voumard, Gardaz, and Assia teamed up again for the following year's contest with the song "L'enfant que j'etais" (The child that I was), but it finished only eighth out of ten entries. For the next three years Voumard and Gardaz continued to compose *chansons* for Switzerland's ESC entries: in 1961 "Nous aurons demain" (Tomorrow we'll have), sung by Franca di Rienzo, took third place, while the following year a male singer, Jean Philippe, ranked only tenth with "Le retour" (The return). In 1963 Voumard and Gardaz had their final success when "T'en vas pas" (Don't leave), sung by Esther Ofarim, finished second, only two points behind the winning Danish song. The song's accompaniment with eighth-note triplets was a characteristic feature in many popular songs of the late 1950s and early 1960s, as in many of Piaf's *chansons*.

Esther Ofarim, who was born in Safed, Israel, was the first of a number of non-native Swiss singers performing for Switzerland. With her husband, Abi Ofarim, she had won the Tel Aviv song contest in 1961, then gained recognition in Germany and elsewhere in Europe. The Greek singer Yovanna represented Switzerland in 1965 and took eighth place with another *chanson*, "Non, à jamais sans toi" (No, forever without you), which strongly recalls Piaf's "Non, je ne regrette rien" and many of Gilbert Bécaud's early songs.

In the mid-1960s came a transition away from the postwar *chanson* tradition towards more contemporary musical styles from further abroad. In 1966 Madeleine Pascal finished in sixth place with "Ne vois-tu pas?" (Don't you see?), and her voice recalls the new French *chanson* stars of the 1960s, notably Françoise Hardy and Marie Laforêt. The simple but memorable melody was again accompanied by an eighth-note triplet figure, but now a rock beat indicates the influence of the British beat movement. Similarly, Switzerland's 1967 entry "Quel coeur vas-tu briser?" (Whose heart will you break?) is an upbeat rock number that has a similar rhythmic structure to some Beatles songs of the period, notably "Penny Lane" and "All You Need Is Love," as well as a trumpet interlude that recalls the widely popular style of Herb Alpert—but the song finished last, with zero points. Three years later, another *chanson* entry was "Retour" (Return), written and performed by Henri Dès (one of the few male performers for Switzerland). This song, which finished fourth, situates itself somewhere between "Ob-la-di, ob-la-da" by the Beatles and a *chanson* by Joe Dassin, who was also very popular at the time.

American folk music and war protest songs were also contemporary influences on Swiss ESC entries of the time. In 1971 Peter, Sue & Marc made their first appearance with "Les illusions de nos vingt ans," a "flower power" song with the message that "you, who have lived your lives, who have had your dreams, let us now have our dreams and live our lives." Though sung in French, it is clearly not a French *chanson*,

---

Rosa Mina Schärer) was already known to a wider German audience, as in 1951 she gained substantial success with Paul Burkhard's song "O mein Papa" from the 1939 musical comedy *Der Schwarze Hecht* (revived in 1950 as *Das Feuerwerk*). Assia not only competed for Switzerland, but also in the German national preliminary in 1956. In Germany she entered with the song "Ein kleiner goldner Ring" (A little golden ring); in Switzerland, together with the two above-mentioned songs, she entered "Sei doch nicht so eifersüchtig" (Don't be so jealous), "Le bohémian," and "Addio bella Napoli" (Goodbye, beautiful Naples).

recalling instead the music of Bob Dylan and Joan Baez. In the style of their role model—Peter, Paul & Mary—the trio sings in three-part harmony, and a guitar and tambourine underline the folk character. Of Peter, Sue & Marc's four appearances in the ESC, this song was their least successful one, coming in twelfth, but it did jump-start their very successful career in Switzerland and Germany (with fifteen LPs and total sales of one million records) as well as Canada (with the anti-whaling song "Moby Dick"). The following year, in 1972, Véronique Müller represented Switzerland with another folk-style song, "C'est la chanson de mon amour" (It's the song of my love), performing it with a very "natural," unpretentious voice, and occasionally embellishing the melody in the manner of a country singer. "C'est la chanson de mon amour" ranked eighth that year, outdistanced by another more traditional French *chanson*, "Après toi" (After you), performed by Vicky Leandros for Luxembourg.

With "Vivre" (To live), sung by Carole Vinci in 1978, a decade began in which Switzerland gradually advanced towards winning the ESC solely with French *chansons*: "Vivre" took ninth place; "Cinéma" (1980), fourth place; "Amour, on t'aime" (Love, we love you, 1982), third place; "Pas pour moi" (Not for me, 1986), second place; "Ne partez pas sans moi" (Don't leave without me, 1988), first place. "Cinéma," for example, was a collaboration by experienced ESC artists: Peter Reber (of Peter, Sue & Marc) composed the music, Véronique Müller wrote the lyrics, and Paola (who had sung "Bonjour, bonjour" for Switzerland in 1969) performed. The song includes a reference to Charlie Chaplin, who had died a year before in Vevey, Switzerland. The verse and chorus have almost an identical melodic and harmonic structure, which results in a continual repetition of the same musical material. Reber also used this compositional technique in "Io senza te," the 1981 entry sung by Peter, Sue & Marc, and the formula worked twice—both songs finished in fourth place.

Switzerland's "magic formula" for ESC success in the 1980s can be credited to composer Atilla Şereftuğ and lyricist Nella Martinetti. The Turkish-born Şereftuğ was briefly a member of the Pepe Lienhard Band. The Swiss-Italian Martinetti had a successful career in Switzerland as an entertainer, singer, and songwriter. With her song "Bella musica" (Beautiful music) in 1986 she won the first Grand Prix der Volksmusik (Grand Prize for Folk Music), an immensely popular song contest in Germany, Switzerland, and Austria primarily for "Alpine country music." Martinetti had collaborated with Peter Reber on "Io senza te" (Peter, Sue & Marc) for the 1981 ESC, and wrote the lyrics for "Io così non ci sto" (I don't like it this way) in 1983. However, her two songs written together with Şereftuğ proved to be outstanding successes: "Pas pour moi," performed by the Italian-born Daniela Simons, finished second in 1986,[13] and "Ne partez pas sans moi," performed by the Québécoise Céline Dion, came in first in 1988. The latter song, of course, has become one of the most popular ESC favorites of all time, and next to the Swedish group ABBA Dion

---

13 1986 was the year of the French *chanson* performed by female singers in the ESC. In addition to "Pas pour moi," the top three songs that year were "J'aime la vie" (I love life) performed by Sandra Kim, who won the contest for Belgium, and "L'amour de ma vie" (The love of my life) performed by Sherisse Laurence, who sang for Luxembourg and finished third.

has remained practically the only ESC performer to launch a sustained international career.

Both of these successful love ballads—"Pas pour moi" and "Ne partez pas sans moi"—feature similar musical "hooks," a fanfare-like opening on the upbeat of the anthemic chorus, and the frequent use of suspensions and appoggiaturas in the chorus melody. In "Pas pour moi" the verses and chorus contrast each other musically and textually. In the verses the singer describes the kinds of affairs she wants to avoid ("easy dates" and "tricks," "the follies that one regrets later in life") with a low and rapid, almost spoken delivery, while the chorus, with its soaring *cantabile* melody, reveals her wish not for "a one-night stand" but for "love, the way it used to be, [and] tender feelings" (Example 4.1). "Ne partez pas sans moi" features an even more triumphant chorus, also signalled by a fanfare-like upbeat figure echoed later by the synthesizer (Example 4.2).

Example 4.1

Example 4.2

Switzerland's high scores in 1986 and 1988 prompted some imitation in subsequent years. Sereftug's fanfare-like opening on the upbeat of the chorus and liberal use of suspensions and appoggiaturas were also employed in "Canzone per te" (A song for you), Switzerland's 1991 entry by Swiss-Italian composer Renato Mascetti (Example 4.3). It seems more than a coincidence that some of Martinetti's lyrics ("Take me far away from here," followed by the chorus "Don't leave without me") are also echoed in Mascetti's song ("Take me away with you, don't ever

Example 4.3

leave me"). "Canzone per te" finished in fifth place. In 1993 Switzerland made a further attempt to repeat Céline Dion's success, not by re-employing the winning compositional formula but by "importing" another Canadian singer with a similar voice, Annie Cotton. Her *chanson*, "Moi, tout simplement" (Quite simply myself), finished in third place, but this was the last time Switzerland was successful in the ESC with a French love ballad. "Mon cœur l'aime" (My heart loves him, 1996) and "Dans le jardin de mon âme (In the garden of my soul, 2002) both proved to be disastrous entries, ending in 16th and 22nd place respectively.

After the *chanson*

Switzerland's low scores in the ESC during the second half of the 1990s and early 2000s could be credited to uninspired songs or weak performers,[14] but more likely indicate something about the rapidly growing constellation of ESC participants and the changing tastes of a predominantly younger audience. The long-time dominance of the French *chanson* in Eurovision dwindled after the 1980s.[15] "Ethnic pop" became increasingly trendy, and newer East European countries could exploit their rich musical heritage for their ESC contributions. Compared to the rhythmically complex and melodically compelling sounds of these "exotic" folk styles, Swiss folkloristic emblems such as the alphorn and yodel were decidedly unfashionable.

For these reasons Swiss television networks (SF DRS, TSR, and TSI) began looking eastward instead of continuing to promote "home-grown" artists. They chose not to organize a Swiss national preliminary in 2005, but instead decided to send the Estonian girl-group Vanilla Ninja to the competition held in Kiev. (In its short ESC history, Estonia has been extremely successful, finishing first in 2001, third in 2002, fourth in 2000, and fifth in 1996.) The Swiss strategy was partly successful: Vanilla Ninja competed with the catchy English-language song "Cool Vibes" and finished in a respectable eighth place. Not surprisingly, the Estonian jury gave the Swiss entry twelve points, just as Latvia gave twelve points and Lithuania gave eight.

Vanilla Ninja continued a tradition of non-Swiss artists representing Switzerland at the ESC, beginning with the German Christa Williams in 1959, the Israeli Esther Ofarim, the Greek Yovanna, the Italian-born Gianni Mascolo and Daniela

---

14   After Annie Cotton, Duilio finished 19th with "Sto pregando" (I am praying) in 1994, Kathy Leander 16th with "Mon cœur l'aime" (My heart loves him) in 1996, Barbara Bertà 22nd with "Dentro di me" (Inside Me) in 1997, Gunvor 22nd (last place) with "Laß ihn" (Let him) in 1998, Jane Bogaert 20th with "La vita cos'è" (What is life?) in 2000, and Francine Jordi 22nd with "Dans le jardin de mon âme" (In the garden of my soul) in 2002. Piero Esteriore and The MusicStars failed to qualify for the 2004 ESC when their song, "Celebrate," ranked 36th.

15   Between 1956 and 1983, there was a French song among the top four scores every year except 1974, then during the 1980s a little less frequently. After 1993 there were only two French *chansons* among the top four scores, in 1995 (France, 4th place) and 2001 (France, 4th place). It is interesting to note that the most successful singers of *chansons* in the ESC were women, among them 11 contest winners between 1956 and 1988; only two men won first place with French songs (in 1958 and 1961).

Simons, the Austrian Egon Egemann, and the French-Canadians Céline Dion and Annie Cotton. What started more or less unintentionally in the 1960s has become a deliberate strategy. For the 2006 contest held in Athens, Swiss ESC organizers managed to round up six artists from six different countries: the group "six4one" consisted of the promising Israeli singer Liel Collet, Andreas Lundstedt from the Swedish band Alcazar, Tinka Milinovic from Bosnia-Herzegovina, Keith Camilleri from Malta, Marco Matias from Portugal, and Claudia D'Addio, born in Zurich to Italian parents. The hope was that their song, written by the extremely experienced German composer Ralph Siegel and lyricist Bernd Meinunger, would impress the jury of the six countries from which the six singers of the group originated. Unfortunately for Switzerland, however, this particular gambit failed: only Malta gave the song much support.

Perhaps "six4one" did contribute to the weakening of Swiss national identity in the ESC even more than in earlier years when a Persian trumpeter played the alphorn or a Turkish-born composer and Swiss-Italian lyricist wrote a French love ballad performed by an Italian-born singer. The phenomenon continued in 2007, when the highly popular and experienced "Eurodance"-producer DJ Bobo (René Baumann) was selected from 200 applicants to perform in Helsinki. His emphasis on finally representing Switzerland as a "real" Swiss seems misleading, since he was born to an Italian father and his song "Vampires are Alive" is sung in English with a video that strongly recalls Michael Jackson's "Thriller" (1983). Switzerland as a united country representing its national identity in the ESC is ultimately a myth, for it appears much more like a multicultural conglomerate, a microcosm of the ESC itself.

Chapter 5

Chasing the "magic formula" for success: Ralph Siegel and the Grand Prix Eurovision de la Chanson

Thorsten Hindrichs

From the very first Eurovision Song Contest (ESC) in 1956, German composers have contributed songs rooted in a genre called *Schlager* (literally, "hits"), a type of popular song composition mainly determined by strategies for commercial success. These songs typically have catchy melodies and a predictable musical structure.[1] The themes and topics of *Schlager* lyrics rely heavily on everyday experiences of the largest possible segment of buyers of records and, in earlier decades, of sheet music. Because of their compositional accessibility and the primary goal of achieving economic success, *Schlager* songs (and their composers, singers and fans, as well) have had to deal with numerous prejudices and complaints.

One of the most common assumptions about *Schlager* songs is that they follow simple musical and lyrical formulas and are rather a phenomenon of *Gebrauchsmusik* (that is, "useful" or "utility" music) than a matter of "true art."[2] From a musical point of view the observation of simplicity seems accurate, but overlooks the challenges of composing in such a manner. Since a *Schlager* song is usually meant to become a chart hit, it has to appeal to as large an audience as possible; any unusual or complicated musical style could possibly curtail a song's success. Furthermore, attempting to compose a hit inevitably means imitating and varying older songs which already have enjoyed a certain popular success, so the main challenge is how to imitate a hit song without prompting the claim of sheer plagiarism.[3]

Since Eurovision composers intend to reach a target group extending far beyond German-speaking audiences, the challenges become even more complicated on a broader European level. Any successful contest performance must appeal to as many

I would like to thank Daniel P. Balestrini, Horst Dewald, Jan Feddersen, Albert Möller, Anno Mungen, and Ivan Raykoff for their help and suggestions.

1 Peter Wicke, "Schlager," in *Die Musik in Geschichte und Gegenwart: Allgemeine Enzyklopädie der Musik*, ed. Ludwig Finscher, 2nd ed. (Kassel: Bärenreiter, Metzler, 1998), vol. 8, col. 1064–5.

2   See Reimund Hess, "Die musikalischen Merkmale," in *Schlager in Deutschland*, ed. Siegmund Helms (Wiesbaden: Breitkopf & Härtel, 1972), pp. 41–64.

3   See Werner Mezger, *Schlager: Versuch einer Gesamtdarstellung unter besonderer Berücksichtigung des bundesdeutschen Musikmarktes* (Tübingen: Tübinger Vereinigung für Volkskunde, 1975), pp. 283–4.

European listeners as possible, which means that it has to cross certain national and cultural borders, whether by means of language, musical taste, visual appearance or zeitgeist – that is, "the spirit of the times": references to contemporary events, trends, opinions, and cultural concerns. The German composer Ralph Siegel (b. 1945), a significant contributor to the ESC for many years, has taken on this challenge of translating a song's meanings into a pan-European language through musical/aural and visual codes meant to be understood by audiences all over Europe.

This chapter takes a closer look at Siegel's strategies for composing his Eurovision contributions over the past three decades. Since Siegel's songs work on more levels of meaning than exclusively musical ones, this chapter considers how meaning can be conveyed through a synthesis of musical/aural, textual, and visual elements closely tied to contemporary musical tastes and the prevailing zeitgeist. Siegel once described this tactic of composing as his "great formula" for success,[4] and this chapter examines if, when, and why this formula really proved successful.

Table 5.1   Ralph Siegel's compositions for the Eurovision Song Contest, 1974–2003

Year	Title	Performer(s)	Lyricist	Nation, Rank
1974	Bye Bye, I Love You	Ireen Sheer	Michael Kunze	Luxembourg, 4th
1976	Sing Sang Song	Les Humphries Singers	Kurt Hertha	Germany, 15th
1979	Dschinghis Khan	Dschinghis Khan	Bernd Meinunger	Germany, 4th
1980	Theater	Katja Ebstein	Bernd Meinunger	Germany, 2nd
1980	Le papa pingouin	Sophie & Magaly Meinunger	Pierre Delanoë, Jean-Paul Cara	Luxembourg, 9th
1981	Johnny Blue	Lena Valaitis	Bernd Meinunger	Germany, 2nd
1982	Ein bißchen Frieden	Nicole	Bernd Meinunger	Germany, 1st
1985	Children, Kinder, enfants	Ireen Sheer, Margo, Malcolm & Chris Roberts, Franck Olivier, Diane Solomon	Bernd Meinunger, Jean-Michel Bériat	Luxembourg, 13th

---

4   Chris Melville, "eurosong.net talks to Ralph Siegel" <www.eurosong.net/reports/ralph.htm> Accessed 28 October 2004.

1987	Laß die Sonne in dein Herz	Wind	Bernd Meinunger	Germany, 2nd
1988	Lied für einen Freund	Maxi & Chris Garden	Bernd Meinunger	Germany, 14th
1990	Frei zu leben	Chris Kempers & Daniel Kovac	Michael Kunze	Germany, 9th
1992	Träume sind für alle da	Wind	Bernd Meinunger	Germany, 16th
1994	Wir geben 'ne Party	MeKaDo	Bernd Meinunger	Germany, 3rd
1997	Zeit	Bianca Shomburg	Bernd Meinunger	Germany, 18th
1999	Reise nach Jerusalem	Sürpriz	Bernd Meinunger, Deniz Filizmen, Cihan Özden	Germany, 3rd
2002	I Can't Live Without Music	Corinna May	Bernd Meinunger	Germany, 21st
2003	Let's Get Happy	Lou	Bernd Meinunger	Germany, 12th

Since first participating in 1974 with "Bye Bye, I Love You," Ralph Siegel has contributed 17 songs to the ESC, more titles than any other composer. During this time his *Schlager* songs have reached almost every position in the competition – from his greatest triumph in 1982, when Nicole's "Ein bißchen Frieden" (A little peace) went to number one, to his "personal Waterloo" in 2002, when Corinna May's "I Can't Live Without Music" finished in 21st place (see Table 1). Upon surveying Siegel's ESC record, the following four periods can be distinguished:

1. the "early years," when he made his first contributions in 1974 and 1976;
2. the "golden age" from 1979 to 1982, when Dschinghis Khan, Katja Ebstein, Lena Valaitis and Nicole successively achieved fourth, third, second, and first place, with Siegel contributing two different songs in the 1980 contest;
3. a comeback with five contributions between 1987 and 1994 (highlighted by a third place for MeKaDo in 1994); and
4. Siegel's attempts to deal with the challenge presented by "comic" participants such as Guildo Horn and Stefan Raab since 1998.

The son of operetta singer Ingeborg Döderlein and the highly successful *Schlager* composer Ralph Maria Siegel, Siegel was raised in a European musical culture of the 1950s and 60s that was influenced mainly by rock 'n' roll, blues, and jazz. His teenage efforts at composition attempted to establish a certain distance from the enormously popular songs his father composed ("Caprifischer," "Ich hab' noch einen Koffer in Berlin," and many more), and he "tried to prove to his father that 'with jazz and better music' one could earn money as well."[5] But still, when he took over his father's music publishing firm in the late 1960s, Siegel came to realize that the largest part of the firm's profit resulted from his father's song royalties rather than from his own more "pretentious" compositions. With his family's musical background in mind, and facing the economic needs of his own music business, Siegel helped to create a new *Schlager* sound that combined contemporary popular music and youth culture with the traditions he inherited from his father. By the early 1970s Siegel had become one of the leading German *Schlager* composers.

After 30 years of participating in the ESC, and despite having experienced (at least what he considered to be) more failures than successes, Siegel confessed, "I'm addicted to the Grand Prix. It's like a drug, to be honest. Month after month I work towards the competition, puzzling, brooding, revising."[6] Perhaps because of this mindset, Siegel's way of handling defeat has been characterized by complaining about any kind of unfavorable circumstances (be it an incompetent jury or a singer's weak performance) instead of taking the blame on himself.[7] Nevertheless, Siegel has kept trying to repeat the success of Nicole's victory in 1982: "I won't say the word 'never' again. I have said that a few times in the past few years, but I admit that I can not tell what the future will bring – if the situation and the feeling is right, and I have a song that I really want to enter with," he stated in an interview.[8] Apart from Siegel's personal conviction, his way of trying to plan an ESC success is quite remarkable: "Then in 1994, we came up with a great formula," he said, referring to MeKaDo's song in that year's contest in Dublin.[9] This choice of words suggests that Siegel might be considered as much a producer as a composer.[10]

What does this formula look like then, if it exists at all? For one thing, Siegel prefers simple melodic lines. Parts of his catchy melodies are built of broken triads, like the chorus of "Dschinghis Khan" (Example 5.1), or the same motif expanded by just one passing note in the chorus of "Johnny Blue" (Example 5.2; originally in F minor).

---

5   Jan Feddersen, "Ein Handwerker der Emotionen," in *L'Allemagne Deux Points: Ein Kniefall vor dem Grand Prix*, ed. Milena Fessmann, Kerstin Topp, and Wolfgang N. Kriegs (Berlin: Ullstein, 1998), p. 33. All translations in this chapter are by Daniel P. Balestrini.

6   Jan Feddersen, "Ein Gespräch mit Ralph Siegel," in *Ein Lied kann eine Brücke sein: Die deutsche und internationale Geschichte des Grand Prix Eurovision* (Hamburg: Hoffmann und Campe, 2002), p. 280.

7   Jan Feddersen, "Ein Handwerk der Emotionen," pp. 36–7.

8   Melville, "eurosong.net talks to Ralph Siegel."

9   Ibid.

10   Unfortunately the importance of the role of music producers still seems to be underestimated in scholarly discourses on popular music.

Example 5.1

Dschin,   Dschin,   Dschin - ghis Khan___

Example 5.2

Blue,   Blue   Blue, John - ny Blue___

Siegel's second method of building melodies uses sequences of short three- or four-note motives, as can be heard in the chorus of "Theater" (Example 5.3), as well as in "Ein bißchen Frieden" (Example 5.4).

Example 5.3

The - a-ter, The - a - ter, der Vor-hang geht auf,   dann wird die Büh-ne zur Welt!

Example 5.4

Ein bißchen Frie - den, ein bißchen Son - ne, für diese Er - de, auf der wir woh - nen.

In some cases Siegel combines both techniques – broken triads and sequencing – in one song; "Dschinghis Khan" provides an impressive example. The opening phrase of the chorus outlines an A minor triad, followed by a sequential three-note figure moving downward stepwise and repeated three times (Example 5.5).

Example 5.5

Dschin, Dschin,   Dschin-ghis Khan,___ he Rei-ter, ho Rei-ter, he Rei-ter, im-mer wei-ter

Similarly, the verses consist of two rather short linear phrases, each repeated once. The first phrase is built of paired repetitions of single notes leading five steps down. The second phrase is a little more complicated since it consists of two descending broken triads, each embellished by a repeated passing note (Example 5.6).

Example 5.6

Sie rit–ten um die Wet–te mit dem Step–pen - wind, _____ tau - send Mann, _____ die
und ei - ner ritt vor - an, dem folg–ten al - le blind, _____ Dschin–ghis Khan, _____

Hu–fe ih–rer Pfer–de, die peit–schen dem Sand, _____ sie tru–gen Angst und Schre–cken in je–des Land _____

Siegel's tunes are easy to sing and, most importantly, they are easy to remember. This is even more the case when he establishes additional "sing-along" melodies that accompany the main melody of the chorus, as in the last part of "Ein bißchen Frieden" with the line that translates "Sing my little song along with me" (Example 5.7).

Example 5.7

Sing mit mir mein klei - nes Lied
Ein bißchen Frie - den, ein bißchen Son - ne, für die–se Er - de, auf der wir woh - nen

Siegel's compositional technique refers to the very basic ways of creating melodies that remind one of the musical structure of children's songs. Certainly a highlight of simplicity is the chorus of "A Miracle of Love" (performed by Marco Matias and Nicole Süßmilch), Siegel's contribution to Germany's national preliminary competition in 2005. Here the melody consists of a simple D major scale leading downwards from an octave leap on A (Example 5.8).

Example 5.8

All we need is a mi - ra - cle of love

The harmonic structure of Siegel's songs is simple, rarely comprising more than the three basic chords of a full harmonic cadence. Surprising or uncommon harmonic shifts are missing completely, but the common modulation of a whole step upwards, right before the last chorus, can be found in "Johnny Blue" and "Ein bißchen Frieden." The form of his songs is generally strophic. While such melodic, harmonic, and formal elements represent rather conventional qualities of German *Schlager* songs in general, Siegel reduces them more frequently to the very basics than most other established composers.[11]

---

11 It is surprising that Siegel has had so little impact on other German *Schlager* composers; one of the rare examples that reveals a quite similar way of composing with sequences of short motives and broken triads is Michael Reinecke's "Aufrecht geh'n" (Walking upright), performed by Mary Roos in the 1984 ESC.

It is in two other realms that Siegel's productions stand out in comparison to other *Schlager* songs: their aural and visual performance. At least since Albin J. Zak's *The Poetics of Rock*, "sound" must be seen as a category of its own in popular music.[12] In his songs Siegel works with this category of sound in two different ways. One way is to adapt the sound and rhythm of contemporary pop music. The Les Humphries Singers' "Sing Sang Song" (1976) clearly refers to a clichéd "flower power" sound as heard in the 1968 musical *Hair*, for example, and Dschinghis Khan undoubtedly takes over the disco sound of the late 1970s. MeKaDo's "Wir geben 'ne Party" (We're having a party, 1994) uses the synthetic techno sound of the early 1990s with a bumping bass,[13] recalling the songs of DJ Bobo as well as rap elements, while Sürpriz's "Reise nach Jerusalem/Kudüs'e seyahat" (Journey to Jerusalem) copies the ethno-pop sound that became extraordinarily popular in Germany when the Turkish superstar Tarkan hit the European charts in 1999 with his song "Simarik."

Siegel also uses particular aspects of sound to support the message of a specific song. "Theater" (1980), for example, is accompanied by a cabaret-like upright piano and orchestra, recalling Liza Minelli's rendition of "Cabaret" in the 1972 film version of the Broadway musical. Nicole sings "Ein bißchen Frieden" accompanying herself on an acoustic guitar, creating the image that she is just like any other sincere and innocent teenage girl sitting in her bedroom worrying about "the bomb." The blue mood of "Johnny Blue" arises especially because Lena Valaitis sings it with a warm and mellow timbre while she is accompanied by a blues harmonica.

Valaitis's clothing underlined the song's blue mood as well, since the dress she wore onstage at the ESC was colored black and blue. Siegel seems to be one of the first *Schlager* composers to understand the importance of the visual element in a contest disseminated via television. Furthermore, with the integration of this visual element into his "magic formula," Siegel's role as producer is not limited only to the arrangement of the music alone. He is known to plan and control all aspects of a song's performance – the choice of the appropriate singer, the creation of the relevant image, the clothing, the choreography, and the performance itself. The visual appearance and performance spectacle of Dschinghis Khan is of particular interest here because it was the first band in the history of pop music to have been cast *after* its song had been worked out by the composer in advance: "the original idea was [to compose a song] for the Grand Prix where people have to perform on an international stage, and there's a jury, and they don't understand what the song's about ... so we thought: let's present a song not only with aural but with visual elements, too," Siegel explained in an interview.[14]

At this point it is useful to consider Andrew Goodwin's remarks on a "musicology of the image," and to examine the song "Dschinghis Khan" with regard to two of

---

12 Albin J. Zak, *The Poetics of Rock: Cutting Tracks, Making Records* (Berkeley: University of California Press, 2001).

13 Rhythm can be regarded as a subcategory of "sound" here, which is why it is missing in the preceding remarks on the musical structure of Siegel's songs.

14 Christian Stöffler, *Wer weiß, wohin der Weg mich führt* (Hamburg: NDR TV, 1997).

Goodwin's five "sources for the iconographies stored in popular cultural memory."[15] One of these categories Goodwin defines as "visual signifiers deriving from national-popular iconography, perhaps related to geographical associations prompted by the performers." This is what Siegel probably intended when he dressed up the members of Dschinghis Khan with exotic costumes and had them dance in quite a martial way that alludes to something like a Cossack sabre dance— though this kind of "national-popular iconography" is rather what Siegel believed Mongol warriors might have looked like, not prompted by actual historical evidence.

The driving rhythm of "Dschinghis Khan" and the warlike "hoo, ha" calls of the singers during the introduction and the short bridges between verse and chorus help to create what Goodwin calls "images associated purely with the music itself" that are "already present in the music itself."[16] Goodwin distinguishes symbolic, iconic, and indexical relations between signifiers and signifieds that generate what he calls the "inner speech of musical-visual associations,"[17] following a linguistic concept of Valentin Nikolaevič Vološinov.[18] The driving rhythm of "Dschinghis Khan" might be read as a symbol for a martial habitus, whereas the short fill-ins from the violins, which sound like a whip-lash, can be read as iconic signs for a furious cavalry charge, and the short breaks of the tom-toms, heard in the first verse, as signifying "die Hufe ihrer Pferde" ("their horses' hooves"). The "hoo, ha" shouts seem indexical signs of masculinity, just like the "ho-ho" and "ha-ha" laughter suggests a wild drinking session ("Let's get some more vodka, ha ha ha ha, for we're Mongol warriors, ho ho ho ho, and the Devil will catch us soon enough").

Conveying the meaning of the lyrics through supplementary aural and visual codes strengthens their impression for a German-speaking audience, but proves even more useful in the wider context of the ESC, where one must cross the borders of foreign languages to gain European-wide reception and success. This translation of meaning becomes an essential part of Siegel's formula for composing ESC songs.

---

15   Goodwin's five categories of iconographic sources are 1) "personal imagery deriving from the individual memories associated with the song," 2) "images associated purely with the music itself," 3) "images of the musicians/performers," 4) "visual signifiers deriving from national-popular iconography," and 5) "popular cultural signs associated with rock music." Central to the understanding of a "musicology of the image" is the idea that "these levels of iconography are *already* present in the music itself," thus the aural and visual together facilitate our understanding of a pop song's meaning. Andrew Goodwin, *Dancing in the Distraction Factory: Music Television and Popular Culture* (Minneapolis: University of Minnesota, 1992), p. 56.

16   Ibid.

17   Ibid., pp. 58–9. Following Goodwin, a symbolic relationship exists where a musical convention has been established; for example, certain half-tone scales might symbolize "exotic otherness." Iconic signs work through resemblance: for example, the sounds of an electric guitar might resemble a machine gun (as in Jimi Hendrix's "Machine Gun"). Indexical relations create a causal link between what is seen/heard and what is concluded from this observation: for example, where there is "scratching" there must be a DJ with turntables.

18   Valentin Nikolaevič Vološinov, *Marxism and the Philosophy of Language*, trans. Ladislav Matejka and I.R. Titunik (New York: Seminar Press, 1973), pp. 115–23, especially p. 118.

The synthesis of music, sound, and visuality that provokes the "inner speech of musical-visual associations" is surely the most important part of Siegel's concept of composing a successful ESC song, as in the cabaret-like "Theater," the motherly timbre of Lena Valaitis singing "Johnny Blue," and Lou's cheery image in "Let's Get Happy." Indeed, Siegel seems to be the first German *Schlager* composer to understand the importance of a well-balanced relation between performer, image, song, sound, visual appearance, and the spatial arrangement of setting in order to create the ideal *mise-en-scène* for the performance.

This integration of visual imagery applies not only to the meaning of a song's lyrics, but to higher levels of association as well. Generally Siegel seems to prefer white clothes for the singers and groups he produces, perhaps in order to symbolize a certain innocence or sincerity or to give the audiences a neutral projection surface for their own interpretations.[19] The rather kitschy arrangement of Bianca Shomburg's "Zeit" (Time) in the 1997 ESC might have been Siegel's attempt to remind the audience of another grand dame of Eurovision, Céline Dion, who had won the contest in 1988 for Switzerland and reached worldwide fame; her biggest success was recording the title song of the movie *Titanic*, which was released that same year. During her appearance at the contest Shomburg wore a black suit and a white blouse with big ruches, an outfit very similar to Dion's outfit in the 1988 contest. Since Shomburg had won the *Sound-Mix-Show* on German television some months earlier with Céline Dion's song "Think Twice," this connection can hardly be coincidental.

In addition to his synthesis of musical and visual signs, Siegel's formula also involves choosing the subjects for his songs from what he believes to be the contemporary zeitgeist. "Dschinghis Khan," for example, reflects a kind of adventurous exoticism in vogue in Germany during the late 1970s (for example, the television series *Sandokan*, about an Indonesian freedom-fighter, gained enormous popularity in early 1979).[20] In "Johnny Blue" the song's protagonist plays harmonica just like Bernd Clüver's protagonist in the then-still popular *Schlager* song "Der Junge mit der Mundharmonika" (The boy with the harmonica) – but besides that reference Johnny is blind, a detail that relates the song to the 1970s disability rights movement and society's growing awareness of handicapped people. Nicole's victory in 1982 reflected the contemporary political atmosphere in Europe, where "Ein bißchen Frieden" moved an audience that shared her fear of nuclear war during the early 1980s.[21]

Siegel's most remarkable attempt at capturing the zeitgeist was his original concept for the song "Zeit." Although Bianca Shomburg sang this song in the

---

19   Katja Ebstein (1980), Nicole (1982), Wind (1987), Sürpriz (1999), and Lou (2003) wore almost all white clothes; although Maxi and Chris Garden wore black suits in 1988, they still played a white grand piano.

20   Germans' predilection for "exotic" countries (mainly eastern and southeastern Asia, and a rather unspecified concept of the South Seas) in the late 1970s was motivated rather by a fictional fascination with the foreign Other than by reasons of cultural and/or political rapprochement.

21   See André Port le roi, *Schlager lügen nicht: Deutsche Schlager und Politik in ihrer Zeit* (Essen: Klartext, 1998), pp. 203–209.

competition, he had initially hoped Esther Ofarim would perform it.[22] Thus not only the Klezmer-like arrangement of the song, but also the plan to have a Jewish singer represent Germany in the ESC certainly highlights his quest for a winning formula[23] that failed only because Ofarim's management demanded a fee that obviously reached far beyond Siegel's usual limit.[24] This was a period of heated debates in Germany on racism, anti-Semitism, the Holocaust and political relations with Israel, prompted, for example, by the return to Germany of many Jewish *Russlanddeutsche* (Russian Germans) after the collapse of the Soviet Union, the infamous arson attacks on refugees and immigrants in Hoyerswerda and Mölln in the early 1990s, and the charged discussions around the building of a Holocaust memorial in Berlin.

Whereas the songs of Siegel's "golden years" in the 1980s were able to catch certain aspects of contemporary life, his later attempts with the zeitgeist formula were less successful. After 1989 the ESC was broadened by cultural and geographical means, which is why at the turn of the millennium the role of "local" fashions and tastes differed much more than some 20 years before. Admittedly, the appealing Orientalism of Sürpriz' "Reise nach Jerusalem/Kudüs'e seyahat" reached third place in the 1999 contest held in Israel, which might also be due to Siegel's clever strategy of showing a certain solidarity with Turkish immigrants in Germany whose relatives back in Turkey had the chance to vote for Germany. Corinna May's performance in the 2002 contest recalled the subject of blindness already used in "Johnny Blue" in 1981, but the sympathy factor was completely out of fashion in 2002. Lou's "Let's Get Happy" in 2003 might have been Siegel's answer to comic *Schlager* songs like Guildo Horn's "Guildo hat euch lieb" (Guildo loves you all, 1998), produced by Stefan Raab using the pseudonym Alf Igel, or Raab's own contribution in 2000, "Wadde hadde dudde da?" (What do you have there?). Unfortunately, Lou did not succeed in conveying enough happiness to win over the European audience, nor did the lyrics of the song's chorus ("Let's get happy and let's be gay") reach a possible group of addressees, the gay fans who have regularly celebrated the ESC, especially since Dana International won the contest with "Diva" in 1998.[25]

Siegel's "magic formula" for success could be a useful model for understanding his remarkably long-lasting success and popularity in German-speaking countries. His craft at adapting the sounds of contemporary popular music was highly successful during the 1970s and the early 1980s, and during his "golden years" it almost seemed as if Siegel's concept of synthesis and zeitgeist worked out perfectly. But his ability to pursue more recent trends obviously diminished as the years went by. The disaster of 2002, when "I Can't Live Without Music" placed 21st out of 24, showed his formula faltering, as did his arrangement of Malta's contribution "On Again, Off

---

22 Feddersen, *Ein Lied kann eine Brücke sein*, pp. 283, 300.

23 Which *de facto* means not only to construct or refer to a certain pop image, but to include even the singer's private background in the "formula"!

24 Jan Feddersen mentions Siegel's general unwillingness to pay any fees at all to his contest participants: *Ein Lied kann eine Brücke sein*, p. 300.

25 See Elmar Kraushaar, "Showtreppe in Schwarz-Rot-Gold: Nationalgefühl und schwule Identität beim Grand Prix," in Feddersen, *L'Allemagne Deux Points*, pp. 128–32.

Again," performed by Julie Zahra and Ludwig Galea in the 2004 contest.[26] Perhaps Siegel's earliest inclinations towards artsy and popular synthesis have since become his undoing. This might not be for the worst, in the end!

---

26 In trying to mix electronic beats with a sweet string arrangement, this song's wavering between pop sound and *Schlager* sound produced a sound that was neither of them.

Chapter 6

Fernando, Filippo, and Milly: Bringing blackness to the Eurovision stage

Lutgard Mutsaers

In 1964 the Netherlands was the first nation to break the spell of whiteness in the Eurovision Song Contest (ESC) when it selected Anneke Grönloh as its representative. Her roots were in the former colony of the Dutch East Indies (renamed Indonesia) and she belonged to the first wave of postcolonial immigrants to the Netherlands. Anneke Grönloh's participation was a milestone in the relationship between popular music and ethnicity in Eurovision. Until 1964, Eurovision had been an "all-white" environment for the marking of national identities through the performance of a three-minute pop song. In 1966 the Netherlands sent Milly Scott, a jazz singer of Afro-Surinamese background, as its delegate. Scott went down in Eurovision history as the first black singer to compete. Surprisingly, the country kept this monopoly position for a quarter-century within a constantly growing field of competing nations, Europe's changing demographics, and the globalizing world of popular music in which the United States continued to set the tone.[1] Other nations such as France, the United Kingdom, and Sweden followed in these Dutch footsteps long after it would have been considered controversial or progressive to do so.[2]

The selection of so-called "new-Dutch" performers to represent the Netherlands in the ESC has a context of postwar decolonization, which brought successive waves of immigration to the Netherlands and made the country increasingly multicultural.[3]

An early version of this chapter was published in Dutch as "De nieuw-Nederlandse afvaardiging naar het Songfestival 1964–2001," in *Kunsten in Beweging 1900–1980*, ed. Rosemarie Buikema and Maaike Meijer (The Hague: SDU, 2003), pp. 329–43.

1   Of the 46 times the Netherlands participated in the Eurovision Song Contest between 1956 and 2005, the country was represented by Indonesian-Dutch, Afro-Surinamese, or Moluccan performers 14 times, or almost one in three times. The Netherlands did not participate in 1985, 1991, 1995, and 2002; in 2005 the country lost its chance to participate in the contest after the semi-final round two days earlier, but these semi-finals were also broadcast internationally, so the representation issue still applies.

2   In 1990 France became the second country to be represented in Eurovision by a black singer. The United Kingdom followed in 1998. Sweden sent the first black female trio (Afro'dite) to the contest in 2002.

3   The term "new-Dutch" is a translation of *nieuwe Nederlander*, a commonly used expression referring to Dutch citizens and residents of foreign background. The term "Indo" refers to Eurasians of Dutch and Indonesian descent.

Migration from Indonesia began immediately following its independence in December 1949, with several thousand people of mixed Indonesian-Dutch background as well as ethnic Polynesians from the Moluccan Islands arriving over the next ten to fifteen years. Surinam (the former Dutch Guyana on the South American continent) became independent in 1975, which resulted in a migration wave of Afro-Surinamese and Asian-Surinamese to the Netherlands. Migration from the Dutch Antilles, a group of islands in the Caribbean Sea, became a major phenomenon in the 1980s and 1990s. At the end of the 1970s, the Dutch government introduced its policy of "family reunion" through which wives and children of migrant workers, mostly from Turkey and Moroccco, were invited to join their husbands and fathers in the Netherlands; since the 1990s the second generation of these reunited families has manifested itself socially and culturally.

The phenomenon of new-Dutch performers in Eurovision foregrounds not only otherness in terms of ethnicity but also diversity in terms of musical style. In 1964 Anneke Grönloh remained safely within the established musical borders of Eurovision, leaving references to her cultural background out of the picture. Two years later, Milly Scott broke the second barrier also, with her rhythmically daring rendition of a Latin-flavored song. From a historical European perspective, the emphasis on dance rhythms and so-called "jungle" sounds played right into stereotypes about people of African descent that had circulated widely since American popular song and dance first conquered European audiences around 1900.

The claim that racial politics has nothing to do with Eurovision cannot be sustained, but most ESC history books have so far ignored this issue. An exception can be found in the Dutch Eurovision history *Dinge-Dong*, which bluntly states, "Singers with dark skin have a problem; there has never been a winner in that category so far. The explanation is easy: there simply have not been many black competitors. ... There are no signals that there is racial discrimination at play in the national selection rounds, but it remains strange. The regular charts *are* dominated by black artists."[4]

Eurovision functions within a visual medium, and therefore looks are relevant in the overall picture of a national entry. Visible African ancestry is usually a defining factor in the discussion of "blackness," but the Dutch reality defies the simple black/white dichotomy that runs through American music-history writing. In the Netherlands, Eurasians and Mediterranean peoples also represent ethnic difference from the majority of the Dutch population. Eurovision, in its own showbiz way, highlights many different nations and cultures, but at the same time its "whiteness" is still taken for granted. This chapter examines the pioneering role of the Netherlands in this regard.

---

4   Hans Walraven and Geert Willems, *Dinge-Dong: Het Eurovisie Songfestival in de twintigste eeuw* (Amsterdam: Forum, 2000), p. 155. Emphasis in original. Unless otherwise stated, all translations are by the author.

A promising start

The Netherlands was among the seven West European countries to compete in the first ESC held in Lugano in 1956. Five nations entered with two songs by two different performers, while two nations had one performer for both songs. After a secret process of voting by a panel of undisclosed professionals, only the overall winner was announced. This was not an ideal format for live television or the enhancement of patriotic sentiments, so from 1957 onwards Eurovision featured just one performer per nation – which made the task of representing one's country a matter of "do or die" – and a voting system of national jury panels distributing a maximum of 12 points for the best song.

From then on, the event generated more media attention every year, involving audiences in their speculations, critical remarks from commentators, and even fanaticism from its most devoted fans.[5] Eurovision became a platform for national identities, where the performer was held personally responsible for representing his or her country, embodying its musical qualities and displaying its "national" tastes in popular song. According to the ESC mission statement, not the singers but the songwriters were the real competitors, and it was understood that performers only mediated what the composers had created and intended. From the very start, however, television audiences automatically focused on the performers and the spectacle of the show. While the songwriters stayed safely backstage, the singers had to deliver the goods on the spot, live, with a strange orchestra, before a big audience, in the intense heat of the spotlights, and dressed in unusual attire, with itchy pancake in heavy layers on their faces.

In 1957 the Netherlands took first place in Eurovision with Corry Brokken singing "Net als toen" (Just like the old days), accompanied on stage by a classical violinist. Her act projected an old-fashioned type of popular song with a dated sound. The Dutch popular music scene in the meantime was changing rapidly, as in most European countries. Rock 'n' roll bands consisting of young people from the former colony of the Dutch East Indies dominated the new music entertainment scene in the Netherlands in the late 1950s. These Indo-rock musicians were also branching out into continental Europe; the young Beatles playing the nightclub scene in Hamburg knew where to spy for guitar licks, drum rhythms, bass patterns, and performance tricks of the trade.[6]

With a deliberate deafness for exciting new youth music, the traditional Dutch music and media establishment was not amused to see their domain crumble under such "noise." As a result, the rock 'n' roll scene lacked the necessary funding and the interest of viable commercial enterprises such as established record companies, booking agencies, and suitable concert venues. While the sounds and spectacle of Dutch popular music rapidly changed under the influence of this new international

---

5   In 1999 came the introduction of individual televoting, which enabled people at home to take part in the selection process and added enormously to the appeal of the event.

6   Lutgard Mutsaers, *Rockin' Ramona: Een gekleurde kijk op de bakermat van de Nederpop* (The Hague: SDU, 1989); Lutgard Mutsaers, "Indorock: An Early Eurorock Style," *Popular Music* 9/3 (1990): 307–320.

youth music promoted by pirate radio, local ESC officials chose to stick to well-performed and well-produced light popular music in the styles that had been pre-eminent before rock 'n' roll.

One participant in the 1958 national preliminary contest was a classically trained singer of Dutch-Indonesian background, Anneke van der Graaf, who performed well but eventually was not chosen to represent the country in the finals. To play it safe, perhaps, the performer of the previous year's winning song, Corry Brokken, was again picked to represent the nation in 1958, but she tied for last place in that year's contest. The notion that Eurovision could make or break musical careers crept into the consciousness of participants and audiences alike. It made prospective participants more cautious over the years, while audiences increasingly enjoyed the drama and gossip leading up to the national finals and the day of the contest itself.

Cracks in the surface

In 1962, for the first time, the Dutch national preliminary contest had resulted in a new-Dutch act. A male duo of Indo background, The Padre Twins, was chosen to represent the nation with "Katinka." After they were given the sheet music and the lyrics to the song, they suddenly withdrew from the competition without explanation. (A white male duo, De Spelbrekers, then took their place and ended last with zero points, but their version of "Katinka" did well in the home charts afterwards.) Perhaps their decision to withdraw reflected an attitude in the Indo-rock scene that it was not acceptable to sing in Dutch. After the Padre Twins' 1962 English-language hit song "Roses are Red, My Love" on the small independent Artone label, the duo was probably not keen on changing its sound and image, not even just once for the prestigious ESC. This was a generation of new-Dutch immigrants who had living memories of the colonial era and life in another part of the world, which made allegiance to the Netherlands a different story altogether.

At the same time, The Padre Twins suffered unfair competition in the music business from another very popular young male Indo duo, The Blue Diamonds. This brother act was released on Phonogram (Philips), then the major international record company based in the Netherlands. The Blue Diamonds were role models for their own community as well as the young generation of teenagers tuned in to the new international pop sounds. They also refused to sing in Dutch. Phonogram presumably had such influence in the media that The Padre Twins were seldom heard on the radio. The monthly pop music magazine *Tuney Tunes* criticized this situation as early as February 1961. In April that year *Tuney Tunes* wrote that the rivalry had grown into an actual boycott, and radio DJs were quoted saying that The Padre Twins were too shy to be believable as youth idols. "It's a scandal!" wrote *Tuney Tunes*. "Lots of lesser records (also by *Dutch* teenagers) are being pushed by Hilversum, but as soon as a civilized couple of teenagers cuts a record, it is ignored!"[7] The emphasis

---

7   Hilversum is a town close to Amsterdam where the radio and television broadcasting companies are located.

Table 6.1   **"New-Dutch" representation in the Eurovision Song Contest, 1964–2005**

Year	Performer	Song	Points	Ranking
1964	Anneke Grönloh	"Jij bent mijn leven"	2	10th
1966	Milly Scott	"Fernando en Filippo"	2	15th
1970	Patricia & The Hearts of Soul	"Waterman"	7	7th
1972	Sandra & Andres	"Als het om de liefde gaat"	106	4th
1976	Sandra Reemer	"The Party's Over"	56	9th
1978	Harmony	"'t Is Oké"	37	13th
1979	Xandra	"Colorado"	51	12th
1989	Justine Pelmelay	"Blijf zoals je bent"	45	15th
1992	Humphrey Campbell	"Wijs me de weg"	67	9th
1993	Ruth Jacott	"Vrede"	92	6th
1996	Maxine & Franklin Brown	"De eerste keer"	78	7th
1998	Edsilia Rombley	"Hemel en aarde"	150	4th
2000	Linda Wagenmakers	"No Goodbyes"	40	13th
2005	Glennis Grace	"My Impossible Dream"	Out in Semi-Finals	

on the word "Dutch" was an accepted way of putting the issue of ethnicity on the table. By naming and even stressing the norm of whiteness as "Dutch," the "other" was present in terms everybody knew how to read in that context.

As is more often the case in this type of situation, it took a female performer to cross the line. Anneke Grönloh was the nation's best-selling solo pop singer of 1962 and 1963; she sang in Dutch, and Phonogram released her records. Like The Blue Diamonds, Grönloh was hugely popular in Indonesia also. The British Invasion of 1964 brought a new spectacle of young guys strumming on their electric guitars, shouting their lyrics, and working their audiences, and so although she was an accomplished jazz and ballad singer, and an occasional performer of Indonesian folk songs, Grönloh's career was in danger. Happy to be in the international spotlight and confident in that role, she agreed to represent the nation at Eurovision 1964 with "Jij bent mijn leven" (You're my life), an old-fashioned ballad about male adultery from the perspective of a suffering but faithful wife. Only one ESC history book mentions her Eurasian background specifically,[8] but apart from her looks nothing in her song or her performance style made her stand out as "different." After a disappointing score (see Table 6.1) her career as a hit singer was over.

"Fernando and Filippo"

In 1966, the year the slogan "Black Power" was coined in the United States by Stokely Carmichael, taking the civil rights movement to another level, Afro-Surinamese Milly Scott took the Eurovision stage for the Netherlands. That year's contest was broadcast from Villa Louvigny in Luxembourg, headquarters of the commercial broadcasting corporation Radio Luxembourg, which had promoted rock 'n' roll and merseybeat to an eager young audience all over continental western Europe. The event was broadcast live in all 18 competing countries, and also in a number of East European countries and Morocco. All in all, the ESC reached 230 million viewers that year.

Milly Scott was a jazz singer who also occasionally performed in the "Latin" style, as black singers often found themselves typecast with such music. She entered the Dutch national selection rounds as an outsider. Her song "Fernando en Filippo" (Fernando and Filippo) met with skepticism, and Scott was criticized for a singing style that did not suit the ESC – that is, it was not sufficiently "European," "white" in sound, style, and everything else. Even after "Fernando en Filippo" won the national competition, the song itself still harvested harsh verdicts ("the most commercial melody with the most unworthy lyrics"), but Scott's performance was suddenly praised as "full of temperament, fresh and swinging."[9] "Perhaps 'Fernando en Filippo' can be a surprise success, because it's got a spicy rhythm," the national pop magazine *Muziekparade* remarked in its March issue.[10] "Temperament," "fresh," "swinging," "spicy," and "rhythm" signify what was unspeakable at the time: the stereotypical connotations of sensual physicality and liberated sexuality associated with the body and voice of a black woman. The Austrian Eurovision history book *Merci, Jury!* considers "Fernando en Filippo" a "pitifully bizarre composition" and insists that it could not have been "a case of racism" that Scott's performance scored so low (with two points, ending in 15th place), implying that the quality of the song itself was to blame.[11] With her inescapably different looks and movements (the latter were choreographed, not "spontaneous"), Milly Scott stepped out of the confines of performing the Euro-whiteness that Eurovision had so far managed to establish.

"Fernando en Filippo" tells of two guitar players from a place called Santiago; viewers might have assumed that this was in Mexico because of the outfits of the two men who performed with Scott in the Eurovision show. *The Complete Eurovision Song Contest Companion* calls "Fernando en Filippo" "a daft little number about

8   Leif Thorsson, *Melodi Festivalen* (Stockholm: Premium Förlag, 1999), p. 48.

9   Louis In 't Zandt, "De geschiedenis van het Eurovisie Songfestival, deel 12, 1966: Merci Jury in Luxemburg," *Eurovision Artists News* 1998–9, no. 2 (1998): 10–12.

10   "Milly naar Luxemburg!" *Muziekparade* (March 1966).

11   Jan Feddersen, *Merci, Jury! Die Geschichte des Grand Prix Eurovision de la Chanson: Zahlen – Daten – Stories* (Vienna: Döcker Verlag, 2000), p. 51.

two Mexicans, who were on stage, complete with ponchos and guitars."[12] These Mexican clothes, however, signify a more general Latin American sensibility to go with the music, and the song is actually situated in Chile, as the lyrics make clear (the port town of San Antonio lies within a few hours driving distance of Santiago). It is not too far-fetched to see in the connection to Chile (and the similar-sounding "chili" pepper, *capsicum pubescens*) a symbol of the hot temperament that Milly Scott's blackness was supposed to embody on stage. Scott went "Latin," shaking her hips, and inserted an improvised scat ad lib (*ronki-tonk-tikitiki-tonk*) as her own contribution in the song's instrumental bridges. For a jazz singer this was standard practice, but in the mid-1960s world of mainstream pop music, this was daring, even revolutionary.

Music, lyrics and politics

After Milly Scott, the differences between songs sung by white and non-white contestants were primarily a matter of lyrical content, not musical style, so these would be obvious only to listeners who understood Dutch. In 1970 the Indo sister act Patricia & The Hearts of Soul (Patricia, Stella, and Bianca Maessen) sang "Waterman." This song about the astrological sign Aquarius referred to the hit song from the contemporary Broadway musical *Hair*. Water is also a symbol for The Netherlands, famously situated below sea level with its dikes and canals. "Waterman, my sign and talisman, from now on you belong to me" could be heard as a love declaration from an immigrant female to a white Dutch male. It could also have referred to encounters that had raised eyebrows and fists during the 1950s when Indo males (especially those who played in a rock 'n' roll band) were hugely successful with white Dutch females.

In 1972 the Indonesian-Dutch singers Sandra Reemer and Dries Holten represented the Netherlands as Sandra & Andres. Their song "Als het om de liefde gaat" (When love is concerned) contains one typically Dutch saying, which translates as, "Just act normal, that's eccentric enough." In 1976 Sandra Reemer again represented the Netherlands, this time with an English-language song ("The Party's Over") that contained no specific references to the nation and its stereotypical characteristics. In 1979, as Xandra, she entered with a Dutch-language song about traveling to Colorado in the American West. This song contained several references to the Dutch stereotype of all-too-carefully watching the pennies. A native Dutch singer might have had little critical distance to those references, whereas Xandra still projected her new-Dutch identity enough to give them added resonance. As a television talk-show hostess, she continued to cherish her nickname of "Kroepoekje" ("little Indonesian shrimp crisp") given to her by her white male co-star.

From 1975 onwards, immigration from Surinam to the Netherlands resulted in half of the newly independent country's population living in Amsterdam. During the same period, the Netherlands was shaken by terrorist actions by a small group

---

12   Paul Gambaccini, Jonathan Rice, and Tony Brown, *The Complete Eurovision Song Contest Companion* (London: Pavilion Books, 1999), p. 38.

of militant Moluccans (from Ambon, part of the former colony of the Dutch East Indies) frustrated by the long-standing tensions between their community and the Dutch government. There were police and media reports of young blacks, including Moluccans, being refused entry to discotheques. A cloud of racial discrimination began to hang over the formerly "liberal" country. In 1978 the Dutch Eurovision entry consisted of the racially mixed trio comprising Afro-Surinamese-Dutch Donald Lieveld, Indonesian-Dutch Rosina Lauwaars, and native Dutch Ab van Woudenberg. Their group's name, Harmony, was well chosen to send a positive message, and their song, "'t is Oké" (It's OK), calls for positive communication, finding oneself in happy company, and never feeling lonely. Over a decade later, in 1989, the Netherlands sent its first Moluccan representative to Eurovision, Justine Pelmelay. Her song "Blijf zoals je bent" (Stay the way you are) had a gospel-like quality, and some of its lyrics could be interpreted as a message to the people of her community in relation to the rest of the Dutch population. The next year France finally joined the Netherlands in sending a black performer to Eurovision, Joëlle Ursull from Martinique, who came in second with "White and Black Blues."

Husband and wife Humphrey Campbell and Ruth Jacott, both of Afro-Surinamese descent, competed for the Netherlands in 1992 and 1993 respectively. Humphrey Campbell performed with his brothers Carlo and Ben, singing the sophisticated "Wijs me de weg" (Show me the way). Ruth Jacott presented the ballad "Vrede" (Peace). Both songs were crafty, musically challenging, lyrically critical and intelligent, taking Dutch-language Eurovision song to another level. Both songs incorporated eternally human and topical issues such as helping one another find a way in society (an issue particularly relevant to immigrants) and calling a halt to war (the current Balkan wars in particular). Considering perceptions of gender and race, the black male trio of 1992 definitely projected a more powerful otherness than the female solo act of 1993; Campbell ended in ninth place, Jacott in sixth. Jacott's ranking was regretted by many who felt that her song and choreography were the best in that year's contest. Her participation in the ESC coincided with the start of a new phase in the national history of the show. By championing the competition, television talk-show host Paul de Leeuw, openly gay and enthusiastically celebrating his lifestyle, almost single-handedly removed the dust that had settled on Eurovision during the 1980s. The radical gay investment in Eurovision in the 1990s resulted in a more "other-friendly" and festive occasion, coinciding with an overall rise in the number of black performers and gay acts not only from the Netherlands.

In 1998 Afro-Surinamese Edsilia Rombley was the first Dutch contestant actually to sing the word "Nederland" (Netherlands) in her song "Hemel en aarde" (Heaven and earth) when she described the coolness of the weather and related it to the coolness of the native Dutch temperament. This created some sort of critical distance, making Edsilia an observer rather than an insider of Dutch culture. At the same time, her immense popularity at the time underscored the decreasing dominance of whiteness for the nation as a whole. As a statement about identity, Edsilia's song is undoubtedly the most directly meaningful of all contributions by new-Dutch performers. It was also the last song to be sung in Dutch in recent years, and the last time the performers were backed by a live orchestra. From then on, the importance of "different" ethnicities has gradually melted away. Especially in popular music and entertainment, the new-Dutch artist is omnipresent nowadays.

In 2000 the Indonesian-Dutch musical-theater star Linda Wagenmakers created a sensation not with her song, which was sung in English and does not refer to anything particularly Dutch, but with her architectural dress that literally covered her backing group. Before her, the 1996 new-Dutch duo Maxine and Franklin Brown had gone completely unnoticed. In the case of Afro-Surinamese Glennis Grace's 2005 entry, "My Impossible Dream," the issue of blackness was revisited in an interesting way. Glennis Grace started her semi-finals performance by raising her right arm while solemnly reciting the well-known mantra, "I have a dream." She failed to reach the finals, which made the adjective "*impossible* dream" all the more poignant. Still, her opening line would have been not credible, and perhaps even verging on blasphemous, if stated by someone who was not black.

A new-Dutch act has never won for the Netherlands, but none has ever come in last place either. The first *winning* ESC entry to include a black performer represented Estonia in 2001, but still provides an interesting angle on the Dutch situation. For that year's contest the Estonian singer Tanel Padar teamed up with Dave Benton, whose real name is Ef'ren Benita. Benton originally comes from Aruba, one of the Dutch Antilles, and had lived in Rotterdam for many years. As soon as this detail became known, the Dutch delegation and media were over the moon: the victory was really (partly) theirs! The Aruban Ministry of Culture, Economic Affairs, and Tourism immediately claimed the victory for Aruba, though the island nation could never have competed in Eurovision anyway.[13] Coincidentally, the low-scoring Dutch entry of 2001 had disqualified the nation from participation in 2002. Suddenly there was talk about the Netherlands proposing to take over the organization of Eurovision 2002 from the "poor" former Soviet satellite Estonia.[14] Not amused by this display of Western superiority and colonialist thinking, Estonia ignored the Dutch offer and hosted a splendid Eurovision show in 2002.

Conclusion

Analyzing the Dutch ESC entries performed by new-Dutch singers, it turns out that Indo performers represented national identity in more old-fashioned or established ways, or sang the average superficial love song in musically unremarkable styles that did not digress from the traditional Eurovision sound. Performers of Afro-Caribbean descent, however, clearly showed a more critical distance towards Dutch culture and a musically more diverse and upbeat sound. This is even more remarkable because almost all performed songs written by white composers and lyricists.[15] Dutch Eurovision history to date (2005) has not yet had a representative from the country's largest immigrant groups, Moroccans and Turks. While the first-generation Moroccan-Dutch rapper Ali B (Ali Bouali, b. 1981 in the Netherlands)

---

13 Geert Willems, untitled article, *De Gelderlander* (14 May 2001).

14 Henk van Gelder, "Noorwegen: weer 0 punten," *NRC Handelsblad* (25 May 2002): 59.

15 With one exception: in 1972 the Dutch entry was written by Dries Holten, who performed as Andres.

was the nation's leading pop artist in the year of the 50th ESC, the contest itself remained a relatively conservative arena in terms of its delegates and their roots.

All of Europe is used to black pop singers nowadays. These performers usually radiate a more "international" identity, bound less by national characteristics, and therefore they communicate more easily to a mainstream audience from many different cultural environments. Eurovision, on the other hand, has long been widely perceived as the last fortress of whiteness in mainstream popular music, mostly because the ESC never set out or claimed to be a youth cultural phenomenon or to be in tune with global trends in popular music. Still not a generational marker in terms of audience (although its performers are usually, though not necessarily, "young"), Eurovision did make an effort to incorporate contemporary trends and topical styles in its entries, increasingly so during the 1990s. It is common knowledge among ESC aficionados and general audiences alike that national references in the form of particular folk sounds or costumes influence the song's winning chances considerably – for a long time in a completely negative way, but in recent years in a much more positive way. It is ironic that the Netherlands in the meantime has buried its national musical folklore so deep in history that this particular option to score points in Eurovision seems lost forever.

Finally, non-white performers and musical styles have not only invaded but also convincingly conquered the fortress of the Old World through the ideal marriage of popular song and mass media, a marriage first cemented in the New World. As a nation precociously promoting liberal attitudes to the extreme, the Netherlands has perfectly played its stereotypical role in this international field.

Chapter 7

Finland, zero points: Nationality, failure, and shame in the Finnish media

Mari Pajala

"Finland, zero points" has become a popular phrase to describe the Finnish Eurovision experience. The television magazine *Katso* wrote before the 2000 national selection, "Next week we once again get to vote for our candidates to be humiliated on an international level. How many times have we already experienced it: *Finlande, zéro point*!"[1] As here, the phrase is often written in (incorrect) French, as a humorous reference to the Eurovision convention of repeating all the votes in English and French. The Eurovision Song Contest (ESC) is represented as a source of negative emotion, a national humiliation. The quote also emphasizes the repetitive nature of this humiliation: on the basis of previous experiences it is anticipated to happen "once again."

The words "Finland, zero points" are of course never heard in the actual ESC broadcasts, but they have popular appeal as a shorthand expression for Finland's perceived position in Eurovision.[2] The Finnish Broadcasting Company YLE has taken part in the contest since 1961, and has seen its representative finish in last place eight times. The best Finnish placing before 2006 was more than 30 years previously, in 1973, when Marion Rung came in sixth. Since then, numerous contestants tried to beat this record, but to no avail until Lordi won the contest with "Hard Rock, Hallelujah." No wonder that feelings of failure and disappointment have a central place in the Finnish image of the Eurovision Song Contest.

In this chapter I analyze popular understandings of Finnish Eurovision failure in terms of the structures of feeling they incorporate.[3] Following Sara Ahmed, I am interested in the ways emotions shape collective, in this case national, bodies.[4] Reading the 2002 contest in relation to comparable cases from 1968, 1981, and 1982, I analyze the affective structures that are used to make sense of Eurovision failure

---

1   *Katso* 5 (2000). All translations are by the author.

2   Finnish songs have ended up with zero points three times, of which two occurrences were in the 1960s when the voting system was different and there were often several countries scoring no points. Instead of being spectacular failures, Finnish entrants have often scored somewhere in the middle rank – or at least that was the case until the end of the 1980s. In the 1990s most Finnish entrants did very poorly, and when the least successful countries had to make way for the new ESC members, YLE ended up missing the contest every two years. These poor showings helped to create the impression that Finland was "always" among the last in the Eurovision Song Contest.

3   Raymond Williams, *Marxismi, kulttuuri ja kirjallisuus*, trans. Mikko Lehtonen (Tampere: Vastapaino, 1988), pp. 149–53.

4   Sara Ahmed, *The Cultural Politics of Emotion* (New York: Routledge, 2004), p. 1.

in the Finnish media. What kind of identifications with the nation do they suggest? How do they construct the relationship between Finland and (western) Europe? My material consists of Eurovision coverage in major Finnish newspapers, evening papers, and magazines as well as the online edition of the largest evening paper, *Ilta-Sanomat*.[5] By placing the 2002 contest in the context of Finnish Eurovision history I hope to show how the repetitive nature of the ESC has enabled particular interpretations of Finland and its relation to Europe. I concentrate on negative affective responses that are common in Finnish media coverage of the contest, and in this way I offer an alternative understanding of the ESC that differs from the prevalent way of approaching the competition as a piece of fun "Eurotrash."

The negative affective relationship between the television spectator, the nation, and Eurovision constitutes itself in two ways: national shame and the melodrama of repeated disappointment. Shame is typically evoked when the Finnish entry is considered poor and expected to fail miserably in the international final; narratives of melodramatic disappointment are constructed when there are high expectations for the Finnish contestant, who then fails to live up to them. A single entry may well evoke both kinds of responses. The ESC is not always taken this "seriously" in the Finnish media – it may also be seen as too trivial to be worth such emotional responses – but even humorous accounts of Finnish Eurovision experience often build upon the themes of shame and melodrama, only from a position of irony or self-conscious distance. Gloom is an essential part of Eurovision entertainment in Finland.

Finland in Eurovision Europe

In 1961 the French presenter began the ESC with the words "Good evening, Europe," and welcomed two new countries, Finland and Yugoslavia, to the contest. In the salutation, "Europe" was equated with western Europe, as the program was not yet broadcast in East European countries. Finland was situated at the outskirts of this initial Eurovision Europe, as neatly illustrated by the map used to introduce the songs of the 1963 contest. It was framed in such a way that it only included parts of Norway and Sweden and a small southwestern corner of Finland. The map is an important visual symbol for Europe, and here it gave a central position to West European countries, marginalizing the north.

Finland's position in relation to the Cold War-era definition of Europe was precarious. After losing the war, Finland didn't become a socialist state, but it did have close relations to the Soviet Union. Finnish foreign policy relied on the ideal of neutrality and represented the country as a kind of borderland between West and

---

5   For the 2002 contest, I have collected material from the following papers and magazines: *Helsingin Sanomat* (*HS*), the largest news paper in Finland, *Aamulehti* (*AL*) and *Turun Sanomat* (*TS*), two of the largest regional papers, *Ilta-Sanomat* (*IS*) and *Iltalehti* (*IL*), the two national evening papers, women's magazines *Anna* and *Me Naiset*, and family magazine *Apu*. For 1982, the material is comparable to that of 2002. For 1981 and 1968 I have had access to the YLE press clippings archive, which includes material from many small and regional newspapers.

East.[6] After the break-up of the Soviet Union Finland began to modify its traditional policy of neutrality and joined the European Union in 1995.

This in-between position was also taken up by Finnish television. The broadcaster YLE was a member of both the Eurovision and Intervision networks, and in this dual role it was keen to represent itself as bridge between East and West.[7] It took part in the Intervision Song Contest, where Finnish participants often did very well, but the Intervision Song Contest never held as much popular appeal and symbolic importance as its West European equivalent. Success in the ESC has been interpreted as a kind of proof of European approval, which can only be granted by West European countries. Since the early 1990s Eurovision Europe has become much wider as former Intervision countries have joined the competition. Despite this, western Europe continues to hold a hegemonic position as the representative of "Europe" proper in Finnish media coverage of the contest.

It has been suggested that a sense of otherness in relation to Europe is a constitutive part of Finnish identity, and that European peoples and cultures represent an ideal that Finnish people struggle to achieve.[8] Cinema scholar Tarja Laine compares the Finnish case to a colonial situation and argues that the "European" elite has had the power to make the Finnish people experience themselves as "Other." Drawing on earlier psycho-historical research, Laine suggests that shame, caused by a denial of social respect and a feeling of inferiority in relation to Europe, has a particularly important role in Finnish culture.[9] Finnish media coverage of the ESC could seem to support this notion of Finland as a "shame culture," but I want to avoid generalizing accounts of "Finnish culture." Finland's troubled relationship to Europe is just one historically important, but not exclusive, discourse about Finnishness: consider the country's success stories such as Finnish design in the 1950s and 1960s – or, more recently, Nokia – which have been interpreted as national triumphs of industry and technology.

Eurovision as national shame

A recurring question around the ESC in Finland has been whether or not one is ashamed of this year's Finnish representative. After Laura, a nationally well-known singer, was chosen to represent Finland in the 2002 contest, *Ilta-Sanomat* asked in its daily readers' poll whether people expected her to do well in the international finals.[10] Shame features in the responses of those readers who didn't believe in

6   For example, Vilho Harle and Sami Moisio, *Missä on Suomi? Kansallisen identiteettipolitiikan historia ja geopolitiikka* (Tampere: Vastapaino, 2000), pp. 183–91.

7   Raimo Salokangas, *Aikansa oloinen: Yleisradion historia 1926–1996, Osa 2* (Helsinki: Yleisradio, 1996), p. 126.

8   Tarja Laine, *Shame and Desire: Intersubjectivity in Finnish Visual Culture* (Amsterdam: ASCA, 2004), p. 8.

9   Ibid., pp. 24–32.

10   A total of 8,567 people took part in the poll, and 78 per cent didn't expect Laura to do well. About 450 comments are available at <www.iltasanomat.fi/arkisto/nettikysely.asp?id=1658> Accessed 25 April 2005.

Laura's chances. "Once again we bring shame upon ourselves with our hillbilly crap in front of the whole world" was one reply; "'Nolla pistettä, nyl points, ziro points' ... One will have to be ashamed once again this year!" another complained. The comments follow conventional ways of expressing shame in relation to the ESC: it is attached to nationality and typically manifested in a confessional mode, most bluntly as "I'm ashamed of being Finnish."[11] There is a sense of being vulnerable to shame when something Finnish is exported for others to see.

Often shame is felt in situations where some kind of cultural norms have been broken. The topic comes up particularly when Finnish entrants are not felt to conform to Eurovision conventions, for example in 1981 and 1982. In the late 1970s and early 1980s the ESC was heavily criticized for its commercialism, standardized show tunes, and meaningless lyrics.[12] In the spirit of this critique, the juries of the 1981 and 1982 national preliminaries favored songs that were deliberately different from current Eurovision styles and closer to rock values. Their chosen entrants, Riki Sorsa with "Reggae OK" and Kojo with "Nuku pommiin" (Oversleep), an aggressive song about nuclear bombs, were much critiqued in readers' letters in the press. A central cause of shame for the readers was the impression that the performers and juries did not take the contest seriously, making fools of themselves and, by implication, the whole nation. The untidy appearance of the male performers and the low quality of music were also called shameful.[13] Twenty years later Laura's song "Addicted to You," with its slightly 1970s retro feel, was criticized for being old-fashioned, and her English pronunciation and daring short and low-cut dress were described as shameful.[14] Both in the early 1980s and in 2002 shame was attached to a sense that the performances didn't live up to Eurovision norms: the songs represented "wrong" styles (reggae, rock, or "old-fashioned" disco) and the performers' looks didn't conform to respectable ideals.

On the other hand, shame doesn't necessarily require violation of norms. It is conventionally distinguished from guilt on the basis that it is more closely linked to an understanding of the self. Whereas guilt follows from specific deeds, shame is connected to what the person *is*. It commonly arises in situations where there is a wish for communication, recognition, and rapport, but for some reason communication is blocked.[15] Accordingly, in discussions of Eurovision it is sometimes exactly this feeling of failed communication that is said to cause shame. "I'm ashamed of being Finnish. Who could understand us when we don't even understand ourselves," a dissatisfied viewer commented on the results of the 1982 national selection.[16] According to one view, the most shameful thing of all is to be ignored by the

---

11   Ibid.

12   Mari Pajala, "'Laulukilpailut vai pelkkää viihdettä?' Käsityksiä viihteestä 1970-luvun lopun euroviisukeskusteluissa," in *Populaarin lumo – mediat ja arki*, ed. Anu Koivunen, Susanna Paasonen, and Mari Pajala (Turku: University of Turku, 2000), pp. 214–38.

13   For example, *IS* (24 February 1981); *IS* (26 February 1981); *Katso* 11 (1981); *Vaasa* (17 April 1981); *IS* (26 February 1982); *Katso* 9 (1982).

14   <www.iltasanomat.fi/arkisto/nettikysely.asp?id=1658> Accessed 25 April 2005.

15   Eve Kosofsky Sedgwick, *Touching Feeling: Affect, Pedagogy, Performativity* (Durham, NC, and London: Duke University Press, 2003), pp. 35–7.

16   *Katso* 9 (1982).

international audience. Thus people may argue that it is better to stand out, even in a way that isn't particularly popular. "Finland has absolutely no reason to be ashamed of Riki or our entry," assured one commentator of the 1981 contest; "Thanks to Riki we were finally noticed."[17] With his pink and yellow harlequin outfit and reggae-light tune, Riki Sorsa certainly stood out from more traditional male Eurovision contestants.

In the case of the ESC, shame has a specific relation to temporality, and it is common to stress that shame is recurrent. This feeling is apparent in nearly every mention of shame in the *Ilta-Sanomat* poll about Laura's chances, as in this example: "It is about that time of the year again when Finland considers that it is in need of an international shaming."[18] Shame is both anticipatory and backward-looking, supported by reference to previous Eurovision experiences. Expressions of shame are typical right after the Finnish national preliminaries, when there is not yet any indication of how the European audience will respond to the Finnish song. The evaluating look of others is anticipated on the basis of one's own negative feelings about the Finnish entrant. This can be read as an example of a situation where feelings create boundaries between self and others, but at the same time unmake them. As Sara Ahmed writes, "what separates us from others also connects us to others."[19] In shame, the ashamed party feels separated from others, but at the same time the emotion is based on an assumption that one knows how they think.

How then does the performance of one artist come to be understood as a national shame? Silvan Tomkins argues that affective investment in the surrounding world makes one vulnerable to feeling shame for others. Even though the actions of other people are the source of a negative feeling, shame is a sign of positive interest in them. Shared shame may thus powerfully enhance the feeling of community.[20] In the case of Eurovision, where contestants are seen as representatives of their country, nationality functions as the uniting factor that spreads shame from the performer to others. By expressing shame, people also express identification with the nation and an interest in the image of the country.

Nationality, however, is not a fixed, already-existing entity through which shame simply moves, but rather "Finnishness" is in part constructed in the expressions of shame. As Sara Ahmed argues, emotions shape communities, such as nations. For example, if others are seen as a cause of pain, a boundary is constructed to separate the self from them, which creates an impression of two separate entities.[21] A comparable process takes place when a television viewer dislikes the Finnish entry and expresses shame about it. The imagined look of the other forces the television viewer to identify with the Finnish entry and forms the collective body – the Finnish people as a whole – that is shamed.

---

17 *AL* (21 April 1981).

18 <www.iltasanomat.fi/arkisto/nettikysely.asp?id=1658> Accessed 25 April 2005.

19 Ahmed, *The Cultural Politics of Emotion*, pp. 24–5.

20 Silvan Tomkins, *Shame and its Sisters: A Silvan Tomkins Reader*, ed. Eve Kosofsky Sedgwick and Adam Frank (Durham, NC, and London: Duke University Press, 1995), pp. 156–7, 159.

21 Ahmed, *The Cultural Politics of Emotion*, pp. 1, 24.

What does the confession of national shame accomplish? What happens when the normative subject – in this case, someone able to speak as a legitimate national subject – admits to feeling shame?[22] Ahmed suggests that national shame is a way of identifying with the nation in a situation where the nation fails to fulfill the demands that are expected from it. When someone is ashamed as a Finnish subject of Finland's failure to live up to the ideal image of the nation, the emotion at the same time confirms the subject's love for the nation;[23] shame doesn't question the importance of the nation but reaffirms it. The ability to express national shame requires the possibility to speak legitimately from the position of a national subject – a position that is not equally available to everybody.

Moreover, national shame serves as a guarantee of good intentions and enables the reproduction of the ideal image of the nation.[24] Thus, when a television viewer writes "I'm ashamed of being Finnish," the confession has a double meaning. It acknowledges that Finnishness has failed to live up to shared expectations, and proves that the writer is both aware of these expectations and, in a way, above the failure. Expressions of shame leave norms unquestioned and paradoxically enable national pride: "Shame collapses the 'I' and the 'we' in the failure to transform the social ideal into action, a failure which, when witnessed, confirms the ideal, and makes possible a return to pride."[25] In the context of the ESC, shame expresses a commitment to imagined West European standards and a troubled national pride.

The melodrama of disappointment

Another typical Finnish account of the ESC focuses on the feeling of disappointment. According to a common view, Finnish Eurovision experience follows a pattern where unrealistically high expectations and media hype are followed by a bitter return to reality: "Finland has always been a favorite before the contest and usually among the five last after it."[26] This is not quite true, but nonetheless melodramatic accounts of disappointing failure have had an important role in Eurovision media coverage.

The cyclical nature of the annual ESC makes it particularly suitable material for Ien Ang's notion of a "melodramatic structure of feeling."[27] Melodrama has been linked to cultural forms that do not follow strictly linear narratives, such as soap operas with their never-ending storylines.[28] The problems that the characters face are not resolved once and for all, but resolution is endlessly postponed. Thomas Elsaesser has characterized the plots of 1950s Hollywood family melodramas as

---

22   Ibid., p. 108.

23   Ibid.

24   Ibid., pp. 108–109.

25   Ibid., p. 109.

26   <www.iltasanomat.fi/arkisto/default.asp?alue=nettikyselyt&id=2023> Accessed 16 March 2007.

27   Ien Ang, *Watching Dallas: Soap Opera and the Melodramatic Imagination*, trans. Della Couling (London: Methuen, 1985; reprint, New York: Routledge, 1996), pp. 61–83.

28   Ibid.

circular patterns in which the characters face a "cycle of non-fulfilment."[29] In a common Finnish interpretation, the ESC is read as a kind of "cycle of non-fulfilment" driven forward by a "desire focusing on an unobtainable object,"[30] that is, the first Finnish victory or at least a good ranking. Every year, the contest promises a chance of improving the Finnish track record, but more often than not the results are disappointing and the expectations must be redirected towards the following year. The Finnish contestant and "Finland" as a whole are positioned as melodramatic characters who struggle to succeed against all odds.

The story built around the 2002 ESC follows the pattern where high expectations result in bitter disappointment. The Finnish national preliminary was of a relatively high profile with some well-known participants. According to critics, the songs were of a better quality than in previous competitions.[31] For the first time, none of the songs was in Finnish, and the songs were also considered less "Finnish" and more "European" in other ways. "No orchestral arrangements, no arty-farties and no purely Finnish *Schlagers*. Even Eurovision has shifted into Euro-time," promised a preview article in an evening paper. Stylistically the songs were said to range from Euro-dance and Anglo-American ballads to Swedish and Italian pop.[32]

Laura's "Addicted to You" was the clear favourite of the television audience, getting more than a third of all votes. Since the last time YLE participated in the ESC in 2000, several Finnish groups (Bomfunk MC's, Darude) had produced international top-ten hits, which created the unprecedented impression that it was actually possible for Finnish artists to succeed in Europe.[33] Accordingly, after the national preliminary there was notable optimism about "Addicted to You," which was characterized as "the first Eurovision song in a long time with which Finland has a chance of doing well."[34]

As the ESC finals in Tallinn drew close, popular magazines and evening papers raised expectations about Laura's chances. The cover of *Me Naiset* women's magazine boldly announced: "Laura matured into a world-class star. Ready for victory!"[35] According to the papers, public relations efforts before the contest had been more wide-ranging than usual for Finnish entrants: much care had gone into the preparation of Laura's look, and she had visited several countries to perform her Eurovision song.[36] During Eurovision week came news that "Addicted to You" had received a lot of positive attention, winning polls in Sweden, Spain, and Tallinn, as well as on the Internet.[37]

---

29 Thomas Elsaesser, "Tales of Sound and Fury: Observations on the Family Melodrama," in *Home Is Where the Heart Is: Studies in Melodrama and the Woman's Film*, ed. Christine Gledhill (London: BFI, 1987), pp. 56–7, 62.

30 Ibid., p. 62.

31 *AL*, *TS* (27 January 2002).

32 *IS* (22 January 2002).

33 *IS* (2 January 2002).

34 *IS* (28 January 2002).

35 *Me Naiset* 11 (2002).

36 *Anna* 21 (2002); *Apu* 18 (2002); *IL* (11 May 2002).

37 *IL*, *IS* (25 May 2002).

In the end, Laura ended up with only 24 points and came fifth to last. The commentator for the Finnish broadcast of the contest called the results disappointing, and speculated in an emotional voice that "tears of disappointment" were not out of the question in Finnish homes. The evening papers made the most of Laura's feelings after the competition. *Ilta-Sanomat* featured a photo of a dumbfounded Laura on its cover with the headline "I CRIED, CRIED, CRIED." In the interview Laura expressed surprise at the results – "Everybody thought that I should have won" – and in the accompanying photo she was pictured drying her tearful eyes.[38] Laura's tears were headline material in other papers as well.[39] Tears bring a sense of melodramatic excess to the accounts of Eurovision; according to cinema scholar Linda Williams, crying is closely associated with melodrama, which turns crying into a spectacle of emotion and also attempts to move the viewer to tears. Typically it is the image of a crying woman that provides the melodramatic excess.[40]

Many commentators stressed that Laura's performance was not bad in itself, and that the results of the competition (particularly the Latvian victory) were surprising. Laura herself wondered, "I don't see what could be done better. Everything went just as it should. Can Finland ever win Eurovision if everything already went exactly as it should?"[41] Laura's words express a feeling that Finnish songs just cannot succeed at Eurovision, no matter what they are like. This sentiment builds on decades of comparable disappointments.

A very similar story had already been built around the ESC in 1968.[42] That year, the Finnish contestant was chosen by television viewers for the first time, which ensured that the winner, Kristina Hautala, was relatively popular. The Finnish press built up expectations before the contest with reports of sales success and positive attention in London.[43] On the night of the contest, Hautala finished last with just one point. The results of the vote were considered surprising[44] and her disappointment was described with empathy: "The poor girl must have melted into tears, for when she was photographed and interviewed for weeks in advance and celebrated as an almost self-evident winner, falling back to earth must have been painful."[45]

As early as 1968 it was possible to see Hautala's poor result as one more chapter in a cycle of "annual national disappointment"[46] that television viewers had to face: "Year after year the citizens of this country sit in front of their television sets waiting and hoping for success in the Euro-arena. Year after year [we have been]

---

38   *IS* (27 May 2002).

39   *AL*, *IL*, *TS* (27 May 2002).

40   Linda Williams, "Film Bodies: Gender, Genre, and Excess," *Film Quarterly* 44/4 (1991): 2–13.

41   *IS* (27 May 2002).

42   In a sense 1968 can be seen as the first really big Finnish Eurovision disappointment. Twice, in 1963 and 1965, Finnish entries had ended up with zero points, but there hadn't really been very high hopes beforehand for either of the songs.

43   *AL*, *HS* (5 April 1968); *TS* (6 April 1968).

44   *AL* (9 April 1968); *HS* (8 April 1968).

45   *Savo* (10 April 1968).

46   *Hufvudstadsbladet* (9 April 1968).

disappointed."[47] By the end of the 1960s, it was already commonly felt that it was very difficult, if not impossible, for Finland to do well in Eurovision. "Kristiina Hautala did what she could. But how can she help the fact that Finland is a remote and small country that has difficulties getting its voice heard among the big ones?"[48] In the decades that followed, this view was strengthened through reiteration.

Accounts of the Finnish Eurovision experience create a sense of powerlessness that is a typical source of pathos in melodrama. According to Ien Ang, the tragedy of melodrama arises from the way characters' hopes are gradually crushed as they become aware of their helplessness in the face of greater forces. A melodramatic structure of feeling is thus characterized by fatalism.[49] The feeling of powerlessness is produced over the years when the reception of songs is interpreted in the context of the wider Finnish Eurovision history; the reading of this history is selective and emphasizes the worst results. This creates an impression of a national destiny that cannot be altered, no matter how good the performances may be. As Marcia Landy points out while discussing the relationship between melodrama and common sense, "melodrama and history feed on familiarity, ritualization, repetition, and overvaluation of the past to produce a déjà vu sense of 'Yes, that is the way it was and is.'"[50] In a melodramatic reading, Finland is seen as an eternal underdog that keeps trying to change its position in the forcefield of Eurovision Europe, but remains powerless to effect that change. Language, cultural differences in musical preference, and a marginal position in terms of geography and politics have been popular explanations given to the situation.

Melodramatic narration in film typically separates the viewpoints of the characters and the viewer so that the viewer knows more about the events than any particular character. The viewer has access to characters' feelings but also sees the larger circumstances that determine their fate.[51] The stories of Finnish Eurovision disappointment offer this kind of an all-seeing position to the viewer. Because the narrative of high hopes and bitter disappointment has been repeated many times, optimism loses its credibility. The television viewer can expect that advance hype will be followed by an anti-climax once again. The Finnish representative gets the role of the melodramatic character whose optimistic comments seem pathetic, for the viewer already "knows" that the singer will end up disappointed. The very conventionality of the melodramatic Eurovision disappointment also makes it potential material for ironic and humorous readings. Through reiteration, the conventions of the scenario

---

47 *Valkeakosken Sanomat* (10 April 1968).

48 *Pohjolan Sanomat* (10 April 1968). The idea of Finland as a "small" country has had an important influence in Finnish nationalistic thought and politics since the nineteenth century. In the Cold War era Finnish security politics emphasized that, in order to remain independent, Finland had to recognize its smallness and take this "fact" into account in its relations to the great world powers. Harle and Moisio, *Missä on Suomi?* pp. 185–6.

49 Ang, *Watching Dallas*, pp. 72–3, 82, 123.

50 Marcia Landy, *Cinematic Uses of the Past* (Minneapolis: University of Minnesota Press, 1996), p. 19.

51 Steve Neale, "Melodrama and Tears," *Screen* 27/6 (1986): 7.

have become well known and can be enjoyed from a position of ironic distance.[52] The exaggerated emotionality of the headline "I CRIED, CRIED, CRIED" can seem both pathetic and ridiculous.

A paranoid structure of feeling

The attempt to explain Laura's failure resulted in some rather paranoid interpretations of the voting process. It was commonly argued that the competition was decided by neighborly voting, for which East European countries were blamed in particular. "The Balkans" were especially singled out as the guilty party.[53] Members of YLE's Eurovision team accused East European countries of dishonest conduct and suggested that they had deliberately traded votes.[54] The corruption charges draw on stereotypical ideas of the Balkans as a primitive and dangerous area at the border of the "symbolic continent" of Europe.[55] It is easy to scapegoat "the Balkans," as the conspiracy theories can build on a long history of representing the area as a "problem" for Europe.[56]

The accusations raised against the Balkans are a response to the changing power balance of the ESC. In the melodramatic understanding of the contest, Eurovision has been seen as a field in which Finland doesn't have equal chances with the dominant West European countries, and melodramatic fatalism has emphasized the seemingly unchanging nature of this situation. However, in 2002 the contest was won by a newly joined East European country for a second year in a row. The success of the Baltic countries seemed to suggest that the power relations of Eurovision were changing and that even small countries on the margins of Europe could do well in the ESC. This development called into question traditional explanations for Finland's failure. In the search for new explanations, paranoid conspiracy theories are one answer.

Another way of responding to the new situation was to modify the melodramatic story of Finland as the eternal underdog. It was claimed that the East European countries now dominated the ESC, and that in their eyes Finland belonged "firmly to the West."[57] In contrast to earlier decades, Eurovision failure now seemed to function

---

52 See Barbara Klinger, *Melodrama and Meaning: History, Culture, and the Films of Douglas Sirk* (Bloomington: Indiana University Press, 1994), p. 142.

53 *AL, IL, TS* (27 May 2002); *HS, IS* (28 May 2002).

54 *IL, IS* (27 May 2002); *IL* (28 May 2002).

55 See Dubravka Zarkov, "Gender, Orientalism and the History of Ethnic Hatred in the Former Yugoslavia," in *Crossfires: Nationalism, Racism and Gender in Europe*, ed. Helma Lutz, Ann Phoenix, and Nira Yuval-Davis (London: Pluto Press, 1995), pp. 105–120.

56 It is questionable whether the Balkan countries actually favored each other that conspicuously. On the other hand, Estonia and the Nordic countries did award each other many votes as often before. When "the Balkans" are represented as the villains of the story, the question of favoritism is removed to a safe distance from Finland. Thus it was possible to represent the Nordic countries as a contrast to the "scheming" Balkans. See *IS* (28 May 2002).

57 *IS* (27 May 2002); see also *IL* (28 May 2002).

as a proof of Finland's belonging to the West.[58] The sheer number of East European countries was emphasized, and they were represented as a kind of flood that was taking over the competition.[59] It was even claimed that Eurovision would soon start to resemble the "good old Intervision Song Contest."[60] The power of East European participants was exaggerated in a way that seems rather paranoid.

Shame and melodramatic readings of failure both have something paranoid about them. Indeed, I would argue that a kind of paranoid structure of feeling serves as a unifying feature in negative affective responses to Eurovision in the Finnish media. Here I don't use paranoia to refer to a pathological psychological state, but to a manner of interpreting the world. Eve Kosofsky Sedgwick has analyzed paranoia as a way of knowing: the primary aim of paranoia is to avoid unpleasant surprises, which means that any bad news must always already be known beforehand, and paranoia is thus by nature anticipatory.[61] Expressions of shame after national preliminaries and the melodramatic way failure is expected from Finnish entrants exemplify this attempt to avoid negative surprises. If one "knows" from the beginning that Finnish representatives cannot do well, one doesn't have to be disappointed when they end up at the bottom of the scoreboard.

Conclusion: Finland 292 points

After Laura's poor showing in 2002 it was suggested that Finland should no longer participate in the ESC. Both the evening papers held Internet polls about whether or not Finland should discontinue its participation. "Finland's reputation as a pitiful Eurovision country has long roots. Saying goodbye to the competition might save Finland from becoming a laughing stock," one of them suggested, appealing to a wish to avoid negative experiences.[62] In both polls, the vast majority (78% and 84%, respectively) of the respondents held the opinion that Finland should leave the contest.[63] Many claimed that neighborly voting by East European countries spoiled the competition, and it was suggested that European Union members should have a contest of their own.[64] Even prominent members of YLE's Eurovision team argued that it was not worthwhile to participate in the ESC in its present form. As an alternative they suggested that the Nordic broadcasters could set up a new

---

58   This opinion is hardly supported by the voting results, as three of the six countries that actually voted for "Addicted to You" belong to the "East."

59   *IS* (27 May 2002).

60   *IS* (28 May 2002).

61   Eve Kosofsky Sedgwick, "Paranoid Reading and Reparative Reading; or, You're So Paranoid, You Probably Think This Introduction Is about You," in *Novel Gazing: Queer Readings in Fiction*, ed. Eve Kosofsky Sedgwick (Durham, NC: Duke University Press, 1997), pp. 9–10.

62   *IS* (28 May 2002).

63   *IL* (28 May 2002); *IS* (29 May 2002).

64   <www.iltasanomat.fi/arkisto/default.asp?alue=nettikyselyt&id=2023> Accessed 16 March 2007.

competition of their own.[65] These responses manifested a wish to turn away from a potential source of distress and search for safety in the company of the the country's closest West European allies and neighbors – a logical paranoid reaction.

At the same time, the melodramatic representation of Finland as a stubborn anti-hero offered its own pleasures. This image of Finland was made more widely recognizable through the international media attention given to the Finnish representative Lordi before the 2006 ESC, when Lordi's monster show was represented as the defiant response of a country long troubled by its unsuccessful Eurovision history. Lordi's spectacular victory then provided a happy ending to the melodramatic story of Finnish Eurovision efforts. In Finland Lordi's success was greeted by huge media excitement, and the winners were celebrated as national heroes everywhere from the popular press to the government. The volume and emotional tone of the response attests to the affective power that the ESC has acquired over the decades as a symbol of European recognition. The fact that Lordi received a record of 292 points, made up of votes from almost all participating countries, was treated as a special source of joy. The media response also shows how close national shame and pride can be to each other: after decades of talk about shame, it was possible to turn Eurovision into a source of national pride overnight.

---

65   *IL, IS* (27 May 2002).

Chapter 8

The socialist star:
Yugoslavia, Cold War politics and the
Eurovision Song Contest

Dean Vuletic

During the Cold War the cultural and political identities of the multinational federation of Yugoslavia were performed on the stage of the Eurovision Song Contest (ESC).[1] Yugoslavia was the only socialist East European country to take part in this contest, which started out as a manifestation of West European cultural cooperation, and its anomalous position in Eurovision is explained by the unique geopolitical position that Yugoslavia occupied in Europe during the Cold War. In 1948 Yugoslav leader Josip Broz Tito refused to submit his country to Soviet political dominance, and for the rest of its existence Yugoslavia pursued an independent foreign policy between East and West that saw it become a founder of the Non-Aligned Movement. After Yugoslavia broke with the Soviet Union it pursued a rapprochement with the that was accompanied by an increasing openness towards Western cultural influences; as a consequence, the regime allowed Western popular music trends to develop more freely in Yugoslavia than its counterparts did in other parts of eastern Europe.[2] Because of these political considerations, Yugoslavia was also able to engage in

---

1   There were, of course, three "Yugoslavias": interwar, royal Yugoslavia (known officially as the Kingdom of Serbs, Croats, and Slovenes until 1929) from 1918 to 1941; postwar, socialist Yugoslavia from 1945 to 1991; and a rump Yugoslavia comprising Serbia and Montenegro from 1992 to 2003. In this chapter, the term "Yugoslavia" refers only to socialist Yugoslavia.

2   For a comparative discussion of the history of popular music, especially rock, in postwar eastern Europe, see *Rocking the State: Rock Music and Politics in Eastern Europe and Russia*, ed. Sabrina Ramet (Boulder, CO: Westview Press, 1994), and Timothy Ryback, *Rock Around the Bloc: A History of Rock Music in Eastern Europe and the Soviet Union* (New York: Oxford University Press, 1990). Although Yugoslavia's openness towards Western cultural influences from the 1950s onwards gave it the semblance of being the most liberal country in socialist eastern Europe, popular music in Yugoslavia was still subject to censorship when it challenged the ideology and politics of the regime. In his study of censorship in Yugoslavia from 1945 to 1991, Marko Lopušina maintains that the Yugoslav regime never compiled lists of songs that could not be broadcast or performed, but that it was instead radio, television, and press editors, concert organizers, and record company officials who imposed political censorship on artists and songs that were deemed ideologically or politically inappropriate. In addition, artists, composers, and songwriters engaged in self-censorship, be it for genuine ideological or political convictions or because they wanted to maintain job security. Marko Lopušina, *Crna knjiga: cenzura u Jugoslaviji 1945–91* (Belgrade: Fokus, 1991), pp. 14, 243–4.

cultural cooperation with the West through the ESC earlier than other East European countries: while they only began entering Eurovision after the fall of their state socialist regimes in 1989 and 1990, Yugoslavia took part in it from 1961.

Participation in the ESC presented Yugoslavia with the challenge of how to express its non-aligned, multinational, and socialist characteristics, together with the traditional and modern elements of its identities, in a musical form to a predominantly West European audience. Yugoslavia's Cold War politics, cultural policy, and modernity were consequently captured in the lyrics, music, performances, and videos of the songs that it contributed to Eurovision. They also shaped the Yugoslav public's perceptions of the contest's significance, as many Yugoslavs considered participation in the contest to be beneficial for the international promotion of their country – especially for tourism – and the development of its popular music industry. However, as Yugoslavia's Eurovision entries continued to be marked by poor results in the 1960s and the 1970s, Yugoslavs questioned whether their popular music production was "Western" and "modern" enough to compete with that of western Europe, and whether a Yugoslav popular music style that incorporated folk influences was culturally just too different for West European tastes to be successful in the contest. These concerns reflected a wider debate in Yugoslav society concerning the nature of Yugoslavia's cultural and political identities during the Cold War period, identities that popular music reflected, promoted, and shaped.

By the 1980s Yugoslavia appeared to have addressed some of these issues in Eurovision at least by sending songs that conformed to international popular music styles, and this approach contributed to its victory in the 1989 ESC. However, as Yugoslavia was achieving this cultural success on the European stage, citizens and political leaders were questioning the value of common Yugoslav cultural and political identities and emphasizing instead the primacy of Croatian, Serbian, Slovenian, and other national ones. And just as Yugoslavia's distinct Cold War character found expression at Eurovision, so too was its disintegration played out in the contest in the early 1990s: as one of the last international cultural events at which Yugoslavia appeared as a united country in 1991, Eurovision provided a stage on which the Yugoslav federation sang its final song.

Popular music and Cold War politics

The Yugoslav Communists came to power after having led the antifascist Partisan resistance movement during World War II. Upon assuming control they endeavored to create a supranational Yugoslav identity that would unify the constituent nations but also acknowledge their diversity: this Yugoslavist cultural policy was based on the ideas of "brotherhood and unity" among the nations and a Yugoslav brand of socialism.[3] In the musical sphere this policy determined what could be performed and produced: for example, immediately after the war, themes that emphasized national differences within Yugoslavia were ignored in music and superseded by a

---

3   Andrew Baruch Wachtel, *Making a Nation, Breaking a Nation: Literature and Cultural Politics in Yugoslavia* (Stanford, CA: Stanford University Press, 1998), p. 9.

focus on the wartime struggle of the Partisan movement, socialist development, and Yugoslavism.[4] Instead of songs that imitated Western styles or were nationalist or religious in content, revolutionary songs, Partisan marching songs, traditional folk songs and Russian songs were privileged in the years immediately after the war.[5] Ideological commissions urged songwriters to compose lyrics that incorporated socialist realist symbols and themes (such as the hammer and sickle, tractors, plows, heavy industry, labor, and happiness),[6] and the performance of songs that were considered ideologically or politically inappropriate by the Communists could be punished by the loss of one's job, imprisonment, or penal labor.[7]

In the first years of the postwar era the Yugoslav Communists also attacked Western popular music as culturally degrading, ideologically inappropriate, and politically threatening. Western-style popular music had been developing in Yugoslavia in the interwar period and was largely influenced by American and German trends, which could be heard in the dance orchestras, *Schlager* (sentimental popular songs) and jazz cultivated in the 1920s and 1930s.[8] However, from 1945 to 1948 cultural and political relations between Yugoslavia and the West were strained as they found themselves in opposing ideological camps and with competing interests in such issues as the Greek Civil War and the status of Trieste.[9] Western popular music was at this time perceived by the Yugoslav Communists as a weapon in the battle between capitalists and communists, and the commitment to communism of anyone who performed or listened to such music was rendered questionable. Top officials of the Yugoslav regime led the charge against Western popular music and publicly condemned it as a "Western conspiracy" that corrupted youth and swindled people of their money.[10] In 1947 Milovan Djilas, a leading party ideologue and vice premier in the Yugoslav government, published an article in which he declared that "America is our sworn enemy, and jazz, likewise, as its product."[11] Taking their cue from the statements made by the state leadership, Yugoslav cultural, political, and social organizations waged a battle against Western popular music in the late 1940s: agitprop committees

4   Ibid., p. 146.

5   Petar Luković, *Bolja prošlost: prizori iz muzičkog života Jugoslavije 1940–1989* (Belgrade: Mladost, 1989), p. 9; Ljerka V. Rasmussen, *Newly Composed Folk Music of Yugoslavia* (New York: Routledge, 2002), p. 40.

6   Luković, p. 12.

7   Sabrina P. Ramet, *Balkan Babel: The Disintegration of Yugoslavia from the Death of Tito to the Fall of Milošević*, 4th ed. (Boulder, CO: Westview Press, 2002), p. 128.

8   Krešimir Kovačević, *Muzičko stvaralaštvo u Hrvatskoj 1945–1965* (Zagreb: Udruženje kompozitora Hrvatske, 1966), pp. 88–9; Rasmussen, p. 7.

9   Tvrtko Jakovina, *Američki komunistički saveznik: Hrvati, Titova Jugoslavija i Sjedinjene američke države 1945–1955* (Zagreb: Profil, Srednja Europa, 2003), pp. 20–223; David L. Larson, *United States Foreign Policy Toward Yugoslavia, 1943–1963* (Washington, DC: University Press of America, 1979), pp. 82–179; Lorraine M. Lees, *Keeping Tito Afloat: The United States, Yugoslavia, and the Cold War* (University Park, PA: Pennsylvania State University Press, 1997), pp. 1–41.

10   Luković, pp. 40, 46.

11   Cited in ibid., p. 11.

banned concerts and plays that had "decadent Western music,"[12] and advisory boards were formed on all radio stations with the job of censoring music that used the English language or was considered "capitalist," "decadent," or "kitsch."[13]

After 1948, though, when Moscow severed its alliance with Belgrade, the Yugoslav Communists' hostile attitude towards Western popular music began to soften. Russian songs became subject to political censorship on Yugoslav radio and, as Yugoslavia turned to the West for economic and political support, Western popular music began to receive more airplay.[14] From the early 1950s jazz concerts were organized with the support of state cultural institutions, and associations of artists and composers of popular music were formed: in 1953 the Udruženje jazz muzičara (Association of jazz musicians) was established in Belgrade, followed by the Savez kompozitora zabavne i džez muzike (Federation of composers of pop and jazz music) in Zagreb in 1956.[15] By the late 1950s Yugoslav record companies had licensing agreements with their Western counterparts, and Yugoslavia's major popular music producer, the Zagreb-based Jugoton, was distributing the songs of Elvis Presley.[16]

In the 1950s, then, Western popular music became less politicized in Yugoslavia in the sense that the regime no longer considered it to be so much of a cultural and political threat. But as consumer culture, the entertainment industry and the mass media expanded in Yugoslavia,[17] the sociopolitical force of popular music was harnessed to give expression and form to cultural, political, and social identities. This was especially evident in the popular music festivals that were established from the 1950s, which the ethnomusicologist Ljerka V. Rasmussen describes as "the single most powerful public forum for the presentation, production and definition of Yugoslav popular music"[18] (a significance that Eurovision would also have for it at the international level). The Zagreb Festival was the first popular music festival established in Yugoslavia,[19] but it was the Opatija Festival that began in the Croatian town of the same name in 1958 that was the most important festival in

---

12   Cited in Lopušina, p. 23.

13   Ibid., pp. 23–4, 26–7, 32, 246; Luković, p. 12. With the censorship of Western popular music on Yugoslav radio, people instead tuned in to Radio Luxembourg, the Voice of America and other international broadcasts to listen to it, or they accessed it at foreign cultural and diplomatic missions in Yugoslav cities. Cited in Luković, pp. 10, 29.

14   Lopušina, p. 243; Luković, p. 33. For a discussion of the opening up of Yugoslavia, especially Croatia, to American cultural influences in the late 1940s and early 1950s, see Jakovina, pp. 456–77.

15   Luković, pp. 15, 17, 24–5, 29, 34–5.

16   Rasmussen, p. 49. Jugoton was established in 1947, and in 1952 another important Yugoslav record company, Produkcija gramofonskih ploča Radiotelevizije Beograd (PGP RTB, Production of Gramophone Records of Radio-Television Belgrade), was set up. Ibid., pp. xxix, 42–3.

17   Ibid., p. 42; Maroje Mihovilović, "Jer što je nama Eurovizija?" *Start* (24 March 1976).

18   Rasmussen, pp. 41–2.

19   In 1953 Horizont (Horizon) – the musical section of the leading youth organization in Croatia, the Narodna omladina Hrvatske (National Youth of Croatia) – organized the first dance melody competition in Yugoslavia, and the Zagreb Festival developed from it.

Yugoslavia for the next two decades,[20] and for a time it was there that the Yugoslav entry for Eurovision was selected. As the bulletin for the 1976 Opatija Festival puts it, "the role of the festival is not small. As the one and only all-Yugoslav festival it is particularly significant for the development of all that comprises the popular music of the nations and nationalities [of Yugoslavia]. In this regard the festival has a sociopolitical significance…"[21]

With these developments on its popular music scene the foundations were laid for Yugoslavia to enter Eurovision, but in the very first years of the contest it was not yet able to do so because television services in the country were too limited.[22] Television broadcasting did not develop simultaneously in all of the Yugoslav republics and provinces, each of which would eventually come to have its own television center situated in and named after its capital. The first experimental broadcasts were made in 1956 by Croatia's TV Zagreb, followed by Serbia's TV Belgrade and Slovenia's TV Ljubljana in 1958.[23] After this the Jugoslavenska radiotelevizija (JRT, Yugoslav Radio & Television) network was formed, and it could participate in Eurovision and other televised productions of the European Broadcasting Union (EBU), of which Yugoslavia had been a founding member in 1950.[24] The limited development of the mass media in Yugoslavia in those years – especially a component of it that focused on entertainment – also meant that there was little coverage of Eurovision in the Yugoslav press in the late 1950s.[25]

Yugoslavia made its Eurovision debut in 1961 in Cannes with Ljiljana Petrović singing "Neke davne zvezde" (Some ancient stars); she later recalled that "the appearance of Yugoslavia aroused much interest … as the first socialist country at the festival of European popular music."[26] Although the word "stars" appeared in the title of Petrović's song, this was not symbolic of any political message: the theme of the song – like that of almost all of the Yugoslav entries from 1961 to 1992[27] – was

---

Kovačević, p. 89; Siniša Škarica, *Pjeva Vam Ivo Robić: Izvorne snimke (1949–1959)* (Zagreb: Perfekt Music for Croatia Records, 2001), pp. 57–60, 69.

20   Rasmussen, p. 41.

21   Cited in Zvonko Kovačić, "Čestitke prije i poslije," *Studio* (28 February 1976). Yugoslavia's ethnic groups were divided into the categories of "nations" and "nationalities," with the former being those that had traditional territorial homelands within Yugoslavia (Bosnian Muslims, Croats, Macedonians, Montenegrins, Serbs, and Slovenes) and the latter those with territorial homelands beyond Yugoslavia's boundaries (including the Albanians, Czechs, Hungarians, Italians, Ruthenians, Slovaks, Turks, and Ukrainians).

22   Momčilo Karan, "'Zvezde' na sedmom nebu," *Oslobodjenje* (3 May 1990).

23   "Povijest," Hrvatska radiotelevizija, <www.hrt.hr/povijest/povijest_hrv.html> Accessed 30 March 2005; "Prošlost," Radio-televizija Srbije, <www.rts.co.yu/ rts_istorija. asp> Accessed 30 March 2005.

24   "50 Years of EBU," Hrvatska radiotelevizija, <www.hrt.hr/ebu/ebu50-sve.html> Accessed 3 April 2005.

25   Momčilo Karan, *Pesma Evrovizije: od Ljiljane Petrović do Željka Joksimovića* (Belgrade: Svet knjige, 2005), p. 5.

26   Cited in Karan, "'Zvezde' na sedmom nebu."

27   Indeed, of all the songs that Yugoslavia sent to Eurovision in this period, only one of them – "Moja generacija" (My generation), performed by Korni grupa (Korni Group) in 1974

instead one of love. In this case it was about a woman pining for lost love, and it did not differ remarkably in style and theme from other songs that were performed at Eurovision in 1961. A Yugoslav socialist consciousness did, however, influence the aesthetics of Petrović's performance: after the lyricist of her song, Miroslav Antić, had told the singer that she should look "humble and worthy of the socialist country from which I come," Petrović appeared on stage wearing a simple dress with a brooch.[28]

Nul points

Yugoslavia came eighth out of 16 contestants in 1961, but the following year it came fourth with Lola Novaković and her song "Ne pali svetla u sumrak" (Don't turn on the lights at twilight). Novaković was overjoyed with the result, for she believed that it showed that Yugoslav popular music could "successfully contend with that created by songwriters in western Europe."[29] But after 1962 Yugoslavia performed poorly in the contest: in 1964, for example, Sabahudin Kurt came last and received no points for his song "Život je sklopio krug" (Life has come full circle).[30] In the subsequent years that it took part in Eurovision in the 1960s and 1970s, Yugoslavia appeared mostly in the bottom half of the scoreboard, and it would only surpass the relative success of the early 1960s in the 1980s. These low rankings occurred despite the fact that Yugoslavia was sending its most popular artists to Eurovision, and they prompted the Yugoslav media and music industry to question why Yugoslav popular music was not successful in western Europe, and whether the country should continue to participate in the contest.

In the debates over Eurovision that took place in the Yugoslav media in the 1960s and 1970s, the principal reasons advanced for Yugoslavia's participation in the contest concerned the international promotion of the country and the development of its popular music industry. Yugoslavia used Eurovision not only to show that it was a socialist East European country that was open to cultural exchange with the West, but also to promote itself as a tourist destination for West Europeans. In the postwar period Yugoslavia derived much of its hard currency earnings from a tourist industry concentrated along its Adriatic Coast, and most of its visitors came from western Europe. Eurovision gave Yugoslavia the opportunity to promote its tourist attractions to a television audience that by the 1970s was counted in the hundreds of millions, and many of its Eurovision entries consequently promoted a romantic, Mediterranean image of the country through their lyrics and music. For example, in 1963 and 1965 Vice Vukov performed the songs "Brodovi" (Boats) and "Čežnja" (Yearning) respectively, both of which incorporated images of the sea; in 1983 Daniel Popović's song "Džuli" (Julie) was about a summer romance with a foreign

---

– had an overtly political theme. Its lyrics express the difficulties that Yugoslavs faced during the Second World War, and emphasize how much life has improved in Yugoslavia since.

28   Cited in Nataša Smaić, "Broš iz potaje," *Eurosong 90: Pjesma Eurovizije (Studio, posebno izdanje)* (April/May 1990).

29   Cited in Karan, *Pesma Evrovizije*, pp. 11–12.

30   Karan, "'Zvezde' na sedmom nebu."

woman, while in the 1985 song "Ja sam za ples" (I wanna dance) by Novi fosili (New Fossil) a tourist in Yugoslavia invites a local woman to dance on the beach. When Yugoslavia's Eurovision songs were promoted through films and videos they were usually set in coastal locations, too: for example, the video for the 1984 entry "Ciao amore" (Bye, love), sung by Izolda Barudžija and Vlado Kalember, was filmed on the Montenegrin coast, and Barudžija appeared in it bathing topless (while this reflected Yugoslavia's liberal attitudes towards nude bathing, it also caused a Eurovision scandal when Turkish state television refused to broadcast the video because of Barudžija's nudity).[31]

The other advantage of ESC participation that commentators in the Yugoslav media emphasized was the opportunity that it provided for the Yugoslav popular music industry to develop itself through contact with the West European industry and its markets.[32] However, as Yugoslavia continued to achieve poor results in the contest, commentators began to ask the interrelated questions of whether Yugoslav popular music was just culturally too different for the tastes of West European audiences, especially when it incorporated folk influences, or whether it was just not "modern" – which in their discourse was practically synonymous with "Western" – enough to succeed in such a market.[33]

This discussion about whether Yugoslavia's Eurovision entries should conform to international popular music styles or incorporate the sounds of Yugoslavia's folk musics was symptomatic of a wider debate in Yugoslav society on the nature of Yugoslav cultural and political identities in the context of Cold War politics and postwar modernization. While non-aligned Yugoslavia had emerged as a major center of popular music production in eastern Europe and one that was open to Western trends, could socialist economics and Yugoslav aesthetics present a challenge to the popular music industry of the West at Eurovision? In the 1960s and 1970s Yugoslav artists and record companies and JRT complained that they were just not strong enough to compete against the productional and promotional capacities of their West European counterparts, whom some even accused of unfairly influencing the results of the contest.[34] They also believed that Yugoslavia's cultural and geopolitical characteristics hampered its success at Eurovision, especially because it was the only East European and Slavic participant and could not rely on the cultural and regional affinities that other countries (such as those of the Romance-language and Scandinavian blocs) could when it came to voting.[35] The journalist Maroje Mihovilović cynically articulated the geopolitical challenge that Yugoslavia faced at

---

31   Kosta Čakić, "Izolda izranja iz vode," *Danas* (1 May 1984).

32   M. Goluža, "Realan plasman za 'Vše rože sveta,'" *Vjesnik* (10 April 1967).

33   Mustafa R. Gafić, "Sudjelovati, nego šta," *Studio* (12 February 1976); G.I., "Eurovizijska kuhinja nota," *VUS* (13 August 1969); cited in Karan, *Pesma Evrovizije*, p. 26; Zvonko Kovačić, "Želja jedna – ukusa sto," *Studio* (13 March 1976); Branka Malčić, "Tko to, u Evropi, pjeva?" *Vjesnik* (22 February 1981).

34   "Naše pjesme, naši košmari," *Start* (13 May 1989).

35   Momčilo Karan, "Poraženi 'Ambasadori,'" *Oslobodjenje* (5 May 1990); Fran Potočnjak, "Izgubljena milijarda," *Studio* (11 March 1978). More recently, other participants have also criticized the Balkan countries for voting for one another. For examples of this at the 2004 ESC, see Ana Petruseva, "Old Friends Serenade Serbia in Istanbul," *Balkan Crisis*

Eurovision: "we are a proud nation, we know that some geographical and historical circumstances have apparently pushed us into the background of the European cultural and pseudocultural community, and that bothers us. But we know that some neopolitical events nonetheless have a major significance for national self-affirmation."[36]

Yet there were other commentators who suggested that Yugoslavia's unimpressive performance at Eurovision was due not so much to the talents or intrigues of the West Europeans but instead to problems with the way that Yugoslav entries were selected. Juries from each of the television centers chose Yugoslavia's ESC representatives through specially-arranged preliminary contests or at the Opatija Festival, but each television center also nominated a share of the candidates for the selection. A number of journalists suggested that Yugoslavia was not sending its best songs to Eurovision because of competition among the television centers of each republic and province, which would cast their vote for outsiders in order to thwart the success of favorites from other television centers and increase the chances of their own nominees.[37] According to this view, the selection process for Yugoslavia's Eurovision songs thus turned into a contest for power, prestige, and resources among the television centers and the republican and provincial interests that they represented.

In the 1960s and 1970s these rivalries reflected political conditions in Yugoslavia at the governmental level, as devolutionary reforms handed more power to the republics and provinces at the expense of the federal center. Indeed, these reforms meant that by the mid-1960s the forging of a supranational Yugoslav identity was no longer the premier goal of Yugoslav cultural policy, and with increasing decentralization the republics and provinces were given greater reign to develop their national cultures.[38] A consequence of this was the cultural revival that developed in Croatia from 1966 which motivated a national political movement known as the *maspok* (a Croatian acronym for *masovni pokret*, or "mass movement"), and the period that it marked was dubbed the Croatian Spring. The *maspok* articulated the cultural, economic and political grievances that Croatia had regarding its position within Yugoslavia, and it called for increased autonomy for Croatia within the federation.[39] These issues were also articulated in the popular music of the time, especially in the patriotic songs of the pop star Vice Vukov, who had represented Yugoslavia twice at Eurovision in 1963 and 1965. When Tito quashed the Croatian Spring in December 1971 because he believed that the demands of the *maspok* had gone too far and were threatening

---

Report 499 (22 May 2004), via Institute for War and Peace Reporting, <www.iwpr.net/index. pl?archive/bcr3/bcr3_200405_499_2_eng.txt> Accessed 30 March 2005.

36   Mihovilović, "Jer što je nama Eurovizija?"

37   M. Goluža, "Rezultati nezdrave klime," *Vjesnik* (22 March 1965); Karan, *Pesma Evrovizije*, pp. 16, 33; Zvonko Kovačić, "Čestitke prije i poslije," *Studio* (28 February 1976); Kovačić, "Želja jedna – ukusa sto."

38   Wachtel, *Making a Nation, Breaking a Nation*, pp. 173–5.

39   Marcus Tanner, *Croatia: A Nation Forged in War* (New Haven, CT: Yale University Press, 1997), pp. 190–202. As part of the national revival, there was a resurgence in the display of traditional national emblems, and patriotic songs that had been suppressed by the communist authorities were openly sung again. Ante Čuvalo, *The Croatian National Movement: 1966–1972* (New York: Columbia University Press, 1990), p. 161.

the unity of Yugoslavia, the Yugoslav authorities forbade Vukov from performing concerts and recording music, and he went into exile in Paris.[40]

By the late 1970s Yugoslavia still had not managed to improve its rankings on the Eurovision scoreboard, and in 1976 it again hit bottom when the group Amabasdori (Ambassadors) came last with the song "Ne mogu skriti svoju bol" (I can't hide my pain). At this point JRT decided that it, too, could no longer hide its pain and decided to withdraw from the contest, and from 1977 to 1980 Yugoslavia did not take part in it. Among the claims made by JRT to justify its decision were that big international record companies dominated the contest, and that it promoted "kitsch."[41] However, there was a significant public response to JRT's decision that attested to the popularity of Eurovision in Yugoslavia: television viewers sent in letters stating that, despite the rankings of Yugoslav entries, the contest was still a good opportunity to get together around the television and socialize, and others emphasized the benefits that Eurovision provided for the international promotion of Yugoslavia and the development and exposure of its popular music industry.[42] In 1978 the Zagreb-based entertainment weekly *Studio* began a campaign to convince JRT to re-enter the contest, and it even offered to cover the financial cost of Yugoslavia's Eurovision entries if only JRT would reverse its decision![43] *Studio* and other popular entertainment magazines from all over Yugoslavia conducted a poll among their readers on whether Yugoslavia should again participate, and of the 107,181 votes that they received, 97.5 per cent of respondents were in favor of Yugoslavia returning to Eurovision.[44] All of this convinced JRT to reapply to enter the contest in 1980, and after its readmission was approved by the EBU Yugoslavia resumed its participation from 1981.[45] Although some changes were made to the process by which the Yugoslav entry was selected – for example, through a specially-organized contest instead of at the Opatija Festival

---

40 When the Croatian Spring was quelled Vukov's name appeared on a list of its chief offenders, who were labelled the "Counter-revolutionary Committee of the Fifty." Vice Vukov, *Pogled iza ogledala* (Zagreb: Nakladni zavod Matice hrvatske, 1999), p. 7. However, unlike others on the list, Vukov managed to avoid arrest because he was on a concert tour in Australia at the time. When he returned to Yugoslavia in 1976 after exile in Paris, he was still considered a "nationalist" and "politically inappropriate," and he was only allowed to perform in public again in the late 1980s. Lopušina, pp. 57, 79; Vice Vukov, *Tvoja zemlja: sjećanja na 1971* (Zagreb: Nakladni zavod Matice hrvatske, 2003), pp. 79–80, 102.

41 Cited in Karan, *Pesma Evrovizije*, p. 30; cited in Zvonko Kovačić, "Uskoro i službeno!" *Studio* (6 May 1978); Salih Zvizdić, "Lice i naličje 'Pjesme Evrovizije,'" *Vjesnik* (18 June 1976).

42 Karan, "Poraženi 'Ambasadori'"; cited in Zvonko Kovačić, "Na vjetrenjače ne treba jurišati!" *Studio* (2 April 1977); A.V., "Što kažu stručnjaci? Da!" *Studio* (8 April 1978); "Rekli ste – da!" *Studio* (1 April 1978).

43 Redakcija *Studio*, "'Studijev' prijedlog Programskom odboru JRT" (11 March 1978).

44 *Studio*, "Većina ili 97,53% rekla je DA!" (29 April 1978). The other magazines that participated in the poll were Belgrade's *Radio TV revija* (Radio TV Review) and *TV novosti* (TV News), Ljubljana's *Stop*, Sarajevo's *VEN* and Skopje's *Ekran* (Screen).

45 D. Vesović, "Povratak na 'Pesmu Evrovizije,'" *Politika ekspres* (11 November 1980).

– television centers continued to nominate the contestants and their juries still chose the winner.[46]

Twelve points

It was in the 1980s that Yugoslavia experienced its greatest successes at Eurovision, with the crowning achievement being its victory in Lausanne in 1989 and the hosting of the contest in Zagreb the following year. This was happening, however, at the same time that Yugoslavia was facing economic and political challenges that threatened the unity of the federation: these included an economic crisis marked by high inflation and unemployment; uprisings in Kosovo that demanded greater political rights for its Albanian population; a nationalist revival in Serbia; and increasing liberalization in Slovenia, which also called for democratic and market reforms at the federal level.[47] The decade began with the death of Tito on 4 May 1980, which symbolized the passing of a generation of Yugoslav leaders who had shared a common experience in the Partisan movement. In 1985 Yugoslavia did not participate in Eurovision because the contest fell on the anniversary of the death of Tito[48] – which brings one to the conclusion that he only ever prevented Yugoslavia from taking part in Eurovision posthumously. But throughout the 1980s the unifying power of Tito, the Partisans, and other definers of Yugoslavia's collective identity was increasingly challenged as intellectuals, politicians, rock musicians, and others broke established taboos, questioned the legitimacy of sustaining myths, appealed to national sentiments, and called for the federation to be reformed.

Although Yugoslavia's success at Eurovision increased its prestige on the international popular music stage, it did not always transcend its internal divisions, and even served to highlight differences among the republics. From 1983 to 1990 all of Yugoslavia's Eurovision entries were provided by TV Zagreb, although this did not mean that all of TV Zagreb's candidates were Croats since contestants were sent to the Yugoslav selection by the television center that served their place of residence.[49] But it did reflect Croatia's position as the major center for popular music production in Yugoslavia as well as the differences that existed within theYugoslav music industry, with Croatian and Slovenian record companies focusing more on popular music and Bosnian and Serbian ones on folk.[50] Among TV Zagreb's Eurovision entries was Daniel Popović, a Montenegrin living in Zagreb, who came fourth at the 1983 ESC with "Džuli." The song was a European hit and sold some 350,000 copies in its English version,[51] and Popović was compared in press reports

---

46 "To je naš izbor," *Studio* (28 February 1981).

47 For a discussion on the developments in the 1980s that led to the disintegration of Yugoslavia, see Ramet, *Balkan Babel*, pp. 3–77.

48 Zvonko Kovačić, "Od zvijezda do ludosti," *Eurosong 90: Pjesma Eurovizije (Studio, posebno izdanje)* (April/May 1990).

49 Zvonko Kovačić, "Europa pojma nema," *Studio* (21 February 1992).

50 Cited in Rasmussen, p. 152, 170.

51 In 1984 it was reported that Popović's single had sold 800,000 copies in Yugoslavia, too. Cited in Zlatko Franjić, "Priča čudnih otkrića," *Večernji list* (31 March 1984).

at the time to Shakin' Stevens.[52] Thereafter TV Zagreb provided a string of successes for Yugoslavia at Eurovision: at the 1987 contest the group Novi fosili came fourth with "Ja sam za ples," and the following year Srebrna krila (Silver Wings) came sixth with "Mangup" (Rascal). Yugoslavia's high rankings on the Eurovision scoreboard in the 1980s were attributed to the fact that all of these songs followed international popular music styles and did not incorporate folk elements.[53] As Daniel Popović put it in reference to his success in 1983, "Džuli" showed what "needs to be sent to the Eurovision contest, … that we should not always push some kind of folklore,"[54] and "that songs have to be produced according to some sort of European standards and that we have to lean towards Europe, and not it towards us."[55] The success of this approach was crowned in 1989 when the group Riva (Boardwalk) from the Croatian port city of Zadar won Eurovision with the song "Rock Me."[56]

Now that Yugoslavia had proven that it could win Eurovision, it faced the challenge of demonstrating that it was capable of organizing the 35th ESC despite the economic and political problems that it was experiencing.[57] Although there was some debate in the Yugoslav press as to which city would be the best place to host the contest, Zagreb was chosen as Riva had been entered by TV Zagreb, and also because the Croatian capital had the appropriate facilities to host the contest, particularly its Vatroslav Lisinski Concert Hall.[58] As with every Eurovision, the 1990 contest had its share of problems: for example, the comperes Oliver Mlakar and Helga Vlahović resigned just three days before the event took place, but ended up hosting it after all; and when the first entry, the Spanish duo Azúcar Moreno, took to the stage the singers' ear plugs did not work and they could not hear the band start, so they had to begin their performance all over again.[59] But apart from this the Zagreb contest was generally judged a success,[60] and it showed that Yugoslavia could achieve West European standards in the production of such an event. As the author Brian Hall writes about watching the 1990 contest on television with friends in Belgrade:

---

52   Ibid.; Željko Suhadolnik, "U medjunarodnom muzičkom sazvježdju," *Vikend* (6 May 1983); Katja Šutić, "Boom, Džuli, Boom," *Studio* (7 May 1983).

53   Ante Ivković, "Najljepša Riva u Europi," *Svijet* (12 May 1989).

54   Cited in Suhadolnik.

55   Cited in Šutić. Lepa Brena, who with the band Slatki greh (Sweet Sin) was favored to win the 1983 preliminary with the newly composed folk song "Sitnije, Cile, sitnije" (Finer, Cile, finer), represented an opposing view: at the time she said that "at Eurovision imitations, something sixthhand, don't pass," and that she and Slatki greh "were focused on producing a Yugoslav song. No rock, ballad, chanson, nothing of that which we steal from the side. But rather that it be something of our own. Why should we pretend, we are a peasant nation, or more exactly a peasant-worker one…" Cited in Karan, *Pesma Evrovizije*, p. 38.

56   Boro Šantić, "Vremeplov 1989: A što sad?" *Eurosong 90: Pjesma Eurovizije (Studio, posebno izdanje)* (April/May 1990).

57   Rene Bakalović, "Plesnim korakom iz mraka," *Danas* (14 November 1989).

58   A. Ivković, "Dobar glas daleko se čuje," *Večernji list* (13 May 1989); Dubravko Stojsavljević, "Šou i kako ga steći," *Studio* (19 May 1989).

59   Zvonko Kovačić, "Goli pred Evropom," *Studio* (11 May 1990); Zvonko Kovačić, "Zvuk i svjetlo ljudskog faktora," *Studio* (18 May 1990).

60   "Pohvale Zagrebu," *Večernji list* (8 May 1989).

as the broadcast began, as the camera swept dizzyingly down from the ceiling of the specially designed hall in Zagreb and across a stage lit by flashing floor panels while computer graphics swirled across the screen, a sigh of relief went around the room. It looked professional. It looked like Europe.[61]

The Zagreb contest even introduced an innovation to Eurovision, a mascot in the form of an animated figure called "Eurocat," which reflected Zagreb's status as the location of a world famous school of animation.[62] Financially it did well, too, recording the highest earnings of any Eurovision held up until then.[63]

The 1990 ESC took place on 5 May, a day after the anniversary of Tito's death and, coincidentally, on the birthday of Karl Marx; perhaps more meaningful for the time, however, was that it also fell on the Council of Europe's Europe Day. Indeed, it was a pleasant historical coincidence that the only East European country in Eurovision won the contest in the year that saw the fall of state socialism in eastern Europe, and the Zagreb contest was the first Eurovision that was broadcast directly to the other countries of eastern Europe and the Soviet Union.[64] The contest itself was marked by a number of politically themed songs that reflected the historic changes occurring in Europe, best demonstrated by Toto Cutugno's song about European integration, "Insieme: 1992" (All together: 1992), which won the contest for Italy. But for Yugoslavia these historical events presented a challenge, for the ending of the East-West division of Europe meant that the unique geopolitical position on which it had partly staked its *raison d'être* was no longer relevant. And while some republics, especially Slovenia and Croatia, were calling for economic and political reforms in Yugoslavia that would bring it closer to western Europe, others – particularly the president of Serbia, Slobodan Milošević – were more resistant to such change.

Goodnight, Europe

While the Zagreb contest embodied hopes for a new, post-Cold War Europe, there was also a less optimistic moment in it that portended events to come. When the voting took place the telephone lines functioned clearly to every European city except Zadar, where the Yugoslav jury was based;[65] that the Yugoslav phone lines could make connections with Europe but not within their own country was a bad omen for the disintegration of Yugoslavia. Around the same time that Eurovision was held in Zagreb the first multiparty elections of the postwar period took place in Croatia and brought Franjo Tudjman's nationalist Hrvatska demokratska zajednica (HDZ, Croatian Democratic Union) to power. Slovenia and Croatia held referenda on

---

61 Brian Hall, *The Impossible Country: A Journey Through the Last Days of Yugoslavia* (London: Secker & Warburg, 1994), p. 45.

62 "Eurovizijske zgode i nezgode," *Studio* (11 May 1990).

63 Goran Radman, the executive producer of the 1990 ESC, later declared that the Zagreb contest had managed to cover 64 per cent of its costs through earnings from the event. Cited in N. Mikac, "I Talijani nam zavide," *Večernji list* (15 December 1990).

64 Miroslava Jandrić, "Šarmantni mačak," *Vjesnik* (7 July 1990).

65 Hall, *The Impossible Country*, p. 46.

their secession from Yugoslavia in December 1990 and May 1991 respectively, with the results in both republics overwhelmingly favoring independence.[66] And on the very same day that the Yugoslav national preliminary contest for the 1991 ESC took place in Sarajevo on 9 March – the last preliminary in which the television centers from all six republics participated – large demonstrations in Belgrade protesting the antidemocratic policies of the Milošević regime (particularly its control over TV Belgrade) were suppressed with tanks.[67]

The significance of the Yugoslav preliminary in 1991 was of course minor when compared to the violent quelling of the Belgrade protests, but it too reflected the political divisions that were pulling Yugoslavia apart. The winner was the TV Belgrade candidate Baby Doll who sang "Brazil" – a title that suggested that Yugoslavia was not moving with the beat that had been set by the various Europe-themed songs at Eurovision in the previous year. The selection of Baby Doll prompted a scandal, as some television centers – especially Hrvatska radiotelevizija (HTV, Croatian Radio & Television), as TV Zagreb had been renamed in 1990 – believed that the voting had been politically motivated. They accused the television centers of Serbia and its allies Montenegro, Kosovo, and Vojvodina – all of which were now led by governments loyal to Milošević – of uniting forces behind TV Belgrade's entry in order to prevent a victory by HTV's candidate Daniel Popović, who was the favorite to win.[68] At the 1991 ESC in Rome two commentators were sent from Yugoslavia, one from TV Belgrade and the other from HTV; reflecting the divisions in the country between the republics whose governments were opposed to Milošević's politics and those that were pro, the HTV commentary was broadcast in Croatia, Bosnia-Herzegovina, Macedonia, and Slovenia, and that of TV Belgrade in Serbia, Montenegro, Kosovo, and Vojvodina.[69] Baby Doll came second to last in the 1991 contest, receiving only one point for her performance.[70]

By the 1992 ESC the Jugoslovenska narodna armija (JNA, Yugoslav People's Army) had waged wars against the secessionist republics of Slovenia and Croatia – where it aided Serbian forces that opposed Croatian independence – and attacked both Zagreb and Zadar. Although JRT had invited all of the former Yugoslav republics to participate in the national preliminary, Croatia and Slovenia did not send entries as their independence had received widespread recognition from the international community by January 1992, and there was also no Albanian candidate from Kosovo due to the tensions in that province between Albanians and Serbs.[71]

66 Ramet, *Balkan Babel*, pp. 59–60.

67 Laura Silber and Allan Little, *Yugoslavia: Death of a Nation*, rev. ed. (New York: Penguin Books, 1997), pp. 119–25.

68 Zvonko Kovačić, "Jugovizija umire od stida," *Studio* (15 March 1991); Mirela Kruhak, "Sve se zbilo iza kulisa," *TOP* (18 March 1991); Mirela Kruhak and Damir Strugar, "Sve je bilo lažirano?" *TOP* (18 March 1991); Dražen Vrdoljak, "Yuga umire pjevajući," *Večernji list* (12 March 1991).

69 "Hrvatska pjesma na Euroviziji," *TOP* (27 January 1992). However, HTV did not broadcast Eurovision live in 1991 due to fighting that had started in Croatia just before it.

70 Silvije Tomašević, "Baby Dol [*sic*] s drugug planeta," *Studio* (10 May 1991).

71 Igor Gobac, "Srbovizija ide na Euroviziju," *Globus* (3 April 1992); Vesna Latinović, "Digi lu, digi lei," *Glas Slavonije* (30 March 1992); Branka Otašević, "Ko će na 'Pesmu

Chosen to represent Yugoslavia was a Serbian "newly-composed folk song" called "Ljubim te pesmama" (I'm kissing you with songs), and its victory reflected the status of different styles of popular music in Serbia at the time. As the sociologist Eric Gordy has observed, the genre of newly-composed folk music was favored in the early 1990s by the state-controlled media under Milošević's nationalist regime, which marginalized more international styles of popular music, especially rock.[72] The performer of "Ljubim te pesmama," Ekstra Nena, regarded the 1992 ESC as a politically important event for rump Yugoslavia, since "it wasn't at all easy for us to appear at this moment in front of the eyes of the world and receive applause."[73] At her Eurovision press conference she tried to convince journalists "that our government and president were against all forms of violence and armed conflict," and during the contest she "took pains to present my country to Europe and the world as beautifully as possible – with an expensive, elegant wardrobe, proud demeanour [and] glamorous performance."[74] But the song of this Serbian siren was not seductive enough for Europe, and for the rest of the 1990s rump Yugoslavia did not take part in Eurovision due to the international sanctions imposed upon it for its roles in the wars in Bosnia-Herzegovina and Croatia. Because of this JRT also lost its active status in the EBU, and Serbia and Montenegro would only return to Eurovision in 2004 after rejoining this organization.[75]

The other successor states of Yugoslavia took steps to enter Eurovision immediately after they were internationally recognized as independent in 1992. That they were faster to enter the contest than their neighbors in East Central Europe was due to the decades of experience that they had already had in Eurovision, as well as a desire to promote themselves as newly independent states on the international stage and to present themselves as enthusiastic participants in manifestations of European cooperation. The broadcaster HTV had planned to enter the 1992 ESC in Malmo but was not able to do so because it had not yet been admitted into the EBU.[76] The year after, though, Bosnia-Herzegovina, Croatia, and Slovenia all made their debuts on the Eurovision stage, and Croatia and Bosnia-Herzegovina entered songs with themes that reflected their experiences in the wars that had begun in their countries in 1991 and 1992 respectively, and which only ended in 1995. The Bosnian entry "Sva bol svijeta" (All the pain of the world), sung by Fazla, was about a man who

---

Evrovizije,'" *Politika* (2 February 1992); *TOP*, "Hrvatska pjesma na Euroviziji."

72   Gordy defines "newly composed folk music" as "the use of styles and structures borrowed from various folk forms combined with pop instrumentation and arrangements. It is distinguished on the one hand from "authentic folk music" (*izvorna narodna muzika*) in which performers seek to reproduce music from folk traditions, and on the other from "turbofolk," in which instrumentation and arrangements borrowed from commercial dance and disco music dominate while a few folk elements remain." Eric Gordy, *The Culture of Power in Serbia: Nationalism and the Destruction of Alternatives* (University Park, PA: Pennsylvania State University Press, 1999), pp. 104–5.

73   Cited in Karan, *Pesma Evrovizije*, p. 60.

74   Ibid.

75   Radio-televizija Srbije, "Odeljenje za medjunarodnu saradnju," Radio-televizija Srbije, <www.rts.co.yu/cipa/ Medjunarodno.htm> Accessed 3 April 2005.

76   J. Vukelić, "Eurosong bez HTV-a," *Večernji list* (10 April 1992).

remained in Bosnia during the war and was sending out a message to his love who now lived somewhere else. Croatia's song was "Don't Ever Cry," performed by the group Put (Way), and it spoke of a young man, Ivan, who had died in the war; the song called for peace and ended with the line "Don't ever cry, my Croatian sky" – a rare expression of patriotism in the lyrics of a Eurovision song.

Over a decade after the end of the wars in Bosnia-Herzegovina and Croatia, all of the Yugoslav successor states are now regular participants in Eurovision, and it appears that the common experiences that they have shared at the contest and in popular music are influencing their voting. At the 2004 ESC Serbia and Montenegro received 12 points from Bosnia-Herzegovina, Croatia, and Slovenia – countries with which they had been at war in the 1990s – for Željko Joksimović and the Ad Hoc Orchestra's song "Lane moje" (My darling). Goran Svilanović, Serbia's former foreign minister, optimistically told HTV at the time that Croatia's 12 points for Serbia would "help improve relations between the countries in the region."[77] While Eurovision is marked by international politics, Svilanović's comment shows that it can also be a force in politics, too – just as it reflected, promoted, and shaped the cultural and political identities of socialist Yugoslavia.

---

77   Cited in Petruseva, "Old Friends Serenade Serbia in Istanbul."

Chapter 9

Lithuanian contests and European dreams

Bjorn Ingvoldstad

In *Modernity At Large: Cultural Dimensions of Globalization*, Arjun Appadurai identifies electronic mediation and mass migration as two primary determinants of what he dubs "the global now." He posits that these media "compel the transformation of everyday discourse. ... they are resources for experiments with self-making in all sorts of societies, for all sorts of persons ... [and they] provide resources for self-imagining as an everyday social project."[1] Mass migration complicates this negotiation of self, since the combination of movement and media has yielded deterritorialized viewers – both those who have left their country of origin to live and work elsewhere, but also those who stay behind, whose very notion of "home" can shift dramatically. For Appadurai, "this mobile and unforeseeable relationship between mass-mediated events and migratory audiences defines the core of the link between globalization and the modern."[2]

This chapter discusses one application of this linkage: how popular music consumption can demonstrate the continuing negotiations of identity in a locale where post-Soviet transformation, European integration and globalization are taking place concurrently. In particular, I look at the "imagined communities" of both "Lithuania" and "Europe" as articulated through the 2001 Eurovision Song Contest (ESC) – considering both the Lithuanian national preliminary contest held in Vilnius on 14 February, and the international contest held in Copenhagen on 12 May.

The ESC is a particularly fruitful site to grapple with Appadurai's take on globalization because it is a place where notions of both Lithuanian national identity and a more nascent pan-European identity converge, where producers and audiences alike must negotiate what it means to be a part of Europe as Lithuanians. In a very real sense, the ESC sells the notion of "Europe," but does so in a way most often understood as "low culture," quite dissonant to the prevailing discourses surrounding European history and culture. At the same time, the contest receives considerable attention from (and indeed is run by) national media networks, and in the Lithuanian case includes commentary by a noted musicologist, giving its coverage a particularly ambivalent high/low frame. None of the people I spoke with – in the capital, Vilnius, and in the small town of Šeduva (population 2,500) – would admit to liking the ESC, much less having an emotional investment in it, yet they were quite familiar with the contest, particularly knowledgeable about Lithuania's dismal results to

---

1   Arjun Appadurai, *Modernity At Large: Cultural Dimensions of Globalization* (Minneapolis: University of Minnesota Press, 1996), pp. 3–4.

2   Ibid., p. 4.

date, and notably anxious about how Europe would perceive the county through whichever act performed in Copenhagen. Many were quick to write off the ESC as mere entertainment, but their continued concern over the contest's ramifications belied a deeper questioning of the nation's position within Europe.

In this chapter, I am particularly concerned with the articulation between consumption and identity, and the meanings negotiated by Lithuanian audiences via this Europe-wide contest: their understanding of the Lithuanian nation and the status of their language vis-à-vis EU and NATO membership and the increasingly universal embrace of English. Both media coverage and everyday conversation in Lithuania point to another key tension in understanding Eurovision: that of center and periphery. The contest has always raised the distinction between "provincial" versus "European" culture, with Lithuanians asking themselves "are we a vital part of Europe, in touch with trends and fashions, with performers who can hold their own across the rest of the continent, or are we (still?) a backwater country unable to keep up with foreign competition?" Actually, a closer look at popular music trends in Lithuania reveals a more complicated "musicscape" in which notions of center and periphery are challenged if not confounded. When accounting for the full range of languages in use, from English to Lithuanian to Russian to Spanish, the popular music scene in Lithuania underscores how rich and complicated the notion of national identity can be.

Language and identity

In the late 1990s I lived in the central Lithuanian town of Šeduva as a secondary-school English teacher; several years later I returned as an ethnographic media researcher. During my time in Lithuania, I encountered a number of surprises in terms of the circulation and consumption of popular music that challenged my hypotheses, assumptions, and even desires. My initial shock could be termed "the shock of the known": in the same way my heart would both sway and sink upon coming across *another* McDonald's or Irish pub, I felt ambivalent about how Britney Spears and Eminem were as ubiquitous in the Baltics as they were in Bloomington. On the one hand, knowing that a decade previously there had been nuclear missiles aimed at Lithuania from the United States (and, until 1972, *vice versa*), there was a beauty in the fact that we now had elements of a shared culture. On the other hand – and I fully acknowledge the Orientalism of this statement – I wanted Lithuania to be somehow *different*, and became disheartened when it first appeared that it was not.

Slowly, though, I realized how much richer the country's popular music scene really was. I was introduced to a wide range of current Lithuanian bands: the Morrissey-like yelps of Lemon Joy, the retro beatbox breakdancing of Sel, the Celtic rock of Airija, the ska-funk of Bix, the Gothic pop of Antis, and the New Wave keyboard washes of Foje. I listened to the radio and borrowed cassettes from friends. I practiced my Lithuanian by attempting to translate song lyrics. I watched the concert film *Kažkas atsitiko* (Something happened, 1986), which included Foje's song "Laužo šviesa" (The light of the fire), identified by many as a crucial allegorical track from the early days of the independence movement. Increasingly, I realized that while there was certainly a presence of "global pop," there was also, despite a host of economic difficulties, a strong local and national music scene in Lithuania as well.

Simultaneously, I also noticed that everyone at parties, discos, or road trips could (and would) sing along to a particular English-language band, even those who had never learned English. The group, a duo from Germany called Modern Talking, sounds similar to early Erasure with occasional Bee Gees-esque falsettos. At the time, Modern Talking was an extremely popular band in Lithuania and throughout eastern Europe, but virtually unknown in the United States. Similar Europop bands perched firmly on (or just beyond) the periphery of American pop-music consciousness – Scooter, Aqua, Eiffel 65, Captain Jack, and so on – may not have much staying power or prolonged worldwide exposure, but they certainly have a presence in Lithuania. To a native English speaker, Europop lyrics can often seem simplistic, if not downright nonsensical, aspiring to sound as if from the American Midwest but often betrayed by non-native accents.[3] Yet I found that these same lyrics became an entry point or a way of identification for many people to feel part of a larger international English-speaking community.

English is not the only foreign language at play in Lithuania. The significant presence of Russian pop in Lithuania was a surprise for me – and for those who strictly understand the Russian language as a colonizing force of empire. While Lithuania's geopolitical position vis-à-vis Russia has certainly changed since the early 1990s, the response to Russian culture is much more nuanced than I'd imagined. Russian, of course, was the common tongue used by a diverse set of ethnic groups throughout the former Soviet Union. Children in Lithuania grew up learning Russian from the first grade, if not in preschool, but the paucity of ethnic non-Lithuanians in the countryside meant Russian's conversational utility was minimal (though bureaucratic interactions and trips to larger towns and cities might necessitate speaking Russian). Beyond the school, radio and television programming was in Russian. Thus, while daily human interaction was nearly always in Lithuanian, much of the Soviet-era entertainment media was transmitted in Russian. This, in part, helps to explain Lithuanians' continued connection with television programs, films, and popular music from the Soviet era, even among those who strongly supported independence.

This should not be understood as some kind of masochistic nostalgia for the Soviet past or for Russian-language hegemony. Perhaps precisely because people learned Russian fluently as a second language (without the ethnic tensions you might find in Latvia and Estonia, where the percentage of ethnic Russians is much higher), Lithuanians are relatively more comfortable with Russian as the language of popular entertainment. As a result, the country is fertile ground for touring Russian bands. A glance at one of the premiere concert booking agencies shows a fair number of international artists coming to Lithuania, including Russian artists such as glam-rockers Mummy Troll and the phenomenon of the Russian singer known as Vitas,

---

3   As a counterpoint, the "Britpop" scene of the mid-1990s (bands such as Blur, Pulp, and Supergrass, for example) emphasized dense, thoughtful lyrics delivered unapologetically in marked local dialects.

as well as English-language bands whose careers are on the wane: The Scorpions, a-ha, Bryan Adams, and so forth. While these English-language artists had passed their creative and popular peak years ago, now apparently on a "pay-the-rent" tour of backwater Europe, the touring Russian acts seem fresh and contemporary.

In addition to Russian and English, Spanish is another foreign language whose music is receiving significant attention. This phenomenon has nothing to do with language acquisition in school, but rather with migrant labor, including people from Šeduva leaving to work in Spain in significant numbers. Indeed, well before Lithuania's 2004 accession to the European Union and NATO, a significant number of Lithuanians had taken seasonal or quasi-permanent migrant labor jobs in EU countries. This movement of people has resulted in greater movement of media texts as well, perhaps best seen with the growing popularity of Spanish music in Šeduva, including such acts as King Africa and Las Ketchup.[4]

In sum, after the end of the Cold War, Lithuania has not been homogenized into another gray market of global culture, but rather has incorporated international artists and styles alongside its local and national music traditions. My fieldwork did not reveal a pattern of imperialism from West or East, nor a single center-periphery relationship, but rather a complex network of centers and peripheries in which the periphery of one center (say, Vilnius to New York) becomes the center to another periphery (say, Vilnius to Šeduva).

This rather optimistic interpretation, however, comes from a study focused on audiences and reception rather than artists and production. From the viewpoint of Lithuanian recording artists, the situation is considerably more difficult. While many Lithuanian rock and pop musicians have an audience base within the country, none has yet succeeded in becoming an exportable commodity in the way that, for instance, acts from Iceland or Sweden have.[5] The idea of a Lithuanian band making the European charts is still a romantic dream or a woeful delusion. Language is certainly an issue: you might hear a smattering of French or Spanish on European popular radio formats, but "lesser" languages such as Norwegian or Dutch are simply not heard. It is no surprise, then, that the Danish band Aqua performs in English, the *lingua franca* of Europop.[6] Björk's Icelandic tracks with the Sugarcubes or Sinéad O'Connor's occasional performances in Gaelic are exceptions that prove the rule – never released as singles, these songs offer an interesting "extra" for fans.[7]

---

4   Fuelled by the several videos accompanying the CD single of Las Ketchup's "Asereje," the track was a party staple in Šeduva in the summer of 2002, months before garnering international radio play.

5   For an excellent discussion of Sweden's popular music industry and its position in the international market, see Robert Burnett's *The Global Jukebox: The International Music Industry* (New York: Routledge, 1996).

6   While Aqua are regarded as one-hit wonders in America (if they are regarded at all) for "Barbie Girl," they had no less than four #1 singles on the British charts from their 1997 debut album *Aquarium*.

7   Icelandic-language songs were offered as "extra tracks" on the Sugarcubes' debut CD *Life's Too Good* (1988), as well as on 12-inch singles from the album. Previously, Björk sang with the Icelandic-language band Kukl. Sinéad O'Connor speaks the Lord's Prayer in Gaelic

Meanwhile, Lithuanian bands such as Funky and Biplan have attempted to move into the Russian market, but with limited success.

This is not to imply that there aren't a number of bands in Lithuania with a level of success performing in Lithuanian. But Lithuania's relatively depressed economic condition, coupled with its relatively small population of only 3.5 million, creates a trying domestic business market in general and a challenging music business market in particular. Entertainers looking to enlarge their fan base significantly must think beyond national borders. Most often, the ability to deliver songs in English is a prerequisite for success outside the home country. The question remains, then, how to break into this wider market?

Eurovision: a gateway to "Europe"?

The 2001 ESC was the third time Lithuania participated in the contest, and there was a concerted effort by Lithuanian organizers for a better showing than in previous years. Jazz saxophonist Ovidijus Višnauskas had provided Lithuania a dubious debut in 1994; he came 25th with zero points. It took five years for the country to participate again, but the result in 1999 proved painfully similar: a 20th-place finish from Aistė, who adapted a folksong from Žemaitija (a region in western Lithuania), giving it an Enya-esque New-Age treatment which befuddled locals and international viewers alike. For 2001, Lithuanian organizers weren't necessarily looking for an act that could win; in fact, they explicitly urged contenders *not* to win – the fear was that hosting the next year's contest (the privilege and obligation of the previous year's winning nation) might send LTV, the already cash-poor state television network, into fiscal oblivion.[8] Rather, Lithuanian organizers merely hoped for a solid performance, a high enough result to secure an invitation to participate in the 2002 contest.

At the same time, bands from Lithuania were increasingly looking to the ESC as a potential "bridge to Europe."[9] A number of Lithuania's biggest pop and rock acts (such as B'avarija, Rebel Heart, Alenas Chosnau, and Delfinai) began queuing up when LTV announced its plan to have a national preliminary competition that roughly replicated the larger Europe-wide contest. But national media pundits and my Šeduvan neighbors agreed that the two front-runners for the contest were two of the most popular acts in Lithuania: Andrius Mamontovas and Skamp.

Mamontovas is by far the most successful singer and songwriter in the history of Lithuanian popular music, winning innumerable critical and popular awards

---

at the beginning of "Never Get Old" (from *The Lion and the Cobra*, 1988). More recently, her 2002 release *Sean-Nós Nua* features several songs in Gaelic.

8   There was some question as to whether Estonia, winners in 2001, would host the 2002 contest. Only an emergency allocation of funds from the Estonian parliament made hosting the contest in Tallinn a viable proposition.

9   No band from the Baltic States had made an international impact until Brainstorm finished third in the 2000 ESC. The band had achieved major success in Latvia as Prāta Vētra, and was the first in the region to capitalize on the contest as a potential way to access the broader European market. The band has released several albums internationally in English as Brainstorm, but also continues to record in Latvian as Prāta Vētra.

over more than two decades of performing. Starting in 1982, his band Foje was one of the first Lithuanian groups to play in the synthesizer-inflected "New Wave" style popularized by groups such as Depeche Mode and Gary Numan. They were a feature act in the 1986 concert film/video compilation *Kazkas atsitiko* (Something happened) and were a fixture of the annual "rock marches" of the late 1980s throughout Lithuania. All told, Foje released six studio albums in addition to several collections of live tracks, remixes, and unreleased songs, before bowing out with a farewell tour in 1997, including a final outdoor concert in Vilnius' Vingis Park that drew an estimated 60,000 people.

Although he has always shrugged off the label of a "political singer," Mamontovas is tied nevertheless in public consciousness with Sajūdis, the Lithuanian popular-front movement of the late 1980s and early 1990s. Mamontovas asserts that his songs were never meant to be political commentary *per se*, much less discussions about independence; rather, they were more of an attempt to articulate the notion of personal, individual, intellectual, and spiritual rebirth. Like Czesław Miłosz and Václav Havel, he maintained that society will be renewed when every individual within that society is individually transformed and renewed.[10]

While the audience-motivated imperative to "play the old stuff" is seemingly universal, Mamontovas is saddled with associations of a particularly resonant political and social moment; his early recordings have created something of a trap of success, with his subsequent creative work compared unfavorably.[11] Younger music fans, from a new generation fueled largely on hip-hop and techno, take a decidedly ambivalent stance towards his music. The irony is that after a dozen years of re-independence, the personal and societal renewal Mamontovas articulates is perhaps even more distant than before, receding beyond the event horizon along with utopian dreams of quick political, economic, and social transformation. The "return to Europe," seen in the early 1990s as an end in itself and made manifest by Lithuania's accession to the EU and NATO, has brought geopolitical stability but also continued political corruption and increasing economic inequality.[12]

Feeling he had accomplished all he could in Lithuania, Mamontovas began a concerted effort to gain international distribution through a renewed focus on singing and songwriting in English. However, the pattern of his English-language releases has been cautious and irregular: Mamontovas attempted to break into foreign markets, but not at the expense of his domestic fan base. He began experimenting with writing in English in 1991, releasing the occasional English track on otherwise Lithuanian-language albums, and cutting all-English demos. Finally, after four successful Lithuanian-language solo albums, Mamontovas began to work on an all-English project in 2000, but he chose to release it under a new identity: Cloudmaker. Mamontovas explained that he used this name in part because foreigners had a hard

---

10   Personal interview, 2001.

11   My thanks to Janne Mäkelä, whose discussion at IASPM 2001 on John Lennon and the travails of his post-Beatles career in the 1970s articulated a "trap of success" similar to that of Mamontovas' case.

12   The political scandal surrounding the impeachment of President Rolandas Paksas in 2004 is a case in point.

time remembering (much less pronouncing) "complicated" Lithuanian last names. In addition, because he was known domestically as a Lithuanian-language singer, he was worried that these audiences wouldn't accept him performing in English.[13]

Mamontovas, as Cloudmaker, performed his first English-language concerts during the summer of 2000, with two sets at the European Days festival in Helsinki, Finland, and a subsequent club date in Tallinn, Estonia. However, this mini-tour did not culminate with a Cloudmaker show within Lithuania itself – indeed, there has yet to be one. That fall, the self-titled *Cloudmaker* CD became available, hot on the heels of an acoustic Lithuanian-language solo release that summer. Of the ten songs, seven were completely new, two were well-known Lithuanian Mamontovas songs with new English lyrics, and one was a remake of a previous English-language Foje demo. *Cloudmaker* was not available in any Lithuanian stores – only on the Internet at the singer's official website, and at double the regular retail price of a new CD.[14] While nearly all of the members of his Vilnius fan club had copies of the disc, the fact that Mamontovas himself was selling it at such a high cost irked other fans.[15]

While Mamontovas and his generation were heavily influenced by Russian bards such as Vladimir Vysotsky and by British New Wave music, an emerging generation of Lithuanian artists was indebted more to European techno and American hip-hop. Bands such as Sel, Lukas, Skamp, and G & G Sindikatas connected with an audience in the midst of profound social change, and their rise marked the coming-of-age of the first generation of postsocialist Lithuanians. Having grown up in an independent Lithuania, this new generation is still in the process of negotiating how their villages fit into the "global village" and how Lithuanian identity fits with notions of "European-ness."

Skamp is arguably the most critically and commercially successful of the new Lithuanian bands since the mid-1990s. In 2001, the band won three Bravos (industry awards equivalent to the Grammys in the United States) for band, album, and producer of the year; in addition, they held three of the top five singles positions on the year-end chart, including number one.[16] If Mamontovas was attempting to loosen himself from the constraints of being a "Lithuanian singer," Skamp was forced to work surprisingly hard to prove their credibility *as* Lithuanians. Their music is a hybrid of languages and styles, often combining Lithuanian-language hip-hop and English-language blue-eyed soul (sometimes even a smattering of French and German) within the same song. Each of the band's members could be (and were) understood as somehow Other by Lithuanian audiences: Viktoras (Vee) Diawara is half-Malian,

---

13 Personal interview, 2001.

14 For over two years, every track on this album was available via RealAudio streaming at Mamontovas' official Internet web page, <www.andrius.m.tdd.lt>. Since 2003, his webpage has been extensively revamped, including the elimination of audio streaming, at a new address <www.andriusmamontovas.com>. His English-language webpage can be found at <www. cloudmakermusic.com>.

15 I had an opportunity to go to one of the fan-club meetings in preparation for a piece for the Lithuanian Radio, where I was able to talk to nearly two dozen fans in attendance. Several members write an irregular unofficial newsletter, now online at <http://am.area.lt>.

16 For an online version of the Lithuanian Top 20 singles chart, updated weekly, see <www.rc.lt> Accessed 6 May 2007. See also <www.lietus.fm> Accessed 6 May 2007.

with a relatively dark complexion and long curly hair; Vee and Vilius Alesius are Lithuanians who grew up in Germany,[17] which also brings their "Lithuanian-ness" into question in some quarters; Erica Jennings is an Irish national who moved to Lithuania with her family in her mid-teens, and who does not sing or speak publicly in Lithuanian despite having lived in the country for half a decade.

Jennings is perhaps the band's biggest draw and simultaneously its biggest magnet for domestic criticism. A number of Lithuanians I worked with became visibly agitated when talking about Jennings even before it became a question as to whether or not she could (or should) represent the nation at the ESC. Owing to Jennings' emphasis on education and drug-free living, some celebrate her as a role model for young Lithuanians, whom she encourages to pursue their personal dreams. Others question the politics of her minimal Lithuanian language usage, since for many language is a fragile national treasure and the core of national identity.[18] Jennings became a public target for anxieties that through EU and NATO accession the nation would be overrun by Western foreigners whose disregard of the Lithuanian language could lead to its destruction.[19] These fears recall the situation after World War II, when a number of non-Lithuanians (primarily Russians) were brought into the then-Soviet republic by Moscow as a colonizing force, with the local perception that these "outsiders" never bothered or felt the need to learn Lithuanian.

After several successful albums in Lithuania, Skamp began to focus on taking their music to a wider international audience. Their tentative first steps included gigs in neighboring countries such as Germany and Latvia, where they signed a record contract after winning a "battle of the bands" contest. Noting how Brainstorm had managed to parlay an impressive third-place showing at the 2000 ESC into greater opportunities to perform and market their music internationally, Skamp made their bid to become the next Lithuanian ESC entry – but to do so, they would have to best Mamontovas.

---

17 Both attended a *Vasario 16-a gimnazija*, a school system that has been functioning for over a half-century in Germany, a legacy of World War II displaced-persons camps. A debate has recently arisen within Lithuania regarding the continuing funding of a secondary school abroad while local schools continue to face extremely severe economic challenges.

18 For example, old folksongs called *dainas* were one of the primary sites of preservation of the Lithuanian language under centuries of Russian oppression. See Guntis Šmidchens, *A Baltic Music: The Folklore Movement in Lithuania, Latvia, and Estonia, 1968–1991* (PhD dissertation, Indiana University, 1996).

19 Lithuanian and Latvian are the two surviving "Baltic languages." Anatol Lieven notes that "the elimination of the Old Prussians, one of the Baltic peoples, at the hands of the Germans [in the Middle Ages] ... has often been cited in Baltic literature as an awful warning and example of the grim, existential danger facing small nations in the region." *The Baltic Revolution: Estonia, Latvia, Lithuania and the Path to Independence* (New Haven, CT: Yale University Press, 1993), p. 40.

Eurovision 2001

While the ESC invites competition and comparison between nations, it also reveals more subtle struggles within nations. In the Lithuanian context, the contest articulated conflicting notions of "democracy" and political transition both nationally and Europe-wide. The paternalistic attitude of those in power "knowing best" and bypassing the electoral will of the people is a hold-over from Soviet times, but also starkly apparent in the so-called "democracy gap" within the European Union. This paternalism was manifested by the committee that selected Lithuania's ESC entries in previous years, none of which was remotely successful. National organizers promised that 2001 would be different.

This national preliminary contest was touted as an exercise in democracy in which "your vote counts!" whether one chose to phone it in or to vote on the official website. Along with phone and web voting there was also an "expert jury" of several dozen people, though it was unclear to both media pundits and the participants themselves (to say nothing of the general public) just how each of these components would be weighted.[20] The exact formula was publicized the day of the contest: one quarter of the "points" came from online voting, with another quarter from voting either via phone or in person at the contest. In other words, the voting public accounted for only *half* the points, while organizers reserved the other half for their appointed experts. Audiences split their votes fairly evenly, giving Cloudmaker a slight edge, but the jury voted as a bloc for Skamp, thereby making the result a rout for the upstart trio.

Aside from all the talk of democratic empowerment, perhaps the most dispiriting aspect of the contest was how interviewees shrugged off the entire gerrymandered process, either because it didn't matter (in the sense that Lithuania would place poorly in the ESC anyway) or because it was no surprise (in the sense that "the powers that be" would always manipulate the contest to their advantage). This potent mix of defeatism and cynicism was hard to argue against.

Equally dispiriting was the fact that this victory for Skamp did little (at least in the short run) to settle the debate over the band's "Lithuanian-ness." The band even posted this exasperated note on their webpage:

> We are seriously thinking about not participating in the Eurovision contest anymore … (in part) because of the criticism about the fact that two-thirds of SKAMP is not fully Lithuanian. If Lithuanians have a problem with one of their (we emphasize their) best singers being Irish and one of their best producers being half Malian then that's fine

---

20 I was working with the Lietuvos radijas (Lithuanian State Radio) program "Radio Vilnius" at the time, and asked a number of competing bands if they understood the point system. Hardly any of the 15 participants had any idea whatsoever. Andrius Mamontovas diplomatically posited, "I'm not thinking about that right now. I just hope they pick the best." Other than Mamontovas, the other performer fully understanding the breakdown, perhaps not surprisingly, was Viktoras Diawara from Skamp.

with us. We don't feel insulted or anything like that. We just feel we shouldn't bother representing somebody who doesn't want that.[21]

But making an argument for the disassociation of ethnicity from nationality (that Jennings is now a *Lithuanian* singer regardless of her Irish background) was easier than convincing those Lithuanians who, given previous waves of Polonization and Russification, perceive globalization and increased Anglification as the latest threat to the nation. Juozas Liesis of B'Avarija (a popular boy-band which was placed third, the highest showing for an act performing in Lithuanian) gave a rather explosive interview to the nation's main daily newspaper, venting frustration that a band whose singer is not Lithuanian could still represent Lithuania:

> I have nothing against Skamp. But what is happening here, I think it's absurd. … [Jennings] has lived in our country for several years, and she hasn't managed to learn how to speak Lithuanian. … If foreigners are allowed to represent our country, Lithuanian Television needed to take half of their annual budget and hire Michael Jackson for Eurovision. Then Lithuania will take first place for sure.[22]

After all the debate surrounding the national preliminary contest in Vilnius, it was something of a relief when the Copenhagen contest was finally held several months later. Skamp finished a respectable 13th, the highest ranking so far for Lithuania. However, a new scandal broke out during the continent-wide contest. Here, Lithuania had given Estonia ten points (the second-highest score possible) while Estonia had "reciprocated" with zero points for Lithuania. The indignation many Lithuanians felt over this unequal scoring demonstrates another way to understand the ESC in terms of political transition: the way it focuses attention on multinational coalition building – and coalition collapse. Philippe Le Guern, tabulating several decades' worth of ESC scoring results, has identified a pattern of "bloc voting" in which certain countries seem to swap reciprocal votes (for instance, vote trading among Scandinavian countries, between Germany and Austria, and, more recently, among the Baltic States).[23] Lithuanians' perception of the 2001 voting as a snub from Estonia comes in the context of ongoing frustration with tariff rate increases from Lithuanian Telecom (administered by an Estonian) and an Estonian government official's claim that his country was not in fact Baltic but Scandinavian. Thus, as Lithuania was negotiating its identity as a part of Europe, it was also grappling with a more complicated relationship to its former "allies" on a different playing field. The ESC was an occasion for Lithuanians to voice displeasure over their neighbor's

---

21　Skamp's official website is <www.skamp.lt>, available in both Lithuanian and English.

22　Ramūnas Zilnys, "Dvejonės dėl ateities planų apkartino pergalės skonį," *Lietuvos rytas* (14 March 2001), 3. Unless otherwise stated, all translations are by the author.

23　Philippe Le Guern, "From National Pride to Global Kitsch: The Eurovision Song Contest," *The Web Journal of French Media Studies* 3/1 (October 2000), <http://wjfms.ncl.ac.uk/leguWJ.htm> Accessed 22 January 2005. See also "Language, Power Blocs and Unlucky 13," *City Paper* (May 2000), p. 21, <www.balticsww.com/eurovision_analysis.htm> Accessed 22 January 2005.

pretension – made only worse by the fact that Estonia had actually *won* the whole thing.

Epilogue

After the 2001 contest, Skamp redoubled its efforts to parlay Europe-wide exposure into an international record deal. This has included re-recording collaborative singles with Latvian singers for the Latvian market, and the release of *Kingz & Queenz*, a compilation album featured on the Pioneer Living Series on PBS in the United States.[24] The band also enjoyed a marked increase in concert dates outside Lithuania. In an ironic change of perspective, reports in the popular press led to a panic that the band was abandoning their (now) Lithuanian roots or leaving their homeland behind. Skamp was clearly in a frustrating double bind. After a number of media reports speculating on the band's imminent departure, Victor posted this message on the band's webpage in June 2001:

> SKAMP members Erica, Vilius and Vee are planning to move to another country. ... We can't sit in Lithuania; we need new impressions. Everything here is becoming a routine, and we don't want this. Moreover, lately Erica has received a lot of wonderful suggestions from big foreign record companies, which are offering her to start the solo career. I don't think Erica will remain in Lithuania for 2 more years just for SKAMP knowing that she could travel around the world. I also can't stay here only because people recognize me in the streets, while knowing that I could produce and manage various projects.[25]

Skamp's contested status (were they the country's best band, or were they outsiders?) coupled with major success in Lithuania and international attention fueled this sense of impending loss within Lithuania.

While Skamp pondered its options abroad, Mamontovas redoubled his efforts within Lithuania. With minimal to no radio play for the *Cloudmaker* album and no live concert dates, the English-language project was temporarily put on the back burner as Mamontovas recorded yet another Lithuanian-language album, *Visi langai žiuri į dangų* (Every window looks to the sky). Planning began for a major national tour in support of the album soon after the Lithuanian national preliminary contest for the ESC concluded.

And Lithuania did indeed gain accession to both the EU and NATO in 2004. In hindsight, the 2001 ESC served as an important preliminary exercise in "self-imagining" for the nation, highlighting several examples of the contestation of Lithuanian identity and its mapping within both regional and global contexts. The contest was seen by the state television network and participants as a way

---

24 According to the PBS (Public Broadcasting Service) website, the album "mixes urban contemporary and international hip-hop music with positive, inspiring themes on overcoming obstacles and achieving one's dreams." The compilation also includes songs by Bermuda-born Israeli artist Amiel. <www.shoppbs.org/sm-pbs-pioneer-living-kingz-and-queenz-cd--pi-1403135.html#related> Accessed 22 January 2005.

25 "Skamp Leaving Lithuania" (21 June 2001) <www.skamp.lt> Accessed 3 February 2006.

for Lithuania to access European markets. Audiences debated the merits of local performers in terms of their "Lithuanian-ness" and their ability to represent the country internationally. Notions of "democracy" were invoked by organizers of the national preliminary contest, and the results of the Europe-wide competition were impacted by unofficial international alliances. In sum, the 2001 ESC mediated Lithuanians' efforts to transform their own national identity and their place in Europe, prompting both the anxiety of being left behind if the country did not "make the grade" as well as the fear of what it would mean for Lithuania if and when it did finally enter "Europe."

Chapter 10

"Russian body and soul": t.A.T.u. performs at Eurovision 2003

Dana Heller

In 1999, two 14-year-old Russian singers, Julia Volkova and Lena Katina, auditioned for a teen band conceived by Ivan Shapovalov, a 36-year-old advertising executive and former child psychologist. Shapovalov claims that when he first saw Volkova and Katina perform together and sensed the homoerotic energy between them, he decided on the spot to create an "underage sex project," a girl group whose image would depend heavily on illicit sexuality. The group he developed, t.A.T.u. (the acronym stands for "та любит ту" – "this one loves that one"), became an instant success in Russia with the release of their first album, *200 Km/H in the Wrong Lane*. Following the 2002 release of the English-language version, produced by Trevor Horn, the single, "All the Things She Said," rapidly ascended the European pop charts, making t.A.T.u. the first Russian pop performers to reach the number-one spot on the Media and Music Pan-European Singles Chart.

t.A.T.u. shocked Russian audiences and stirred controversy across Europe, Asia, the United States, and the United Kingdom with their diplays of kissing and fondling during performances. The video for "All the Things She Said" depicts Katina and Volkova as school-age lovers on the run from a cold, disproving public gaze. In Russia their alleged sexual relationship was openly acknowledged to be a commercial ploy, a gimmick admitted to by Katina and Volkova in the Russian media, but elsewhere – especially in the UK and US – the singers became embroiled in the politics of identity and sexual morality. Their video was reportedly banned by the BBC's *Top of the Pops* despite producers' denials of any censoring. At locations in London and Tokyo the t.A.T.u. girls were prohibited from filming their new video by city officials who deemed their material disruptive and inappropriate. Even in the group's native Moscow, authorities halted production of the video for the song "Show Me Love" in a confrontation on Red Square that set local militia against a cast of hundreds of girls in plaid skirts and white blouses.[1] During their first tour of the United States, t.A.T.u.'s lesbian affectations and their outspoken opposition to the mounting military crisis in Iraq produced shock and awe of another sort when, appearing on Jay Leno's *Tonight Show*, Katina and Volkova mocked network insistence that they neither kiss nor comment on Iraq by performing in white T-shirts that bore the Russian language message "Хуй Войне!" (Fuck the war!) emblazoned across the front, and by blocking their own faces with their hands as they kissed during a break in their performance. "We are sure that Russia will understand us,"

---

1 Carl Schreck, "Tatu Gets Run Out of Red Square," *The Moscow Times* (16 May 2003): 4.

they remarked in Russian following the performance.[2] The stunt prompted the NBC network to ban t.A.T.u. from any future appearances, but it also helped fuel their international record sales.

"It is really funny that the Tatu campaign in the West goes in a very different way to how it went in Russia," says the Russian music journalist, Artemy Troitsky. "In Russia, this whole lesbian thing has never been taken seriously. When they've been interviewed on talk shows and asked, 'Are you really lesbians?', they've said, 'No, it's a trick, we have boyfriends, we are normal girls, we do this for image.' And the same thing for pedophilia. In Russia this whole issue of dirty old men fancying Tatu in their school uniforms never even broke out. Here, they were just like any other teenybopper pop group with a good gimmick."[3] Despite protests from the Communist wing of government and a failed attempt to have Shapovalov prosecuted, t.A.T.u.'s "gimmick" appeared to win official cultural validation when the group was selected to represent the Russian Federation in the 2003 Eurovision Song Contest (ESC) held in Latvia.

By selecting an already internationally successful pop product, Russia broke from the ESC convention of sending relative unknowns, and showed a willingness to gamble that association with the contest would not taint t.A.T.u's future commercial prospects. "We're going to win Eurovision," Katina told the German magazine *Bild* on the eve of the contest. "We wanted to do this because we are Russian body and soul. We want to blast everything that's been done before with our sexy act."[4] Nevertheless, by selecting an act known for courting controversy as its official representative, Russia seemed to already regard itself as a national and cultural force important enough to flaunt convention by treating Eurovision as an occasion to test the limits of acceptability and challenge the decorous, family-oriented sensibilities of contest producers. For their part, t.A.T.u. did little to dispel this image. "It's not a big deal for us," Katina told BBC News Online. "We were chosen by our country to go. We don't care about their rules at all – we are going to do what we want to do."[5] The strict ESC guidelines only further spurred the duo's defiance as they had to be repeatedly warned not to miss or be late for rehearsals and to contain their behavior on stage during the performance. Although they mocked the guidelines by threatening to perform nude, Katina and Volkova ultimately complied, appearing simply in jeans and T-shirts, which, unlike the T-shirts they had worn on the *Tonight Show*, broadcast no political message.

---

2   *Tonight Show with Jay Leno*, dir. Ellen Brown (episode 2438, 25 February 2003) <http://tvtome.com/tvtome/servlet/GuidePageServlet/showid-10020/epid-233599/>Accessed 11 December 2004.

3   Neil McCormick, "Tatu's Company," *The Sydney Morning Herald* (24 May 2003) <http://smh.com.au/articles/2003/05/23/1053585695725.html?oneclick=true> Accessed 22 February 2005.

4   Roisin Ingle, "Why the Eurovision Must Remain a Cool-free Zone," *The Irish Times* (24 May 2003): 51.

5   Michael Osborn, "Tatu Sneer at Eurovision Dream," BBC News Online (20 May 2003) <http://news.bbc.co.uk/1/hi/entertainment/music/3043557.stm>Accessed 11 December 2004.

With provisional Internet ratings showing t.A.T.u. in the lead, most contest devotees expected Russia to easily take first place.[6] However, the performance of their new single "Ne Ver, Ne Bojsia" (Don't believe it, don't be afraid) came across as inarguably lackluster. In the end, t.A.T.u. came third after Belgium's Urban Trad and Turkey's Sertab Erener, who won first prize with the song "Every Way That I Can." While some music critics pointed to Volkova's alleged vocal-chord injury and canceled rehearsals as the cause of their weak performance, others noted the political implications of Turkey's victory, interpreting it as reward for resisting American efforts to deploy forces from Turkish airbases during the war in Iraq. In any case, some Russian fans cried foul. Several days after the contest, Igor Burenkov, public relations director of Channel One in Russia, cast doubt on the accuracy of the voting results, claiming that t.A.T.u.'s performance had received "unlikely low points" from a number of countries, including Ireland, which had in fact replaced its televoting results at the last minute with jury voting because of slow processing time.[7] Russia threatened a national protest, but its petition for a recount was put to rest when it was confirmed that even an Irish televote would not have changed the results of the contest.

More than providing yet another occasion for the expression of mutual distrust between Russia and the West, the story of t.A.T.u. and their participation in Eurovision reveals the multiple and contradictory ways Russia is currently engaging with concepts of the national and the international, the global and the local. To that end, the controversies that have followed t.A.T.u. to Riga and elsewhere – as well as the seeming inconsistencies of their presentation, marketing, and performances – may be located in the larger context of ongoing debates over the redefinition of post-Soviet Russian national identity and Russia's emerging role on the global mass cultural stage. From this perspective, the t.A.T.u. phenomenon interfaces with aspects of both post-Soviet and international youth cultures; shifts in Russian attitudes toward gender, sexuality, and identity politics; and the contradictory commodification and transnational circulation of distinctive "European" identities that is Eurovision's stock and trade. This chapter is an invitation to consider t.A.T.u.'s ESC performance as a productive flashpoint of East-West misreading and failed translation (not unlike t.A.T.u.'s appearance on the *Tonight Show*) that might account for the duo's very different reception in Russia and the West. It also highlights some of the ways in which post-Soviet appropriations of international pop styles wittingly or unwittingly mock the moral pieties and hypocrisy of Western democratic societies while coyly asserting the uniqueness and innate superiority of "Russianness" and its foundational mythologies.

For example, we might take Shapovalov's response to the BBC video controversy as typical of t.A.T.u.'s tendency to mock the presumed cultural hegemony of the West, as well as the social and spiritual health of the countries that sought to sanitize the teen group's image. "England is sick like America," he told BBC reporters, "and

---

6   Stanislaw Waszak, "Russia's Tatu Set to Sing, as Stage Set for Eurovision Song Contest," Agence France Presse, English version (24 May 2003).

7   "Channel One: Eurovision is Political Contest," News Agency Rosbalt RU (28 May 2003) <www.rosbaltnews.com/2003/05/28/62753.html> Accessed 11 December 2004.

the only thing to do is provide a cure. ... We will heal the country with music."[8] Such oblique comments rhetorically reference the Russian nationalist belief, carried forward from Russian Orthodoxy, that it is the unique mission of the Slavic people (and especially the descendants of ancient Holy Rus) to save the world. At the same time, his comments reflect the Russian pop-music industry's far more recent sense of liberation from earlier economic, political, and social restraints and its beneficent arrival in the world of commercialized global media. Similarly, in t.A.T.u.'s Eurovision performance we find many of the contradictory impulses and elements that describe Russia's current identity crisis and struggle to locate itself in relation to its past.

Culture and resistance

Russian pop and rock music has a long, rich history despite Soviet government efforts to regulate the listening activities of teenagers, and the harassment endured by "unofficial" pop artists and groups in an environment of official state hostility toward purveyors of Western-style decadence. The collapse of the Soviet Union and the subsequent commercialization of Russian youth culture created tremendous nostalgia for Soviet-era pop music and for the powerful sense of oppositional resistance that was inherent in its production and consumption. Since 1990, the Russian pop industry has expanded exponentially to include a wide range of styles and products, many of them imitative of Western trends and lacking any discernible originality and artistry. The result is that contemporary Russian pop is both loved and despised by Russians themselves; however, it still retains importance in its ability to speak meaningfully to the "everyday concerns" and fantasies of Russian youth, and particularly to a post-Soviet generation for whom competitions such as the ESC represent Russia's greater engagement with the West in music styles, as well as in fashion, cultural movements, and consumer goods.[9] Even when it is regarded as imitative of Western styles, indigenous Russian-language pop nevertheless provides occasions for greater emotional affinity and furnishes the background to the everyday lives of young people as it reverberates across open-air markets, at music kiosks outside metro stations, and in night clubs and *tusovki* (informal parties or gatherings). From a consumer standpoint, it is one of many choices available to Russian youth in the post-Soviet marketplace.

However, while Russian youth no longer feel cut off from the international mass-cultural sphere, their sense of inclusion – as Hilary Pilkington's ethnographic research shows – has been experienced less as an exchange than as a "one-way cultural flow, that is from the West to Russia."[10] As one of Pilkington's young subjects bluntly puts it, "Everything here is from the West. ... Young people get everything

8   Rob Walker, "t.A.T.u.: The Underage Sex Project with a Hit Record," *Slate* (11 February 2003) <http://slate.msn.com/id/2078409/> Accessed 24 March 2005.

9   Hilary Pilkington, *et al.*, *Looking West?: Cultural Globalization and Russian Youth Cultures* (University Park: Pennsylvania State University Press, 2002), p. 199.

10   Ibid., p. 201.

from the West."[11] While such a super-abundance of cultural access serves as an ongoing reminder of Russia's accelerated entrance into the global infrastructure, it has also come to represent structures of domination and authority against which post-Soviet Russian identity must assert itself. "The whole of Russian culture is based on resistance to something," explains another of Pilkington's interviewees, "and it is clear that if there is nothing to resist then the culture disintegrates."[12] For many Russians, young and old, resistance to the West continues to serve as a force that holds Russian culture together, a resistance that has strengthened with the disappearance of the Soviet state as a principle antagonist. Since the fall of the Soviet Union, the one-sided cultural dominance of western Europe and the United States has become not only a source of resistance but also resentment, arising largely out of the conviction that while Russians possess tremendous creativity they have not yet mastered the skill of translating those energies into commercially viable global commodities.

The selection of t.A.T.u. for participation in Eurovision 2003 loudly proclaimed, among other things, that this was no longer the case. For all the consternation and condemnation he elicited within Russia, Shapovalov had managed to manufacture an appealing act, infused with propulsive pop rhythms and clean vocal harmonies and framed by an image calculated to offend religious and cultural conservatives as well as progressives, feminists, and gay activists. The group's narrative of defiant girl-on-girl passion playfully evoked both heterosexual male fantasies and youthful fantasies of rebellion and alienation while titillating the international tabloid media. Finally, or so it seemed, Russia's fundamentally ambivalent eye on Europe would be matched by a European gaze that at once desired and disparaged Russia's t.A.T.u.

For many fans, part of the joy of watching Eurovision year after year is in witnessing the annual collision of cultures, economies, and politics that the contest stages. The ESC famously registers the subtle and not-so-subtle dissolutions and redrawing of boundaries that unite and divide blocs of interest, a process determined as much (if not more) by the performances of nation-states as by the performances of representative artists. For example, amidst suspicions that Turkey's 2003 victory was the result of that nation's resistance to the American-led war in Iraq, some critics in the United Kingdom and Spain regarded their countries' unusually low scores as payback for their governments' support of the invasion. Indeed, such speculation was rampant in Britain after the group Jemini set a new record low by receiving zero points.[13] With the triumph of Ukraine's Ruslana in the 2004 ESC only months before the "rigged" presidential election that prompted revolutionary social upheaval and a re-election that handed victory to the reformist candidate, the stage was set again for speculation that more than musical performance is judged, cautioned, and rewarded at Eurovision.

---

11   Ibid., p. 202.

12   Ibid., p. 201.

13   Matt Wells, "Nul Points: UK Out of Tune With Europe," *Guardian Unlimited* (26 May 2003) <www.guardian.co.uk/arts/news/story/0,11711,963573,00.html> Accessed 22 February 2005.

Russians who believe that Europe and the West in general remain determined to see the country chastened and humiliated were wont to assume as much in 2003, and responded with indignation at t.A.T.u.'s third-place ranking. Both inside and outside Russia, t.A.T.u.'s provocative, transgressive image was contextualized unflatteringly with various international legal, economic, and human rights issues, in relation to which Russia has acquired a reputation for bad behavior: the country's controversial trafficking in sex tourism; the exploitation of unregulated child labor; and Russia's pirating of Western properties, in this case "liberalism," in terms that mock the "sacred cows" of diversity, equality, and tolerance. Of course, in the end Katina and Volkova adhered to the rules of the contest during their Riga performance and never crossed the line of sanctioned deportment. However, t.A.T.u.'s performance leading into the competition – their missed rehearsals, their rumored withdrawal, their brash and insolent behavior before the international media, and their promotion of a faux-lesbian eroticism linked to the national "body and soul" of Russia – inevitably became part of what Eurovision audiences saw and responded to at the contest. Some spectators in attendance at Skonto Hall reportedly jeered at t.A.T.u. during their performance, which consequently prompted Katina and Volkova to blame their poor showing on homophobia.

While it is true that t.A.T.u. has been subject to homophobic invective at public appearances as well as in the Russian and international media, their claim that homophobic attitudes determined their ESC outcome is difficult to ascertain. Homophobia may have helped t.A.T.u. rationalize their disappointing performance; however, if t.A.T.u's third-place finish is viewed as a disappointment, it is the sort of disappointment that nevertheless fuels Russia's resistance to the West, thus strengthening the sense of Russian cultural sovereignty. The version of the song that t.A.T.u. performed at Eurovision is important in this sense. Unlike Alsou Safina, who won second prize in 2000, and the Russian boy-band Premier Ministr, which took 10th place in 2002, t.A.T.u. chose to perform in their native language, ignoring the governing ESC logic that "those who want to win sing in English."[14] In this sense, t.A.T.u.'s Eurovision performance broke decisively with Russian performances of the past, for while previous performances had staged the spectacle of Russia speaking to the West, t.A.T.u.'s performance staged the spectacle of Russia speaking to Russians – at the same time strategically courting the Western gaze that t.A.T.u. publicly claimed not to care less about. The group directed a message to Russians that communicated national pride, a challenge to the hegemony of the West, and indifference to the "assumed rules of the globalization process."[15] Thus the global and the local interacted in ways that already presumed such interactions to be far more alienating for Russians than for Western audiences accustomed to English-language versions of international pop products.

---

14   Philippe Le Guern, "From National Pride to Global Kitsch: the Eurovision Song Contest," *The Web Journal of French Media Studies* 3/1 (October 2000) <http://wjfms.ncl.ac.uk/leguWJ.htm> Accessed 11 December 2004.

15   Cordula Gdaniec, review of Hilary Pilkington's *Looking West?: Cultural Globalization and Russian Youth Cultures*, H-Net (July 2003) <www.hnet.msu.edu/reviews/showrev.cgi?path=188041059800639> Accessed 22 February 2005.

In this sense, t.A.T.u.'s participation in Eurovision 2003 was as much reflective of contradictory dialogue within Russia as it was reflective of contradictory dialogue between Russia and an ever-expanding Europe. Musically, t.A.T.u.'s dance tunes are composed of standard synthesized cadences and their lyrics weave narratives of fearless resistance, emotional suffering, and youthful rebellion in a manner entirely consistent with the global pop styles marketed to local youth cultures. Nevertheless, t.A.T.u.'s signature defiance – which describes not only their lyrics but their public personas and their notoriously uncooperative, diva-like behavior before the international media – is reflective of a stylized performance of post-Soviet Russianness as disobedient, disdainfully proud and infinitely powerful. "People are much freer [in Russia] than in the West," explains Yevgenia Debrianskaia, former dissident and queer activist, "because here we spit on any rules, we break them whenever we want. This is exactly what freedom is."[16] The significance of t.A.T.u.'s ESC performance was that it staged Shapovalov's successful translation of this former Soviet-dissident ethos into post-Soviet profit on the European multinational market. Even more so, it reveled in it.

Gender and resistance

Opposition, in other words, is what t.A.T.u. is all about. Given Russia's history of Soviet sexual conservatism and Orthodox Christianity, t.A.T.u.'s coy lesbian image would seem to contradict Volkova's proclamation that she and Katina are "Russian body and soul." However, part of the logic of that proclamation lies in Helen Goscilo's observation that "from time immemorial, the dominant Russian iconography has projected nationhood as female."[17] From this perspective, it could be said that Russia's successful marketing of native female beauty and power in the competitive global industries of women's athletics – in particular tennis, figure skating, and gymnastics – metaphorically reiterates the power of the state. Anna Kournikova, Maria Sharapova, Oksana Bayul (who is Ukrainian), and Svetlana Khorkina have all functioned, in this sense, as global exports who convey, among other things, a distinctive Russian mythology of superior strength and fecundity rooted in the ideal of the essential female mystique and the primal labors a woman performs. Wendy Varney argues that during the Soviet era, a socialist redefinition of women's labor justified the practice of using female gymnasts "on behalf of the state in pursuit of political, ideological, and economic outcomes." Citing the international rise to celebrity of Olga Korbut, whose career demonstrates an instance of national pride and loss of state control over the image of the Soviet Union, Varney's analysis highlights the ways in which female gymnasts during the Soviet era "had to embody contradictions and somehow resolve them … unwittingly reconciling conflicting

---

16   Laurie Essig, *Queer in Russia: A Story of Sex, Self, and the Other* (Durham, NC: Duke University Press, 1999), p. 142.

17   Helena Goscilo, *Dehexing Sex: Russian Womanhood During and After Glasnost* (Ann Arbor: University of Michigan Press, 1996), p. 32.

notions of traditional and modern; industrial and artistic; delicacy and strength; female 'incapacity' and Soviet accomplishment in spite of such incapacity."[18]

In the post-Soviet era some residue of this complex is retained at the juncture of Russia's commercial reclamation of erotic discourse and its international marketing of femininity, sexuality, and nationality. For example, it is manifest in *Komsomolskaya Pravda*'s photo report "Olympic Athletes Compete in Eroticism."[19] Here, female athletes in the 2004 Summer Olympics from Russia, Germany, Australia, and the United States pose provocatively, many in the nude (with the exception of the American athlete, who appears in a full two-piece bathing suit and assumes no discernibly erotic posture), for a pre-games publicity stunt that highlights ideological relations among gender, scopophilia, international competition, and the laboring body. And in this sense, it is important to consider the t.A.T.u. phenomenon in general, and their Eurovision performance in particular, as gendered labor performed not on behalf of the state but on behalf of Russia's fledgling grab-it-while-you-can capitalism and its investments in the modern sex industry. Shapovalov has indicated as much, claiming that he hit upon the idea for the band after identifying an unmet demand for pedophilic erotic material on the Internet. "People visit pornographic sites above all others," he is quoted as saying. "I analyzed it and found 90% of people using the Internet go to porno sites first, and of these nine in 10 are looking for underage entertainment. This means there is big interest as well as some dissatisfaction – their needs are not being met."[20]

While such statements must be read as facetious (all available evidence shows that it is teenagers, and not pedophiles, who rush to purchase t.A.T.u.'s records), Shapovalov has ascertainably shown his willingness to manipulate and exploit Katina and Volkova for his own purposes. And while the ploy has paid off handsomely, the women who have labored under the banner of Russia's pop music industry, like the elite female athletes who labored under the banner of the Soviet Union, were children when they were first identified and were reportedly forced to work many long hours under the Svengali-like command of their coach/manager. Indeed, until recently it would appear that Katina and Volkova exercised very little autonomy in directing their careers, or so the narrative of their experiences suggests: "As far as we know, before this band was made, Ivan Shapovalov never had anything to do with music business. ... He made us to sign contracts with him, and according to these contracts we didn't have any rights to even speak. We just had to do whatever he was telling us to do."[21]

However, even as it mimes elements of the exploitative power relations that characterize both the Soviet athletic system and the child-porn industry, t.A.T.u.'s

---

18   Wendy Varney, "A Labour of Patriotism: Female Soviet Gymnasts' Physical and Ideological Work, 1952–1991," *Genders* 39 (2004) <www.genders.org/g39/g39 varney.html> Accessed 15 February 2005.

19   "Olympic Athletes Compete in Eroticism," *Utra.Ru* (13 August 2004) <www.utro. ru/gallery.shtml?20040813nakedsports,1,7,,240> Accessed 15 February 2005.

20   Iain. S. Bruce, "Too Much, tATu Young," *Sunday Herald Online* (2 February 2003) <www.sundayherald.com/31089> Accessed 15 February 2005.

21   Walker, "t.A.T.u.: The Underage Sex Project."

narrative suggests resistance to the authoritarianism of Soviet sex and the pedagogization of sexuality that took place in the three decades before *glasnost*. A product of the post-Soviet commercialization of sexual discourse (and in key respects a parody of that process), t.A.T.u.'s same-sex eroticism is constructed to arouse heterosexual male fantasies and to sell records to a younger female audience receptive to explorations of sexual desire that defy regulation and normalization and that speak to queer audiences in terms that champion the authenticity of feeling and object attachment over investments in the politics of identity. "We love each other," Katina and Volkova have repeatedly emphasized when asked if they are really lesbian, in an effort to maneuver around the question of sexual categorization and avoid ensnarement in the tabloid media's culture of confession.[22] The success of t.A.T.u. in Russia is indicative of a changing sexual aesthetic that has taken shape alongside changes in the aesthetics of pop music, youth culture, and fashion, part of which includes an awareness of "queer chic." While it is still difficult to be openly gay or lesbian in Russia (especially outside of the cosmopolitan capitals of St Petersburg and Moscow), t.A.T.u.'s reception reflects the greater openness to bisexuality, homosexuality, and sexual experimentation that has increasingly come to characterize the attitudes of young urban Russian women.[23] At the same time, in other contexts Katina and Volkova have not hesitated to distance themselves from homosexuality, claiming that "it is a kind of sickness."[24] Such inconsistencies did little to dampen the enthusiasm of their global fan base, as evidenced by the plethora of international fan clubs and blogs devoted to them.

Arguably, this artful performativity, which Westerners are apt to read as overt opportunism, has allowed Katina and Volkova to haughtily dismiss and ridicule relentless media inquires into the "truth" of their sexual orientations in a manner that perhaps resonates with a younger generation of Europeans weary of identity politics. Indeed, t.A.T.u.'s faux lesbianism is as much a geopolitical performance as their indignation at being confronted always with the same question, for it is precisely through their lucrative performance of pique and indifference that myths of Russian immunity and superiority to the homogenizing effects of Western identity categories and the moral, social, and political narratives they have engendered are globally reiterated. In Rob Walker's estimation, all this amounts to "a sort of infinite loop of provocation, critique, and hypocrisy" as t.A.T.u. mocks the desires that it mimes while profiting from what the West claims to find offensive in their performance of teen lesbian lust as well as in their belligerent refusals to name themselves in "appropriate" accordance with that performance.[25]

---

22   Elysa Gardner, "From Russia With Love Comes Naughty T.A.T.U," *USA Today* (5 March 2003) <www.usatoday.com/life/music/news/2003-03-05-tatu_x.htm> Accessed 21 February 2005.

23   Elena Omel'chenko, "'My Body, My Friend?' Youth, Gender and Sex," in *Gender, State and Society in Soviet and Post-Soviet Russia*, ed. Sarah Ashwin (New York: Routledge, 2000), pp. 147, 158.

24   "t.A.T.u. Flame Out!" *The Face* (9 December 2003) <http://eng.tatysite.net/press/press.php?id=1168_0_7_0_M> Accessed 21 February 2005.

25   Walker, "t.A.T.u.: The Underage Sex Project."

Conclusion

Clearly, part of t.A.T.u.'s success has been in having it both ways, which arguably made them a natural fit for Eurovision, a competition that pits countries against one another, compelling them to perform their distinctive national identities in the name of European "unity"; participating countries are united less by geography than by media space. Otherwise, the contest serves as a consolidating cross-cultural ritual. The ESC notoriously mingles kitsch and geopolitics as it annually constructs the collective memory of European cooperation while dramatizing the impossibility of escaping the borders and boundaries of nation and culture, gender and sexuality, self and other.

Along these lines, Philippe Le Guern argues that the ESC functions according to the "dual principle of proximity and distance: on the one hand, each nation is put on the map through the media. ... On the other hand it contrasts 'us' and 'them,'" both reflecting and deflecting the tensions, indignations, and mutual glad-handing that is reshaping Europe and its others, old and new. Viewers are drawn together in this process, Le Guern claims, through the experience of simultaneity that the contest's broadcast produces:

> The contest brings together audiences that are geographically and socially heterogeneous but who engage in the same activity in the same instant. It brings to life one of those "imagined communities" ... , conjures up a collective identity, socializes each viewer's singular experience by linking it to that of all other viewers, and creates affective links between them by offering a "home collective experience."[26]

Le Guern's reference to Benedict Anderson's theory of nationalism and "imagined communities" underscores Eurovision's role in shaping national consciousness.[27] In this sense, the ESC can be understood as a dynamic media flashpoint, a site of transnational engagement that allows participating nations to collectively imagine their "Europe" in accordance with their own local needs. At the same time, of course, nations themselves are culturally reimagined by the multinational audience's expectations and interpretations, as well as by the expanding economic, institutional, and social reach of geopolitical alliances.

Recent announcements of the birth of Volkova's daughter, and hers and Katina's severed business relations with Shapovalov, suggest that Russia's t.A.T.u. was only temporary. However, the singer Morrissey in an interview with the British magazine *Word* may have best summed up the subtle evolutionary shift in Russia's relation to Europe that their Eurovision performance represents. When asked his opinion on t.A.T.u.'s cover of the Smiths' "How Soon is Now," Morrissey hailed it as "magnificent," but admitted that he didn't know very much about the singers. "They're the teenage Russian lesbians," the interviewer informed him, to which Morrissey responded, "Well, aren't we all?"[28] Similarly, the t.A.T.u. phenomenon

---

26   Le Guern, "From National Pride to Global Kitsch."

27   Benedict Anderson, *Imagined Communities: Reflections on the Origins and Spread of Nationalism* (London: Verso, 1991).

28   Andrew Harrison, "Home Thoughts from Abroad," *Word Magazine* 4 (June 2003): 8.

tells us much about the misrecognitions of the self that are always already inscribed within the cultural forms of the other. The Eurovision performance from t.A.T.u., like the contest itself, is productive of a critical self-awareness that enables co-existence with others as well as participation in the creation and recreation of the limits of cultural belonging.

Chapter 11

Gay brotherhood: Israeli gay men and the Eurovision Song Contest

Dafna Lemish

Gay, Lesbian, Bisexual and Transgender Pride Day was marked in Israel in June 2000, among other things, by a gathering of activists and politicians in the Israeli Knesset (Parliament). Among the many interviews and declarations presented to busy reporters in front of microphones and cameras, attention was called to an activist waving around a bag with the clear logo of "The Eurovision Song Contest" on it. Pride Day. The Eurovision Song Contest. The Israeli Knesset. How are these related?

Israel joined Eurovision in 1973, and has since won the contest three times and hosted it twice. Inclusion within the contest was perceived as a source of national pride, according Israel legitimacy as a "European" country: Western, developed and respected. Indeed, the discourse surrounding Eurovision in the Israeli media has centered around nationalistic sentiments and a desire for international recognition disassociated from issues of war and politics. On the other hand, a parallel theme emerging from the analysis of the media coverage is a patronizing dismissal of the ESC as musical "kitsch" and a shallow show of glamor.

I have been studying the role of the Eurovision Song Contest (ESC) in the construction of identity through in-depth interviews and content analysis of newspaper coverage.[1] As part of this larger project I gradually learned of the unique relationships that gay men have to this musical competition. This chapter considers the role of the ESC in the lives of Israeli gay men and its contribution to their construction of a distinct cultural identity.

The Israeli gay male community has witnessed a dramatic transformation and mainstreaming since the late 1980s, but is still often confronted with stereotypical and negative portrayals of itself in the popular media and with few realistic or positive representations. The culture as a whole, and media texts in particular, serve

My deep gratitude to Amit Kama, who introduced me to the literature and life of gay men and commented on earlier drafts of this article; to Larry Gross, Aeyal Gross, Dekel Shalev, Moshe Shokeid, and to the many men who shared their deepest thoughts with me. A longer version of this paper appeared as "'My Kind of Campfire': The Eurovision Song Contest and Israeli Gay Men," in *Popular Communication* 2/1 (2004): 41–63.

1 Philippe LeGuern and Dafna Lemish, "The Eurovision Song Contest and Identity," paper presented at CNRS research program "The Questions of European Identity" (Rennes, 2000).

the ideology of compulsory heterosexuality.[2] One strategy through which gay men manage their interaction with the productions of the dominant culture is to selectively attend to validating texts while ignoring those damaging or challenging to their self-perception.[3] The purpose of the present study, based mostly on a focus group as well as individual interviews with gay men,[4] is to examine a second strategy, namely that of appropriating a mainstream cultural event such as the ESC and turning it into an empowering one through specific social practices and interpretive strategies. As Joshua Gamson explains, "In part because gays and lesbians, until recently, were rarely addressed directly as an audience, they have a rich history of turning pieces of heterosexually-oriented popular culture into their own expressions of individual and collective identity."[5]

That the ESC has a unique place in the individual lives of Israeli gay men and the gay male community in general clearly emerged from these interviews. Being an ESC fan was frequently described as part of the common experience of growing up as a gay man. Practices of group viewing such as social gatherings and parties were related by all participants. As Guy, the personal manager of one Eurovision performer, explained,

> The ESC is a competition of gays. In gay clubs they celebrate it, and sing ESC songs there. Today for example, people laugh because the ESC is not an important thing, and they say it remains a competition for gays and elderly.

Several mentioned a famous Tel Aviv gay pub that devotes Sunday nights to Eurovision music and is packed with fans and performer imitators in a cheerful atmosphere defined by some as the "ultimate gay night out." Participants in this study described their engagement with the ESC as a special social event. "It is the Passover of the homos," joked Avi, a musician, "people call each other and ask: So where will you be this ESC? Who are you spending it with?" The ESC thus serves as a site for alternative "families" of close friends, replacing the biological family and creating their own familial celebrations.[6] This phenomenon goes largely unnoticed among heterosexual men (usually non-viewers) and women (often viewers). It is as if mainstream culture were blind to an undercurrent of cultural existence so dominant in the lives of a subordinated community.

---

2   Andrea Rich, "Compulsory Heterosexuality and Lesbian Existence," *Signs* 5/4 (1980): 636–60.

3   See Amit Kama, "From *Terra Incognita* to *Terra Firma*: The Logbook of the Voyage of the Gay Men's Community into the Israeli Public Sphere," *Journal of Homosexuality* 38/4 (2000): 133–62.

4   This study involved 54 interviews with gay Israeli ESC viewers, ESC-related professionals (including the chair of the Israeli fan club and a member of the selection committee), and non-gay ESC viewers; further insights were gained through websites and chat groups surrounding the ESC in general and its gay interest in particular.

5   Joshua Gamson, "Sweating in the Spotlight: Lesbian, Gay and Queer Encounters with Media and Popular Culture," in *Handbook of Gay and Lesbian Studies*, ed. D. Eichardson and S. Seidman (London: Sage, 2002), p. 343.

6   See Kath Weston, *Families We Choose: Lesbians, Gays, Kinship* (New York: Columbia University Press, 1991).

Furthermore, all the gay men interviewed were convinced that this is not a uniquely Israeli phenomenon. Ample evidence of Internet fan clubs, chat lines, visits abroad, and personal acquaintances suggest an international gay bond surrounding the ESC. Moshe, a manager, said, "Most of the ESC fans in Europe are gays. I see it in gays' clubs. People who interview and cover the ESC and people who admire it are gays. From my experience with nine contests I know it for sure."

Like a major competitive sports match, the ESC is a media event that provides an exciting bonding experience for spectators and fans, but a major difference here is the factor of sexual identity. The ESC is to gay men what sport events are to heterosexual men, as several interviewees stated: "the ESC is for gays what the Mondial [International soccer tournament] is for straights ... a kind of a ritual"; "It is the same way some straight men sit in front of the television to watch the finals of the Euro [European soccer tournament] and enjoy it completely." Explanations of this division of interest were cast in terms of gender bias. Gays allow themselves more sentimentality, while non-gay men are attracted to demonstrations of physical power and aggression. "Straights like drama just as much as gays, but the difference is how you actualize it. For straights it is sports, and with gays it is in musical competitions. It is the same kind of excitement, except that gays allow themselves to be more sentimental," explained Amos, a linguistics student. Guy, the personal manager, elaborated: "Gays don't like heavy rock [music] or sports. That's something too masculine and aggressive of course ... There is something much more light and colorful and fun to compete with songs and colorful costumes and paillettes [sequins], rather than with sweat and a ball."

Camping around

A central theme underlying the interviewees' discourse, sometimes overtly and sometimes implicitly, is an attempt to interpret this bond between homosexuality and the ESC in terms of camp sensibility.[7] Camp generally refers to counter-culture tastes that mock and challenge mainstream cultural assumptions and aesthetics, and it is often associated with forms of parody, irony, exaggeration, stylization, nostalgia, humor, theatricality, and artificiality. In particular, camp is greatly concerned with the human body and with gender-related issues, and is often engaged in challenging the dichotomous heterosexual division of the social world. As Barbara Klinger suggests, "Camp acts as a form of expressive rebuttal to the values of dominant culture for those on the margins."[8] Gender play, drag, exaggerated femininity, and androgyny are common camp themes that enact alternatives to the so-called "natural" gender

---

7   Since Susan Sontag's milestone 1964 essay, camp has become a much-debated concept in cultural studies in general and in gay and queer studies in particular. Susan Sontag, "Notes on Camp," in *Against Interpretation and Other Essays* (New York: Farrar, Straus & Giroux, 1966), pp. 263–74.

8   Barbara Klinger, *Melodrama and Meaning: History, Culture and the Films of Douglas Sirk* (Bloomington: Indiana University Press, 1994), p. 136.

order.[9] In his discussion of the role of camp in gay culture, Richard Dyer suggests that because gays were engaged so much of the time in hiding their true selves, they "have developed an eye and an ear for surfaces, appearances, forms—style."[10]

Indeed, the ESC is clearly a site of camp-related pleasure for the participants in this study. Many of the interviewees perceived their viewing of the ESC as a form of practicing camp. Some discussed the theoretical concept itself, others referred to its various meanings without naming it as camp, and others used the related term "kitsch." Examples of this awareness were ample: "the ESC is some kind of … three minutes of 'Look at me!' and the customs that all kinds of people put on, and all the so-called big divas that performed there" described Ohad, an academic. Another gay student, Yoav, explained, "there is something about the music of gay culture in the world, something grandiose and schmaltz and catchy." This musical genre allows for the blurring of gendered qualities and roles, he continued:

> It is this attraction to singers with big voices who give their all in three minutes and leave you completely vibrating … it is part of this immediate connection that homos have to drama … because we are sentimental people … it is the kind of masculinity that says: "I am allowed to be sentimental."

Several interviewees contrasted the pleasure of viewing the ESC against the difficulty of being members of a silenced community. Viewing becomes a "time-out" from everyday hardships and struggles, as Yotam, a 20-year-old soldier, explained:

> It's part of a culture of taking things easily. Enjoy things. Pretend everything is a pleasurable dramatic show. For lots of homos, adolescence was very oppressive. Till now we suffered. Now it is time to party. And if partying—then let's do it all the way with the drama of camp. With all the colors, and the sparkle, and the dancers in the background. That's why camp culture is so dominant in the lives of homos.

His friend, Ori, a lawyer, continued,

> Homos seek this element of access in camp because of being rejected from the mainstream culture. Or maybe it is because a special kind of sensitivity related to the closet and coming out of it. This access, and "I will survive" and the repression of suffering. … Camp is a way of playing out the thing one suffers from, and through it to repress it and control it.

For many of the participants, engagement in camp was also perceived as an advantage over heterosexuality, as Ilan, a graduate student, said:

> You see, someone who is straight, he is not used to crossing the barrier of social conventions. Homos on the other hand, have done it already once in their lives, and after you do it once, the second time is much easier … and that's why it is easier for homos to connect to camp, to transgender, to the feeling of freedom.

---

9   Judith Butler, *Gender Trouble: Feminism and the Subversion of Identity* (London: Routledge, 1990).

10   Richard Dyer, "It's Being So Camp As Keeps Us Going," in *Camp: Queer Aesthetics and the Performing Subject*, ed. Fabio Cleto (Edinburgh: Edinburgh University Press, 1999), p. 114.

Rafi, a media consultant, said, "Camp has an element of shiny ostentation to it; something that is intended to shock you with its richness." These qualities were also obvious to a selection-committee member who is a heterosexual female novelist and journalist: "There are many indications of drag performances in the ESC ... the glamor style, all kinds of exaggerated costumes ... The ESC has all kinds of singers [who look] like they are in the middle of a parody about themselves and they are the last to know it."

The attraction to divas, women "bigger than life," and the struggle over the nature of femininity were a central theme in the interviews. Connecting with the ESC seems to offer an opportunity to connect with the feminine parts of the soul and with the struggle for self-definition, as Yishai, a graduate law student, confessed:

> For me it is related to the way I used to perceive myself as boy-girl. When I was young I was really attracted to dressing like a girl, and female celebrities always evoked in me a kind of identification or a desire to be like them. Although I completely do not want to be a woman and do not feel as a woman or something like that, I think that camp is related to homos' reluctance to talk about what it means to be a woman to them. For me, the connection to women who are bigger than life, women who are absurd or ridiculous or exaggerated and overdone, is related to the preoccupation with what is a woman, and what is a homo in relation to a man and in relation to a woman ... this play of a third gender ... the question of what is the gender of a homo.

Rafi said, "I think it is an expression of cross-gender behavior, because it is kind of not manly to watch these kitsch things, it is much more manly to watch soccer. There is a pleasure of feeling a little bit like the other sex." Alon, a graduate psychology student, added, "I think what attracts gay men in general is the extroverted expression of femininity. Maybe because society around us does not allow us to express these aspects and laughs at us. The ESC probably connects to something psychological very deep, a sense of liberation."

Dyer emphasizes that camp is more a question of how one responds to a text rather than the qualities actually inherent in it. Camp sensibility is therefore often characterized by the ability to maintain an interpretive distance through a "willful misreading" of cultural texts.[11] The ability to distance oneself from the text and adopt a critical position of self-awareness was clearly expressed by many of the interviewees, such as Ori:

> There are those who really want to view the ESC performances seriously, they are still fixated within a 17-year-old mentality, because it is really not good music. But we come mainly to have a little laugh, to talk to each other ... most of the songs do not even deserve to be listened to.

Similarly, Nir, a computer specialist, explained,

> For many gays loving the ESC is built in from childhood. The excitement, the fame, the competition. But later, when they mature, they see it in an ironic light, with self-

---

11 Klinger, *Melodrama and Meaning*, p. 132.

awareness. They know it is crap, they know it is ridiculous and laughable and a silly and terrible competition. But it is lots of fun.

Ilan added, "I like to look at the songs, not because I think they are such great quality. I have this kind of an anthropological perspective. My pleasure is this kind of self-humor, kind of making fun of myself."

The "campfire"

Participation in the ESC as a media event has in many ways become an initiation rite and compulsory event for members of the Israeli gay male community: "it is so much ours, that you can't turn your back on it, it's like you are insulting your own identity," suggested Alon. "It is about gay brotherhood," said Ohad. Even those gays who have little interest in the ESC join in the celebration as an expression of loyalty and identification with a shared cultural territory.They realize that "everyone I know watched it yesterday, it is ours." David, a physician, recalled: "When I came out of the closet I was looking for a 'campfire' to sit around with my kind of group. The ESC was already there. So it was very easy to just join in and feel that you are part of it."[12]

As with other media events, the role of the ESC in solidifying gay identity and consciousness goes beyond territorial constraints and national borders, as Yishai explained: "I think that for all of us, there is this international element. The feeling that being a homo is not something that is just here, in Tel Aviv, and not something that is just in Israel. It is something that is all over the world. ... There is a sense of community, an international homo-community that can be reached through events such as the ESC." Daniel, a humanities student, added, "It is a feeling of freedom in this international bondage ... crossing the borders ... not only the transgender border, but also the border of your own country." Interviewees related personal stories about European acquaintances who call them during the broadcast to share the moment: "He is in Germany, watching at the same time that I am, and we have something in common. He wouldn't have called me about a movie or something," remarked Lior, a gay activist.

Watching the ESC serves also the fantasy of "getting away" from everyday heterosexual reality to a fantasy world "out there." This experience is often associated with actual past trips to Europe. For many of the participants, their first trip to Europe was a liberating experience of initiation into the international gay male community. Watching gays walk hand-in-hand in Amsterdam, visiting a gay club in Munich, or meeting gays in a pub in Barcelona were often formative experiences for young gays finally out of secrecy. This phenomenon is explained by Moshe Shokeid as the "centricity orientation supposition," according to which gay men located in the social periphery long for the global center.[13] While at home they behave according to

---

12   The campfire has a central meaning in forming the collective identity of Israelis, as a bonding experience of members of youth movements, soldiers, pioneers, and the like.

13   Moshe Shokeid, "Closeted Cosmopolitans: Israeli Gays Between Center and Periphery," *Global Networks* 3/3 (2003): 387–99.

the codes of the closet, when they travel abroad they take upon themselves the role of pilgrims to "holy" gay sites. Watching the ESC was for many of them a nostalgic moment of reliving such experiences and reconnecting to Europe "out there" and all that it represents.

For some, Europe and the ESC intertwine in the experiential level, as in the intimate story told by Oded, a journalist: "I went to cover a musical event in the Basques [in Spain], and I had this brief affair with a guy from a little town. He didn't know a word of English. ... And what do you think was the highlight of our meeting? He sang to me the Israeli songs from the ESC and I sang to him the Spanish songs. And that says it all." Others tell about their travels in Europe among ESC fans: "When I traveled the world, I met all kinds of homos. In all kinds of places. In Ireland, for example. Ireland hosted the ESC four/five times. It is the annual event of the homos of Dublin." Several interviewees were humorously pitying the Americans for not having access to the ESC. An original Israeli television drama with gay protagonists, *Baal Baal Lev* (A husband with a heart), expressed this very theme in a moving episode when the protagonist, a gay teenage Eurovision fan, said: "The Americans are so miserable—they've got everything: New York, McDonalds, Madonna, Clinton's daughter Chelsea. But what is it all worth if they don't have the ESC?" This drama was often referred to by interviewees with great sympathy and identification. Several also mentioned British playwright Jonathan Harvey's *Boom Bang-A-Bang*, set during the ESC and named after one of its classic songs, as support for the international gay appeal of this musical event.[14]

Identity and desire

Gay men currently coming of age in Israel can be as tormented as their predecessors over their gay identity and the unique dilemma of "coming out" of the metaphoric closet. Through the responses of 45 gay interviewees, Amit Kama demonstrates the centrality of this existential dilemma in the personal narrative of many gay men and the constant struggle against the sense of self-negation coerced by the dominant heterosexual culture.[15] In my own interviews, many participants' early intimate experiences with love, sex and identity were somehow recollected in relationship to the ESC. The following story was told by Ori:

> I was a virgin. Fully in the closet. And the first guy I met ... we had sex, and we started talking, and he started telling me about himself, and there are piles of ESC video-tapes, one on top of the other ... so I told him that I liked the ESC since I was six or seven, and he said to me, "wow, you could have known you are a homo fifteen years ago!" And I remember myself doing all my life everything in my power to hide the fact that I am a homo, and suddenly he tells me that something I was doing all these years so

---

14   Jonathan Harvey, *The Rupert Street Lonely Hearts Club & Boom Bang-a-Bang* (London: Methuen Publishing, 1995).

15   Amit Kama, "The Quest for Inclusion: Jewish-Israeli Gay Men's Perceptions of Gays in the Media," *Feminist Media Studies* 2/2 (2002): 195–212.

intensively—to love the ESC—is clearly identifying me as a homo! I remember it scared me to death.

Lior recalled:

> One of my early experiences was with this silly, lively guy, and he [told] my other flat-mates that he is collecting all the ESC records and he is missing two of them … and I was so embarrassed … that he is so silly, and what it says about me, that he likes the ESC.

Often those early experiences were fixated on the act of coming out of the closet, as in the following story related by Ofer, a university lecturer:

> When I was about 18, I was still in the closet. And I traveled to the USA and I had a homo friend there, and once we talked and I told him about the ESC and he said to me: "that's kind of a homo thing, right?" And I have to admit that paradoxically I wasn't even aware of it although I was a regular viewer. So he said, "yes, it's like the Oscar Academy Awards for us." And that's when I realized it. When I was in the military, suddenly watching the ESC was a big shame … it was about repressing my homosexuality. And then I met my partner. He took me to a group of friends of his who watched the ESC, and through our love I came out of the closet.

"The first time that I met someone gay at his house, and I can reveal that it was my first sexual experience, he put the ESC on in the background, and he held my hand," Avi sweetly recalled.

A common practice in collective gay ESC viewing is pointing out gay performers and gossiping about the sexual desirability of performers and their backup singers and dancers. Interestingly, interviewees admitted that they apply the same heterosexual criteria for identifying gay men on stage: feminine appearance and mannerism, exaggerated gestures, extravagant clothing, and the like.[16] As Lior explains,

> We say, "oh, it is clear that he is a homo, look at the way he dresses, look at the way he dances, look at the way he moves. Surely he is a homo, and wouldn't it be nice if—," or we laugh at him and make fun and say, "he is so stereotypical, and look at the way he moves."

Gossiping, joking and "drooling" over performers was expressed by discussing their appearance as cute, darling, hunky, sexy, or even fantasizing over a potential sexual encounter. As Larry Gross explains, rumor and gossip have an important role in gay culture as a result of the scarcity of openly gay celebrities.[17] This was often evident even when performers were known not to be gay and therefore not running the risk of being "outed." Lior continues his explanation:

> Even if I know in advance that he is not gay I can fantasize about him. … That dancer from Russia [performing in the 2000 ESC], what do I have with him? Nothing. Even if

---

16　Carl B. Holmberg, *Sexualities and Popular Culture* (Thousand Oaks, CA: Sage Publications, 1998): p. 50.

17　Larry Gross, *Up from Invisibility: Lesbians, Gay Men and the Media in America* (New York: Columbia University Press, 2002).

he is the king of the homos. He is in Russia and I am here. It's a fantasy of laughs. ... It's erotic, it's fun.

For gay viewers of the ESC, the competition offers a rare display of a variety of gay (or potentially gay) role models as well as a demonstration of gay tastes and sexual desire. It's a gay fashion show or beauty pageant, several interviewees suggested.

The case of Dana International

If the ESC is the gay campfire, than Dana International is its torch. A male-to-female transsexual who won the contest in 1998, Dana has become an international celebrity. She has openly identified herself with the Israeli gay male community and regularly committed herself to gay political causes. In her choice of music and lyrics (often written herself) she addresses border-crossings of many kinds, and her politics are multidimensional and often seem contradictory.[18] This study prompted discussion of Dana International's significance both on a personal level for participants as well as for their politics as a group. While all agreed that the Eurovision gay bond has always existed, they nevertheless emphasized Dana's role in openly appropriating this international musical event and solidifying a proud Israeli gay male community.

Dana's victory came after an energetic public relations campaign that pumped the public's curiosity about this sexy transsexual who has suffered many hardships in her struggle to gain stardom and recognition. The year she participated was also the first year the ESC instituted the current system of televoting. The active role of the European gay community in affecting the results of the votes through engagement and "bloc" voting appeared in this study as an accepted given, as Gideon, a soldier, described:

> What warmed my heart was that this was the first year of televoting and there was a huge buzz beforehand among the gay community throughout Europe who promised to vote for her. And when that was realized it was a sense of power. A gay power around Europe.

Interviewees provided lively descriptions of their spontaneous reactions to Dana's victory, such as the following one by Dor, a graduate student:

> It was incredible. Across the street from us, a window across a window, there was another group that viewed it. Each time Dana received points—we heard them. When she finally won, it was hysterical. We opened the windows, and we yelled to each other, and one of them did a striptease, and we all started dancing.

---

18   In one of her interviews to CNN she declares, "I do not represent the Jewish state, I represent the Arabs, the Jews, the Christians. I represent all the citizens of Israel. I represent all that want to be represented by me." Quoted in Ayal Gross, "Queering the International: When Dana Meets Amnesty – A Case of Re-presentation," paper at the annual meeting of the American Society of International Law (1999). See also Zvi Triger, "Dana International and the Eurovision Song Contest: A Case Study of an Empowered Self" (unpublished manuscript), and Amalya Ziv, "Dana International," *Theory and Criticism [Theoria ve'Bikoret]* 12 (1999): 401–11.

Celebrations quickly took to the streets and flowed into Tel Aviv's Rabin Square, the site of major political demonstrations. Hundreds of gays from all over the country spent the night celebrating, singing, dancing, waving rainbow flags, and giving interviews to the press. The following day the Israeli media gave unusual coverage to this demonstration of gay solidarity and pride. The community as a whole came out of the closet that night, as Nir described:

> It was incredible … it was the first time that when the press came people didn't say "Don't take pictures" or turned their faces away. There was this absurd contradiction—being out there, with the rainbow flags, celebrating the fact that Dana, in front of the world says, "I am a transsexual." [This was] coming out normally, in contrast to the way we are used to, so "nobody will see me, and nobody will photograph me," the way we were used to from previous gay events.

This experience was related by many interviewees as a sense of liberation and alleviation: "I felt it was our victory. In totality. Afterwards the atmosphere in the Square was incredible, a sense of liberation." Amos elaborated the following:

> As a homo, one of the things that you know, even before coming out of the closet, is that your most basic desire is something that the consensus rejects. And my longings have always been to be part of a majority. Suddenly with Dana's victory there was a connection of all of those things together.

Clearly, interviewees grasped this victory as political in nature, as Aviv said: "With all due respect to the Aguda [Israeli Association of Gay-Lesbian-Bisexual and Transgender Rights], they didn't succeed in doing what Dana did. They didn't give us the feeling of pride and of power and the resonance that Dana did."

Moreover, as one of the participants explained, it was the empowering experience to be in a mixed crowd of gays celebrating Dana's victory, patriotic heterosexuals celebrating Israel's victory, and fans of a local Israeli soccer team who had just won the championship that same day. Colorful rainbow flags, blue and white Israeli flags and yellow soccer flags were all flapping together in Rabin Square in an intense atmosphere bursting with pride and joy. Alon recalled a personal incident:

> A Beitar [soccer group] fan climbed up a huge pole from somewhere and placed a Beitar's flag, and the rest of the fans held the pole. Exactly across from him there was another pole with the Pride flag on, and someone (who didn't even look gay to me) was climbing on it. The two climbers were facing each other, as if in a competition, to the sound of audience applause. It was an astounding situation—and so symbolic on so many levels. … In my eyes it was the moment that two poles represented not two forms of sexual tendencies, but two models of masculinity one across from the other, and it was not accidental that it was a war between flags. … It was the first time ever that I felt that somewhere in a futuristic world maybe the two can truly stand across from each other as two equal alternatives. And yet, I remember that with all the excitement and intensity, I was looking at the two poles with the flags and hoping so much that the one climbing on the Pride flag will be quicker, will reach higher, will get more applause from the audience, straights and gays together.

Dana International's bond with the gay community worldwide was evident in the many news articles and websites that followed her victory and debated her political and cultural contributions to gay issues. Interestingly, general media coverage of the event seemed unconcerned with this internal debate. Dana was appropriated by the general Israeli society as a proud representative of a free, liberal, democratic society, as was clearly expressed in the news coverage of her victory and the honors given her by cultural and political leaders. This theme was also voiced in the interviews with non-gay participants in the study, such as Noam, a student:

> A day after the victory you could see reports about Israel being open, liberal, that it is a much more open place in comparison to many other European countries … it offered another, very different perspective about Israel. Dana's victory provided an opportunity for a big European public that thought that this country is a religious Jewish state, to understand that this is a free, liberal, democratic country.

Conclusion

According to Simon Frith, music is central to understanding identity because it offers "a sense of both self and others, of the subjective in the collective."[19] Following his argument, my interviews suggest that the attachment to Eurovision provides gay men with a site of personal identity struggle and a sounding board against which to examine themselves in relation to others. In many ways, gay men in this study got to know themselves as a distinct group through their engagement with this particular cultural activity. Enjoying Eurovision music and performances, developing a camp sensibility, celebrating ESC broadcasts in parties, jointly expressing sexual desire, waving rainbow flags in Rabin Square, bestowing on Dana International a spokesperson role—all these are expressions of the notion of identity-in-process.

Scholars have demonstrated that music serves social functions for adolescent youth across cultural borders in their search for individual as well as group identity by aiding their self-expression, independence, and intimacy and by appealing to many of their concerns, such as their sexual drive and rebellious inclinations.[20] Similarly, music plays an important role in the construction of gender identity, particularly in relation to femininity.[21] For gay men, however, the ESC goes well beyond the

---

19   Simon Frith, "Music and Identity," in *Questions of Cultural Identity*, ed. Stuart Hall and Paul Du Gays (London: Sage Publications, 1996), p. 110.

20   Amiram Raviv, Daniel Bar-Tal, Alona Raviv, and Asaf Ben-Horn, "Adolescent Idolization of Pop Singers: Causes, Expressions, and Reliance," *Journal of Youth and Adolescence* 2/5 (1996): 634. See also Simon Frith, *Sound Effects: Youth, Leisure, and the Politics of Rock 'n' Roll* (London: Constable, 1983); W. Gantz, H.M. Garteenberg, M.I. Pearson and S.O. Schiller, "Gratifications and Expectations Associated with Pop Music Among Adolescents," *Popular Music and Society* 6/1 (1977): 81–9; and Keith Roe, "Adolescents' Music Use: A Structural-Cultural Approach," in *Popular Music Research: An Anthology from Nordicom-Sweden* (Göteborg: Nordicom, 1990): 41–52.

21   See, for example, Dafna Lemish, "Spice Girls' Talk: A Case Study in the Development of Gendered Identity," in *Millennium Girls: Today's Girls and their Culture*, ed. S.A. Inness (New York: Rowman and Littlefield, 1998), pp. 145–67; Lisa A. Lewis, "Consumer Girls' Culture: How Music Video Appeals to Girls," in *Television and Women's Culture: The Politics of the Popular* (Newsbury Park, CA: Sage, 1990), pp. 89–101; *Growing Up Girls: Popular*

music—it is also the performer, the act of performance itself, and the stage (both literal and metaphorical) which constitute the site of identity construction. The fact that the ESC as an international musical event is clearly designed for general audience appeal does not stand in the way of appropriating it to one particular cultural enclave. This process was labeled by Larry Gross as "queering the 'straight' text," according to which images seemingly produced by and for the majority are read by the minority audience "against the grain," and are appropriated by the minority as if they had been intended for them.[22]

Beyond a particular local or national identification, however, the transnational nature of Eurovision's "gay brotherhood" illustrates the multiplicity of identities and their fragmented nature.[23] Israeli fans of the ESC are connected to other Europeans by their gay identity, but at the same time that they are proud (or perhaps shameful) of being Israeli. They struggle against attempts to associate homosexuality with femininity, yet they applaud a transsexual woman and claim her their own. They put down the musical taste of "serious" uncritical Eurovision fans, yet they adore that same music as glorified camp. The phenomenon of ESC fandom unveils many potentially contradictory identities, particularly in relationship to Dana International's complex representation. As such, it demonstrates the rich multiplicity of meanings that popular music has in everyday life in general and in perceptions of gender in particular.

Culture and the Construction of Identity, ed. Sharon Mazzarella and Norma Pecora (New York: Peter Lang, 1999); and E.E. Peterson, "Media Consumption and Girls Who Want to Have Fun," *Critical Studies in Mass Communication* 4/1 (1987): 37–50.

22 Larry Gross, "Minorities, Majorities and the Media," in *Media, Ritual and Identity*, ed. T. Liebes and J. Curran (London: Routledge, 1998), p. 95.

23 See Lawrence Grossberg, "Identity and Cultural Studies: Is That All There Is?" in *Questions of Cultural Identity*, ed. Stuart Hall and Paul Du Gay (London: Sage Publications, 1996), pp. 104–26.

Chapter 12

Articulating the historical moment: Turkey, Europe, and Eurovision 2003

Thomas Solomon

After some 25 years of trying, Turkey spectacularly won the Eurovision Song Contest (ESC) in May 2003. For many in Turkey, winning the contest was regarded as a symbol of finally being accepted as a "European" country rather than a "Middle Eastern" one. Not surprisingly, this victory fueled Turkey's aspirations to join the European Union, a political and social project that had been under way since the early 1960s, when Turkey first signed an association agreement with the (then) European Economic Community. While much attention has been paid to the political processes behind Turkey's EU candidacy, less has been said about the role that culture plays in Turkey's European vocation, and how events in the cultural sphere contribute to the complex relationship between Turkey and Europe. Turkey's victory in the ESC in 2003 dramatically showed how important culture can be in Turkey's maneuvering to find its place on the European stage.

But was Turkey's win in 2003 just the result of having the right song and the right performer? Or was it also because it was the right *time* for Turkey to take center stage? That is, did events elsewhere in Europe create conditions conducive to Turkey's spectacular victory? In his own analysis of recent Eurovision contests, Philip Bohlman argues, "As in all competitions, it is not necessarily the best song that wins, but rather one that articulates the historical moment."[1] In this chapter I discuss some aspects of the "historical moment" in which Eurovision 2003 occurred and suggest ways that Turkey's participation in the ESC defined that moment. Developments in other parts of Europe, all involving Turkey in one way or another, seem to have created a political and cultural climate conducive to Turkey's success in Eurovision.

Many thanks to Engül Atamert for reading and commenting on a draft of this chapter, and to Ståle Knudsen, Kjetil Fosshagen, and Siv Dale Gencher for sitting through a reading of the manuscript, and giving their comments and suggestions. I also presented an early version of this research at the 2004 meeting of the Society for Ethnomusicology in Tucson.

1   Philip V. Bohlman, *The Music of European Nationalism: Cultural Identity and Modern History* (Santa Barbara: ABC-CLIO, 2004), p. 9.

English lyrics and musical Turkisms

Turkey has participated in the ESC almost every year since 1975.[2] Turkey's entry came in last place that year, setting a precedent for many poor finishes over the years to come. In the 24 times Turkey participated in the contest before 2003, it finished in the bottom half of the field of contestants all but four times, including three times in last place, two of those with zero points (in 1983 and 1987). The country's poor record was an acute source of embarrassment; Turkish friends have told me about how they used to watch Eurovision in the 1980s and 1990s, pleading to the television that some country—any country—would vote for Turkey's song to spare it the humiliation of again finishing with the dreaded *nul points*. These frustrations and embarrassing failures in the contest are widely seen in Turkey as an allegory of its aspirations to join the European Union and its frustratingly slow movement toward that goal, and proof of the perception, warranted or not, that Europeans do not accept Turkey as a European nation.

In Turkey, the state-run Turkish Radio and Television (TRT) oversees the country's participation in the ESC. The Turkish pop singer Sertab Erener accepted TRT's invitation to represent Turkey in Eurovision 2003 on the condition that she be allowed to perform in English. Already an established performer on the Turkish pop scene since the late 1980s,[3] Sertab's credentials for cosmopolitan connections and international collaboration up to that time included recording a duet with Ricky Martin on the single "Private Emotion" for the Turkish and Middle Eastern release of his 1999 English-language album (for the European edition of the album, Ricky sang the duet with Swedish singer Meja), and singing a duet ("All I Ask of You" from Andrew Lloyd Webber's *Phantom of the Opera*) with popular Spanish tenor José Carreras when he performed in Istanbul in December 1998. For the Eurovision project, Sertab also recorded a bilingual Turkish-English version of her contest song, but the plan clearly was to perform the song entirely in English at the contest, and the promotional video clip used the English-only version of the song.[4]

Sertab's insistence on singing in English set off heated debate in Turkey. A member of the Turkish parliament from the ruling Justice and Development Party publicly confronted the Minister of State whose portfolio included oversight of TRT, demanding to know, "Is it right for Turkey to be represented in this contest with

---

2   For various reasons Turkey did not participate in the contest in 1976, 1977, 1979, and 1994.

3   After finishing classical training as a coloratura soprano in the state conservatory in Istanbul, Sertab became a backup singer for Turkey's famous pop singer Sezen Aksu. She participated (unsuccessfully) in the Turkish Eurovision national finals in 1989 and 1990, and struck out on her own with her first album *Sakin Ol* in 1992. Several successful albums and a string of hit singles and video clips followed through the 1990s into the early 2000s.

4   Many previous Turkish performers had recorded English-language versions of their ESC songs. In the days of 45rpm singles, these English versions were often released as the B-side to the "official" version of the song in Turkish, as in Ajda Pekkan's 1980 B-side "Loving on Petrol" to the contest version of the song "Pet'r Oil" on the A-side. But before Sertab, no Turkish performer had ever performed a whole song in English at the contest itself.

an English-language song?"[5] The head of the Turkish Language Society (Türk Dil Kurumu), a quasi-official entity that tries to act as the nation's language academy, used just about the strongest language possible when he said, "That our country will be represented in the Eurovision song contest by a song with lyrics in English ... will lead to new alienation in our language and every area of our life."[6] Sertab defended her decision, asserting that "the world market requires this. ... To be in line with world standards you need to have English lyrics. Half the world listens to English, why shouldn't they listen to a Turkish artist in English?"[7]

In musical terms Sertab's song "Every Way That I Can," composed together with her partner Demir Demirkan, integrates a number of Turkish musical stylistic elements into the pop song format. While the song is not necessarily in any of the Turkish *makams* (modes in the Turkish classical music system, also commonly found in folk and popular music), the melody of the song does resemble a miniaturization of a typical *makam* performance, starting with a repeated phrase in the lower half of the octave and gradually expanding the range upward in successive phrases.[8] This type of development in which the tessitura starts low and then expands upward is also common in other Turkish popular music genres such as *arabesk*. The arrangement of the song also makes use of typically Turkish instrumental timbres and antiphonal relationships between the instruments and vocal solo. The string section of massed unison violins and cellos often play short figures interpolated between the sung phrases of the melody, a common feature of *arabesk*.[9] The rhythm track used for the song's contest version also includes *darbuka*, a ceramic goblet hand drum of the type found throughout the Middle East, associated in Turkey especially with *arabesk*, gypsy music, and belly dancing. All these features are brought even more to the aural foreground in the "radio mix" of the song that is the first track on the CD single of "Every Way That I Can." The *darbuka* is particularly prominent in this mix of the song in the bridge after the second chorus, where all the other instruments drop out except a rhythm track with hip-hop-style scratching and percussion, which support Sertab's vocal with a belly dance-like rhythm. For the last line of the bridge, all the percussion drops out as well, leaving Sertab's spoken vocal accompanied only by the scratching, highlighting the momentary resemblance to rap. The exotic Turkish elements in the song are thus used as elements within an over-all hybrid style, and seem to be intended not so much for consumption in Turkey, but for distribution, promotion, and consumption outside Turkey—in Europe, where these musical Turkisms would help Sertab and Turkey stand out from a crowded field of 26 entrants.

---

5   "Sertab Erener'in İngilizce şarkısı Meclis gündeminde," *Zaman* (18 April 2003) <www.zaman.com.tr/2003/04/18/televizyon/h1.htm> Accessed 26 October 2004.

6   "TDK: İngilizce şarkı, yeni yabancılaşmalara yol açacak," *Zaman* (26 May 2003) <www.zaman.com.tr/2003/05/26/kultur/h3.htm> Accessed 9 July 2003.

7   "İngilizce şarkı tartışma yarattı," *Hürriyet* (25 February 2003) <http://arama. hurriyetim.com.tr/devam.asp?id=130123> Accessed 25 February 2004.

8   Kurt Reinhard, "Turkey," *The New Grove Dictionary of Music and Musicians*, ed. Stanley Sadie (London: Macmillan, 1980), vol. 19, p. 277.

9   Martin Stokes, *The Arabesk Debate: Music and Musicians in Modern Turkey* (Oxford: Clarendon Press, 1992), p. 168.

Political and cultural factors

The period leading up to ESC 2003 brought to the fore a number of political and cultural factors that influenced attitudes towards Turkey in Europe and may also have contributed to Turkey's Eurovision success. Four factors that especially seemed to have played a role were: 1) the limiting of Turkey's support for the United States in the run-up to the second Gulf War, 2) improved relations between Turkey and Greek Cyprus, 3) the large number of diasporic Turks in West European countries, and 4) the re-drawing of the European political map, with the concomitant emergence of new attitudes toward national culture in Europe more generally.

Anti-war sentiment in Europe was one factor that prompted popular support for Turkey at this time. On 1 March 2003, during the run-up to the American-led invasion of Iraq on 20 March, the Turkish parliament voted unexpectedly, and against the wishes of the political leadership, not to allow the United States to use its Incirlik military base in southern Turkey as a staging area for a ground offensive in northern Iraq. The parliament took this measure despite Washington's offer of $6 billion in economic aid to Ankara as compensation for use of the base, and its not-too-subtle threats to sway the International Monetary Fund to impose financial restrictions on Turkey if the country did not comply with the request. Turkey's refusal to allow the United States to use its soil to launch a ground invasion into Iraq also meant that Turkey was later effectively excluded from participating in the subsequent military occupation of northern Iraq, where Turkey has strategic interests both in protecting the small, ethnically related Turkmen minority and in preventing the Kurds there from establishing their own state, which Turkey feared could encourage separatism among Turkey's own large and restive Kurdish minority.

In short, Turkey had a lot to lose by refusing to allow American ground troops a northern invasion route into Iraq through southeast Turkey. The 2003 ESC, just two months after the invasion of Iraq began, was to a certain extent held in the shadow of this war, and was for many fans and participants a celebration of continental European culture in contrast to American culture. European countries where the general population largely opposed the war, such as Germany, France, Norway, Austria, Belgium, and the Netherlands, interpreted the Turkish parliament's decision as Turkey's way of standing up on principle to American bullying tactics. In all of these countries (except the Netherlands), not only popular opinion but also official government policy opposed the war. And all of these countries gave Turkey 10 or 12 points, the two highest scores possible (see Table 12.1 below).[10] Incidentally, the biggest European supporter of the United States in the Iraqi invasion, the United Kingdom, came in last place with zero points after a painfully out-of-tune performance.

---

10   An exception to this trend was Spain, where the majority of people opposed the war despite the government's official support for it; consistent with its lack of interest in the Turkish entry in previous years, Spain gave Turkey only 3 points.

Table 12.1   Scores for Turkey by country, ESC 2003[a]

Austria	12	United Kingdom	7
The Netherlands	12	Israel	7
Belgium	12	Greece	7
Bosnia & Herzegovina	12	Malta	4
Croatia	10	Iceland	3
Slovenia	10	Spain	3
Romania	10	Ukraine	2
Germany	10	Poland	2
France	10	Russia	0
Norway	10	Latvia	0
Cyprus	8	Estonia	0
Sweden	8	Ireland	0
Portugal	8	**Total**	**167**

[a] Each participating country voted for 10 other countries, giving them a range of 1 to 12 points.

Rapprochement in northern Cyprus was another political factor that may have influenced Eurovision voting in Turkey's favor. In April 2003, coincidentally just one month before the contest, Turkish Cypriot authorities eased decades-old travel restrictions between Turkish-occupied northern Cyprus and Greek southern Cyprus. A stream of visitors crossed the border from both directions, and the international media covered the event with many stories of old friends who had been separated for 30 years finally being able to visit each other and re-establish their cross-border friendships, talking nostalgically of the days when Greeks and Turks lived together peacefully in the same Cypriot communities. Feelings of rapprochement were running especially high around the time of the contest.[11] Many attributed this thawing of the Cyprus conflict as a way for Turkey's EU candidacy to move forward. Greek Cyprus was itself scheduled to become a member in May 2005, with or without northern Cyprus, though there was still hope at this time for a last-minute settlement so that a united Cyprus could enter the EU.

In this atmosphere of rapprochement, Cyprus gave some of its points to Turkey for the first time ever in ESC history.[12] Cyprus did, as usual, give its highest number of points (12) to Greece, but Greece finished the contest in 17th place out of a field of 26. As he announced his country's votes via satellite linkup, the Greek Cypriot announcer created a bit of a stir by making a peace sign with his fingers as he said, "Europe, peace to Cyprus, Turkey eight points." Turkey's final point total in the

11 "Eurovision bugs Cyprus," *Kathimerini* (28 May 2003) <www.ekathimerini.com/ 4dcgi/_w_articles_politics_29281_28/05/2003_30113> Accessed 9 July 2003.

12 This trend continued the following year, when Cyprus gave Turkey 4 points. Turkey (sort of) returned the favor for the first time in 2004 when it gave Cyprus 1 point. The part of Cyprus that votes in the contest includes, of course, only Greek southern Cyprus, since the breakaway Turkish Republic of Northern Cyprus is not recognized by any country other than Turkey and does not participate in the contest.

contest was 167; the second-place winner Belgium got 165 points. Had Cyprus not given Turkey the eight points that it did, Turkey would not have won, so this unexpected support from Cyprus contributed significantly to the equally unexpected victory for Turkey.[13]

Aside from these immediate political situations involving Turkey in early 2003, two longer-term factors also contributed to popular support for Turkey in Eurovision. The first of these is especially closely tied to the introduction of televoting in the ESC. Instead of the traditional jury system, telephone voting (whereby viewers directly call in to vote for the song of their choice) had become the standard means for choosing winning songs by 2003, thanks to technological improvements throughout Europe since its introduction in 1997. (In 2003 only Bosnia and Herzegovina, and Russia still used a jury system to determine their votes.) 2003 was also the first year the official contest rules specifically stated that voting by SMS (Short Message Service) was allowed; providing for voting by SMS became required in 2004.

One of the five countries using televoting for the first time in 1997 was Germany. That year saw a dramatic increase in the number of points Germany gave to Turkey, and started a trend that would last several years. After four consecutive years of awarding Turkey no points at all (1991–96, not counting 1994 when Turkey did not compete and 1996 when Germany did not compete), beginning in 1997 Germany gave Turkey the maximum of 12 points three years in a row (1997–99). After 1999, Germany's points to Turkey steadily decreased (10 points in 2000, 7 points in 2001, and 0 points in 2002), then increased again to 10 in 2003, the year Sertab won for Turkey, and returned to the maximum of 12 in 2004. It has been widely remarked that the sudden swell of support for Turkey from Germany starting in 1997 was the result of the large Turkish population in that country using televoting to vote for their homeland.[14] This impression is supported by the fact that apart from 1997, when Turkey finished third overall in the contest (its best-ever finish up to that point, and only the second time ever it had not finished in the bottom half), the high points Germany awarded Turkey were not paralleled by support from most other countries (Turkey finished 14th out of 25 in 1998, and 16th out of 23 in 1999). The implication was that Germany awarded too much support in 1998 and 1999 to Turkish songs everybody else recognized as inferior, and this support must have come from the votes of the Turkish population living in Germany.[15]

---

13 After the contest, reaction in Cyprus to the voting and to Turkey's victory was mixed. Some Greek Cypriots accused the state-run Cyprus Broadcasting Corporation of rigging the televote. The newspapers *Fileleftheros* and *Simerini* both conducted polls of the Greek Cypriot population asking their opinions about this, and many people wrote that they opposed Cyprus' giving Turkey any points. One reader responded, "Personally, I don't want to forget that half of our country has been occupied for 30 years." The Turkish newspaper *Hürriyet* reported on these polls and quoted (in Turkish translation) many of the respondents under the headline "[Cypriot] Greeks regret 8 points." "Rumlar 8 puana pişman," *Hürriyet* (27 May 2003) <http://arama.hurriyetim.com.tr/devam.asp?id=149478> Accessed 25 February 2004.

14 Paul Gambaccini, Jonathan Rice, and Tony Brown, *The Complete Eurovision Song Contest Companion 1999* (London: Pavilion, 1999), p. 149.

15 If Germany's generally high points to Turkey since 1997 are indeed a result of a large German-Turkish voting bloc, Germany's zero points to Turkey in 2002 bucks that trend and

Statistics on the population of Turks living in western Europe vary widely. Table 12.2 below shows figures from three different published sources for the "top five" European countries with Turkish populations between 2000 and 2002. The figures in the "EU" column are taken from the European Union's *Annual Report on Asylum and Migration* (2001), and include only Turkish nationals (that is, the figures do not include Turks who have become naturalized citizens in their country of residence).[16] The figures in the column "OECD" are taken from the Organization for Economic Co-operation and Development's *Database on Immigrants and Expatriates* (2004).[17] Both the EU and the OECD figures arc compiled mostly from official population censuses or population registers, and presumably do not include Turks living in these countries illegally. The figures in the column "Consulates" were compiled from Turkish governmental sources based on figures from Turkish consulates in European countries; these numbers appear to be high, but may also reflect estimates of undocumented Turkish citizens living in these countries.[18]

Table 12.2   Estimated population of diasporic Turks in five European countries

	EU	*OECD*	*Consulates*
Germany	1,947,938	1,189,250	2,551,000
France	173,051	179,382	350,000
The Netherlands	100,309	181,865	330,000
Austria	98,801	125,026	200,000
Belgium	45,866	70,793	140,000

In relation to voting patterns, all of these "top five" countries with the highest populations of Turkish residents gave Turkey either 12 or 10 points, the highest possible scores, in the 2003 contest. ESC rules on televoting state that one cannot vote for the country one is calling from, but there is nothing to prevent viewers residing outside their country of origin, such as Turks living in Germany, from voting

has to be accounted for by other factors.

16   The European Commission, *Annual Report on Asylum and Migration (2001)* <http://europa.eu.int/comm/justice_home/doc_centre/asylum/statistical/doc_annual_report_2001_en.htm> Accessed 28 February 2005.

17   These figures are the sum of the separate numbers provided by the OECD for both foreign and naturalized Turks in each country, except for Germany, where no breakdown of citizenship status is given and one figure for Turks of "unknown" citizenship is given. This figure appears to be particularly low, as it is generally accepted there are about 2 million Turks in Germany; it may thus reflect only those who have not become German citizens. Organization for Economic Co-operation and Development (OECD), *Database on Immigrants and Expatriates* (2004), <www.oecd.org/document/51/0,2340,en_2825_494553_34063091_1_1_1_1,00.html> Accessed 3 March 2005. Thanks for Hakan Sıcakkan for alerting me to these OECD statistics and sharing with me his compilation of the Turkish data from them.

18   Ural Manço, "Turcs d'Europe: Une présence diasporique unique par son poids démographique et sa complexité sociale," in *Turquie: Vers de nouveaux horizons migratoires?* ed. Altay Manço (Paris: L'Harmattan, 2004), pp. 153–77. Thanks to Ural Manço for sharing these figures with me and alerting me to their publication.

for their home country. Since anonymous televoting does not discriminate on the basis of the nationality or ethnicity of the caller, Turks residing outside Turkey could easily vote to support their home country. During the 2003 contest, TRT (Turkish Radio and Television) commentators even encouraged Turks living abroad and who were watching the TRT broadcast of the contest via satellite to call in and vote for Turkey.[19] The 2003 contest rules also stated that "No household shall be permitted to vote more than three times," and anecdotal accounts from my Turkish friends with families in Germany and the Netherlands suggest that many Turks in those countries take full advantage of the maximum number of votes that can be sent from each landline and cellphone number. The large Turkish diaspora in western Europe thus may have played a role in Turkey's success in 2003. This trend continued in 2004 when Germany, France, the Netherlands, and Belgium all gave Turkey the maximum 12 points.

Perhaps the most complex factor that may have affected the result of the 2003 contest was the re-drawing of the political map of Europe and the continued growth of the European Union, prompting newly emergent attitudes toward ethnic and national cultural expression. Where there had formerly been, for example, one Yugoslav state in the ESC before 1993, there are now five separate nations, each with their own set of points to influence the outcome of the contest. Table 12.1 above also shows the other countries giving the highest points to Turkey in 2003, including Bosnia and Herzegovina (12 points), Croatia (10 points), and Slovenia (10 points). (Macedonia and Serbia & Montenegro did not participate in the contest in 2003.) This trend in voting may be due in part to shared musical and cultural affinities between the Balkans and Turkey, but I think there is also something more complex in play here having to do with the cultural dimensions of ethno-nationalism in Europe.

As Europe pursues its political integration, many countries have begun to place greater value and emphasis on national culture and their uniquely "ethnic" cultural identity as a sort of compensation for the perceived loss of individual state sovereignty. This interest in local "national culture" includes holding an approving attitude toward other European countries' display of their own "national culture." The song that articulated Turkey's historical moment in 2003 prominently featured Turkish musical stylings, as discussed above, and voters loved it. Voters that year similarly favored the second-place winner, the Belgian neo-Celtic folk group Urban Trad, whose performance of the folksong-like "Sanomi" evoked an imagined Belgian Celtic past.

This trend toward rewarding self-consciously "ethnic" styles has continued in subsequent years as well. In 2004 Ukraine's Ruslana won first place with a performance of the song "Dyki tantsi" (Wild dances) that included fanciful costumes and choreography supposed to evoke the ethnic culture of the Carpathian Mountain region of western Ukraine. The performance began dramatically with four people

---

19 My thanks to Engül Atamert for providing this information. This kind of encouragement may seem like a violation of ESC rules, but in 2003 the rules made no explicit prohibition of local on-air voice-over commentators showing partisanship for particular songs. For the 2004 contest, however, a new rule was introduced stating, "Commentators should also refrain from urging the audience to vote for any given song."

raising high and blowing on *trembitas*, three-meter-long horns similar to the alphorn, known as a traditional instrument used by shepherds among the Hutsul Ukrainians in the Carpathians to call their flocks back from pasture. The second place-winner in 2004, Željko Joksimović from Serbia & Montenegro, performed his song "Lane moje" (My sweetheart) entirely in Serbian, but the onstage ensemble prominently included *kaval* (a wooden rim-blown, ductless vertical flute common throughout the Balkans), Turkish *saz* (a long-necked lute closely associated with Anatolian folk music), violin, and West African *djembe* drums. In 2005 Greece's performer Elena Paparizou took first place (fully 38 points ahead of the second-place act) with "My Number One," including a dance interlude in which the sound of the *lyra*, a pear-shaped upright fiddle common in the folk music of Crete, was prominent. It seemed that Greece found the right combination of a solid pop song, English lyrics, and "ethnic" stylings in its music and performance, comparable in many ways to Sertab's 2003 performance.

All of these successes with hybridized songs and performances combining "ethnic" national culture with the pop song formula suggest that ESC voters have begun to favor this kind of hybrid, ethnicized cultural expression, in stark contrast to most of the winning songs in the ESC's earlier history.

The four factors discussed above seem to have fortuitously come together in 2003, resulting in Turkey's surprise victory. Any of these factors by itself would probably not have been enough to boost Turkey into the top position in the final tally of votes. It was thus the unique historical moment of May 2003 that provided Turkey's opportunity, articulated by Sertab's song and stage performance.

Eurovision as Turkey's door to Europe

In Turkey, Sertab's victory was popularly regarded not just as a public relations victory for Turkish cultural production, but also as a vindication of Turkey's political ambitions in Europe. The banner headline in the newspaper *Hürriyet* the day after the contest read "Europe will listen to us more," ostensibly referring to the increased European market space for Turkish pop music that the contest victory would presumably bring.[20] There was an obvious implied subtext, however: *See, we've proven we're Europeans with this— now the EU has to accept our claim to membership.* Front-page headlines in the dailies *Milliyet* (center-right) and *Yeni Şafak* (Islamist) both said of Sertab, "She Conquered Europe."[21] Several Turkish politicians were also caught up in the euphoria that followed Turkey's win, making what cooler heads would quickly recognize were over-enthusiastic claims about the political significance of Turkey's Eurovision victory. Minister of State Kürşat Tüzmen was quoted as saying "This success is a milestone in creating an atmosphere for entry in the EU like we deserve,"[22] while prime minister Recep Tayyip Erdoğan

---

20 "Avrupa bizi daha çok dinleyecek," *Hürriyet* (26 May 2003): 1.

21 "Sertab Erener Avrupa'yı fethetti," *Yeni Şafak* (26 May 2003): 1.

22 "Sertab 'utandırdı,'" *Akşam* (26 May 2003) <www.aksam.com.tr/arsiv/aksam/2003/05/26/magazin/magazin2.html> Accessed 8 March 2005.

was even more optimistic, reportedly claiming, "This result will speed up Turkey's EU process."[23]

There was also a near-obsession with what the press in other European countries said about Turkey's performance and victory in the contest. *Hürriyet* included a summary of favorable coverage in other countries of Sertab's win under the headline "What the Foreign Press Said," including translated quotes from reports in England, Greece, Spain, Germany, and the Netherlands (all of course EU countries).[24] The paper *Radikal* had a similar summary of foreign press coverage as well as a separate story on an article in the London *Times*, quoting *The Times* as saying "The sick man is back on his feet."[25] By stressing how a European newspaper had described this formerly "sick man of Europe" as now being strong and on his feet, this report suggested that Europe finally appreciated the contributions Turkey could make, at least in the cultural field. After winning the contest, Sertab said that her insistence on singing in English had paid off, and she argued that Turkey should from now on compete in English in the contest.[26]

Conclusion

Winning the ESC is probably not going to make any difference in the political wrangling that will eventually determine the fate of Turkey's EU candidacy. But don't try telling that to the average Turk on the street. From a Turkish point of view, popular cultural production and performance have an important role to play in what Turkish sociologist Ayşe Öncü refers to as the "debate on Turkey's eligibility and credentials for Europeanness."[27] And while Turkey's internal debates about its place in Europe will continue, the place it takes on the European stage may continue to be determined as much by events elsewhere in a Europe paradoxically brought together by diaspora and ethno-nationalist sentiment.

In his recent discussion of the many complex ways musical expression is put to nationalist purposes in Europe, Philip Bohlman discusses what he calls the "new Europeanness," defined as "an aesthetics of connection and connectedness" that runs "across historical and geographical borders." This "musical aesthetics of a new

---

23 "Meclis'te Sertab Erener rüzgârı esti," *Zaman* (28 May 2003) <www.zaman.com.tr/2003/05/28/haberler/h6.htm> Accessed 26 October 2004.

24 "Dış basın ne dedi," *Hürriyet* (26 May 2003): 4.

25 "Sertab dünyaya açılıyor," *Radikal* (27 May 2003) <www.radikal.com.tr/haber.php?haberno=76340> Accessed 20 June 2003. "The Times: Hasta adam ayağa kalktı," *Radikal* (30 May 2003) <www.radikal.com.tr/haber.php?haberno=76758> Accessed 20 June 2003. The sentence from the original *Times* article translated and paraphrased here is "the once 'sick man of Europe' seems to be doing rather well these days." "The sick man of Europe," *The Times* Magazine section (30 May 2003): 18.

26 "Bu birincilik başlangıç devamı gelecek" *Zaman* (26 May 2003) <www.zaman.com.tr/2003/05/26/kultur/h2.htm> Accessed 9 July 2003.

27 Ayşe Öncü, "Small Worlds and Grand Projects," in *Turkey and the West: Changing Political and Cultural Identities*, ed. Metin Heper, Ayşe Öncü and Heinz Kramer (London: I.B. Tauris, 1993), p. 263.

nationalism" draws on and accounts for "processes of hybridity that have previously not characterized European music." In the new Europeanness, "tradition is up for grabs" and hybridity is celebrated and aestheticized rather than viewed as the enemy of a pure, essential identity.[28] As a player with a recently increased visibility on the European stage, Turkey also partakes of the representational strategies of the new Europeanness. Artists and cultural producers such as Sertab are acutely aware of this new aesthetics, and play with all the resources available to them in their self-representations, combining and re-combining diverse stylistic elements. Sometimes this articulation works, sometimes it doesn't. It worked spectacularly for Turkey in 2003, with the Eurovision stage in Riga in May of that year being just the right place and time. Sertab's song, couched in the musical language of hybridity, with English lyrics surrounded by Middle Eastern drumming and hip-hop scratching, thus projected a Euro-friendly version of Turkey just at the time much of Europe was predisposed to be friendly with Turkey.

---

28 Bohlman, *The Music of European Nationalism*, pp. 278–9, 280, 281, 285.

Chapter 13

"Everyway that I can": Auto-Orientalism at Eurovision 2003

Matthew Gumpert

"Europe has been an object of desire as well as a source of frustration for Turkish national identity." So begins Meltem Ahıska's essay "Occidentalism: The Historical Fantasy of the Modern."[1] And it is precisely as an object of desire, frustration and fantasy that Europe figures in Sertab Erener's pop hit "Everyway That I Can," which won the 2003 Eurovision Song Contest in Riga, Latvia, with a classic Orientalist performance complete with belly-dancing and Middle Eastern musical themes.

It is hard to overstate the impact Sertab's victory made in Turkey. She was greeted by public and press as a national hero, and congratulated by the prime minister.[2] Sertab's victory was celebrated explicitly as a political triumph, and more specifically a step forward in Turkey's campaign to become a member of the European Union. Ali Bulaç, writing in the paper *Zaman*, characterizes the general reaction to Sertab's victory in the following terms: "Turkey has once again clearly demonstrated that it belongs to the modern Western world. ... This brings us one step closer to membership in the EU."[3] The Turkish paper *Milliyet* put it both more succinctly and more triumphantly: "She Conquered Europe."[4] In these two responses we can hear two contrasting rhetorical registers that have long structured the debate on Westernization in Turkey. Long ago the Ottoman Turks came to the conclusion, vis-à-vis the West, that *if you can't beat them, join them*. But is it possible to do both?

The Eurovision contest is regarded in Turkey as an important platform upon which the nation can represent itself to the West.[5] As victor in 2003, Turkey earned the right to host the ESC in 2004. At a press conference in Istanbul, the Minister for Broadcasting "underlined how important [this] Eurovision is for the Turkish government, which regards the Contest as a unique opportunity to promote Turkey in Europe. This event is ... more important than any other political summit ... in

---

1 Meltem Ahıska, "Occidentalism: The Historical Fantasy of the Modern," *South Atlantic Quarterly* 102/2–3 (spring–summer 2003): 351–79.

2 Similar reactions followed Azra Akın's victory in the 2002 Miss World Beauty Contest in London, or when news reached Turkey that the film *Uzak* [*Distant*] had won the Grand Prize at the 2003 Cannes Film Festival.

3 Ali Bulaç, "Sertab Erener özgürlüğe kanat açtı," *Zaman* (28 May 2003).

4 Nevsal Elevli, *Milliyet* (6 May 2003).

5 The day after the Eurovision finals the paper *Aksam* proclaimed: "Europe gave a standing ovation/Europe on its feet": Turkey watching Europe watching Turkey. "Avrupa ayakta alkışladı," *Akşam* (25 May 2003).

Turkey"—including the June NATO summit.[6] Of course the ESC has *always* been a transparently political event, not only in the sense that singers are encouraged (according to the ESC rulebook) to reflect the national identity of the culture they represent, or in the way host nations use the opportunity (as they do at the Olympic Games) to export their own cultural capital, but in the voting process itself.

But there was something special about the way Sertab's victory was received—and designed to be received—in Turkey. If performances such as Sertab's are instantly recognized in Turkey as part of a program of Westernization, it may also be the case that Westernization in Turkey has always been, in essence, a kind of performance.

Occidentalism

Since the beginnings of reform in the Ottoman Empire towards the end of the nineteenth century, the West, sociologist Meltem Ahıska argues, has been held up either as a model to be emulated or an influence to be repelled—a threat, that is, to "'indigenous' national values."[7] In both cases, imagining a specifically Turkish form of modernity is impossible without some *a priori* notion of the West itself. "Occidentalism" is Ahıska's term for the way the debate over Turkish modernization continues to depend on a conception of the West—whether seen as something to follow or something to fear—understood as prior and primary.

In the first case, modernization is essentially synonymous with Westernization.[8] Here the project of reform is lent a certain urgency by way of two privileged tropes, both of which identify the East as spatially and temporally supplementary with regard to the West. The first trope is that of *deferral*. In this scenario, Turkey is conceptualized as always coming after the West. Turkey, it is said, is a "backwards" nation, is always "catching up" to the West. Thus modernity becomes something eternally delayed, an ever receding goal. This motif of Turkish modernity perpetually

---

6   "Eurovision 2004 Ready to Go!: Press Conference News from Istanbul," <www.eurovision.tv/english/index.htm> Accessed 9 October 2004.

7   Ahıska, "Occidentalism," p. 353.

8   This equation is often seen as marking the birth of modern Turkey. The scope of this question obviously exceeds this essay, and the bibliography on the subject is vast. Perhaps Bernard Lewis' *The Emergence of Modern Turkey* (London: Oxford University Press, 1961) remains the classic formulation. It persists as the axiomatic principle of political, economic, and cultural life in contemporary Turkey. Modernization as Westernization is the *idée fixe* of Turkey's favorite foods, fashions, and television shows. Consider *Avrupa Yakası*, or *The European Side*, perhaps the most popular television sit-com in Turkey today. Implicit in every episode is the tension between "Western" manners and "Eastern" ways. The title refers to the way Istanbul has traditionally been described as divided into European and Asian sides. Even today an Istanbullu working in Beyoğlu but living in Uskudar will say he came "from the other or opposite side." On Westernization and modernization more recently in Turkey, see David Kushner, "Westernism in Contemporary Turkey," in *Atatürk and the Modernization of Turkey*, ed. J.M. Landau (Boulder, CO: Westview, 1984), pp. 234–40. On modernization as a Kemalist axiom, see Andrew Mango's authoritative biography *Atatürk* (London: John Murray, 1999).

trapped in a time lag continues to dominate public discourse, especially as Turkey strives to reach its Holy Grail, an object itself that appears to forever elude its grasp: full membership in the European Union.[9]

The second trope is that of *mimesis*. Here Turkey is conceived of as a copy of the West, a kind of ersatz Europe. Modernity in this scenario is essentially a form of imitation in the Platonic sense: an artificial construct, posing as the real, but doomed to be different from and inferior to it. When prime minister of Cyprus Tassos Papadopoulos was asked under what conditions Cyprus would support Turkey's bid for membership in the EU, he responded that Turkey must behave "like a European state."[10] Cultural identity, when it comes to Turkey, can only be a pale simulacrum of an unattainable original.[11]

The second case for modernization, that which advocates the rejection of Westernization, means, in effect, establishing some distinctive "Eastern" identity. It is an effort that would appear to be self-defeating, since it takes place within the very Orientalist framework—one positing a binary opposition between East and West—that it is attempting to dismantle or escape. That is to say, one can assert some coherent Eastern identity only through the continuing mediation of an absolute and uncritical distinction between East and West. Occidentalism, then, must always be a form of Orientalism. Following this second strategy, Nilüfer Göle, for example, has suggested "a divorce of Westernization and modernization."[12] Critics such as Göle are, in effect, arguing for the viability of multiple and locally inflected forms of modernity.

One may note here that the anti-Western position relies more explicitly on a spatial articulation of difference (East and West are different kinds of places, their difference is geographically and topographically definitive) while the pro-Western stance favors temporal imagery (East and West are in different cultural time zones; East can be like West, only later). Turkey's struggle to fashion a coherent cultural identity, then, one either like or unlike the West, would appear to be a classic case of what Jacques Derrida tried to capture in the notion of *différance*: identity, that is, as

---

9   See Gregory Jusdanis on the idea of "belated modernity" in Greece, in his *Belated Modernity and Aesthetic Culture: Inventing National Literature* (Minneapolis: University of Minnesota Press, 1991). On modernity as a temporal construct closely linked to the enlightenment notion of "progress," see Peter Osborne's *The Politics of Time: Modernity and Avant-Garde* (London: Verso, 1995).

10   William Pfaff, "Where Does Europe End and Asia Begin?" *The Herald Tribune* (1 December 2004).

11   On Turkish modernity as mimesis, see Kevin Robins's "Interrupting Identities: Turkey/Europe," in *Questions of Cultural Identity*, ed. Stuart Hall and Paul du Gay (London: Sage, 1996), p. 67. On the mimetic trope more generally in postcolonial discourse, see Homi Bhabha's "Of Mimicry and Man: The Ambivalence of Colonial Discourse," *October* 34 (1985): 26.

12   Nilüfer Göle, "Global Expectations, Local Expressions: Non-Western Modernities," in *Through a Glass Darkly*, ed. Wil Arts (Leiden: E.J. Brill, 2000), pp. 40–42. See also Nilüfer Göle, *The Forbidden Modern: Civilization and Veiling* (Ann Arbor: University of Michigan Press, 1996).

something always already undone by *difference*, whether understood as *distancing* or *deferral*.

Auto-Orientalism

In both cases, whether Westernization is something to be feared or something to be desired, what has *not* been acknowledged is the role that the West as imagined by the East continues to play in the formulation of a Turkish modernity (whether that modernity is meant to diverge from, or converge with, some equally imaginary Western modernity). Ahıska argues that "in theorizing the construction and representation of Turkish modernity, we can neither unproblematically herald the Western model nor dismiss the fantasy of 'the West.'" The theoretical model Ahıska proposes, that of Occidentalism, would help to "conceptualize how the West figures in the temporal/spatial imagining of modern Turkish identity."[13]

Fair enough; *my* point is that one cannot understand the construction of modern Turkish identity without also understanding how *the East* figures in the Turkish imagination: something that we may as well call *auto-Orientalism*. For the fantasy of (that is, *about*) the West is also the fantasy of seeing *the East through the eyes of the West*.

Any conception of Turkish modernity is thus fated to be both Occidentalist and Orientalist in nature. A generation after Edward Said's *Orientalism* (1995), most of us are familiar with the general outlines of that Orientalist vision. Mark Mazower, in *The Balkans*, offers a cogent summary of the way Western authors tended to view the Ottoman lands, beginning in the seventeenth century: "In the writers of travelers, pundits, and philosophers, powerful new polarities emerge—between civilized West and barbarous East, between freedom-loving Europe and despotic Orient. Sensual, slow-moving, dreamlike—the latter acted as a mirror to the self-regarding Western visitor."[14] We see here the familiar temporal and spatial polarities, and their attendant political and sexual associations, that have always subtended Turkey's efforts to formulate its own cultural specificity.

What does it mean for the East to see itself—and to want to see itself—in this way? What does it mean that at Eurovision 2003, upon a stage designed to project images of cultural identity for all the world to see, and at the very moment it is struggling to define itself as part of Western culture, Turkey represents itself as a harem girl straight from the pages of *A Thousand and One Nights* or the paintings of Delacroix?[15]

---

13   Ahıska, "Occidentalism," p. 353.

14   Mark Mazower, *The Balkans* (London: Phoenix Press, 2000), pp. 8–9.

15   Some in Turkey objected to Erener's willing acquiescence in the role of the harem girl. But, in the same article previously cited from *Zaman* (28 May 2003)—a newspaper that some would call "conservative," but which might more helpfully be termed "progressive-Islamist"—Ali Bulaç celebrates Sertab's appropriation of a role once dictated by the demands and desires of the Western male gaze. Bulaç, however, sees this as a politically progressive gesture, a way of liberating the modern Muslim women from the archaic confinement of the harem and, at the same time, from the Orientalist gaze: "Sertab Erener's first place victory

One of the first buildings Atatürk imagined as an adornment to the new capital of the new Turkish state was a Western-style opera house complete with a Western-style repertoire. (Today's opera house offers a charming example of early Republican modernism with Orientalist overtones—overtones that will be all but silenced in later Turkish architecture.) But without question the favorite opera, here and indeed at almost any opera house in Turkey, is the *Abduction from the Seraglio*. The question is: why? Is this an opportunity to laugh at Orientalism, or embrace it? Exactly what is at stake in this ritual of auto-Orientalism?

"Everyway that I can"

These are the questions raised by Sertab's performance at Eurovision 2003. It is a performance that seems to act out both sides of the debate on modernization in Turkey. By playing, this time willfully, and perhaps even ironically, the very role of the East once dictated by the West, "Everyway That I Can" appears to speaks both for the West and against it. If you can't beat them, join them: so goes the old adage. This song seems to be trying to do both.

In its music the song attempts to steer a middle course between the Scylla of Western pop music and the Charybdis of "traditional" Turkish music. (There is, however, nothing distinctively Orientalist *per se* about the lyrics themselves.) Thus, Western rhythms, chords, instruments, even elements of rap, compete with "Oriental" melodic and modal features borrowed from genres with a more Eastern flavor. The result is a commodified, easy-listening brand of Oriental music, something that, to a Western or a Westernized-Turkish ear, might sound distinctively Turkish yet recognizably of the West, only slightly and safely exotic. This is a musical version of an EU summit: state Orientalism, offensive to no one.[16]

---

at Eurovision broke the chains of the 'traditional Muslim woman' who appears in Orientalist paintings, giving her her own dignity, and wings to fly towards freedom ... Sertab Erener, too, by winning the prize, appears, following the desire of the Western male gaze, to have emerged from the Ottoman harem."

16 Some might call this *postmodern Orientalism*. Whatever you call it, one ought to make a distinction between this kind of manufactured, synthesized auto-Orientalism, and a ground-breaking album like Sezen Aksu's *Işık Doğudan Yükselir* (*The Sun Rises in the East*), which suggests a modernist effort to break away from one past and return to another. The story of Turkish pop and its various borrowings from East and West alike is a subject obviously too vast to treat here, but I think it should be pointed out that Erener's experiment in Orientalism is part of a much larger auto-Orientalist trend in contemporary Turkish music. It is a trend visible (or, rather, audible) in almost every musical genre: in folk music (Arif Sağ), folk protest music (Ruhi Su, Rahmi Saltuk, Zülfü Livaneli, Selda Bağcan, Ali Asker, Mahzuni Şerif, Sadık Gürbüz), contemporary leftist folk music (Grup Yorum, Kardeş Türküler), jazz (Okay Temiz and his group Oriental Wind, Yeni Türkü, Yansımalar, Ahmet Sinan Hatıpoğlu, Jamanladeen Tacuma, Burhan Ocal, Mercan Dede, Istanbul Blues Kumpanyası, Balık Ayhan, İlhan Erşahin, Laço Tayfa), jazz-folk synthesis (Metin and Kemal Kahraman, Koma Amed, Koma Denge Azadi, Babazula, Orient Expressions, Erkan Oğur), Sufi-jazz (Yansımalar, Ahmet Sinan Hatıpoğlu), jazz-rembetiko (Yeni Türkü, Muammer Ketencoğlu), Anatolian rock (Moğollar, Cem Karaca, Barış Manço, Üç Hürel, Edip Akbayram), contemporary rock

And no one would accuse "Everyway That I Can" of being particularly innovative in its own right. That is one of the things that makes it useful for analysis. Pop music itself, one could argue, is by definition both recognizably of some place and infinitely exportable, at home in any piano bar or elevator in the world. Pop music, we might say, like pop events such as the ESC, thus provides a perfect medium for conveying—or perhaps canceling out—competing and contradictory models of cultural identity.[17]

It may be the case that to take such a pop object and turn it into an object of analysis, as I am doing here, is inevitably to restore whatever complexity, structure, or semiotic value that object had originally been designed to suppress. And the pop object, in its very passivity, its coherence, its utter sincerity and apparent simplicity, lends itself all too easily to the complicated and conniving designs of the critic. Or was the object designed, precisely, to be compliant in this way?

The lyrics of Sertab's "Everyway That I Can" would seem to offer a perfect example of this kind of pop object, a surface utterly smooth and utterly simple, fashioned entirely out of clichés. Is there really any "cultural work" going on behind this glossy surface? Isn't this just another pop love-ballad, the familiar plaint of the frustrated lover moving through all the rhetorical registers, from self-pity to rage, from seductive invitations to ominous threats, calculated to win back the beloved? In both its immediate and less immediate context, however, it is difficult not to read it as a thinly veiled rehearsal of Turkey's pleas to be recognized as a European state.

All of us may be familiar, to one extent or another, with a certain form of paranoia, one that seems to go hand-in-hand with the work of hermeneutics itself: the point one is trying to prove becomes visible everywhere; the world itself becomes the confirmation of one's thesis. But Turkey has for so long now been defined by its desire to join the West, and by its suspicion that the West does not desire it in return, that paranoia almost seems to be a way of life. And thus perhaps one is rather more

---

revival (Kıraç, Zuğaşi Berepe), multinational or world music (Burhan Ocal, Laço Tayfa), hip-hop (Aziza A., Sultana), techno and technobesque (a synthesis of techno and arabesque) (Harem, Nez), electronica or electro-ethno music (Mercan Dede, Orient Expressions, Baba Zula), ethno-punk (Replikas), Turkish classical music or musiki (Timur Selçuk), neo-Ottoman revival music (Emre Aracı, Burhan Ocal), Western-style classical music (Ferit Tüzün), and opera (Okan Demiriş). Returning to pop, finally, it would be unfair to close this remark without mentioning the phenomenon of Tarkan. This list is not meant, of course, to be comprehensive. (My thanks to Buket Cengiz for bringing many of the names on this list to my attention.)

17   The description of the 2004 ESC "stage design" from the (Istanbul) "Eurovision Song Contest" website offers an architectural analogy: "*Under the Same Sky*: that's the title given to the stage design for the 2004 Eurovision Song Contest in Istanbul. 36 stars from various cultures and religions will compete ... united under that same 'sky'. ... The design is reminiscent of Turkey's world-famous architectural monuments ... Istanbul conjures up images of fairy tales from the Arabian Nights ... . The centre of the stage, like the nave of a cathedral or the main prayer room of a mosque, is the focus of attention..." "Under the Same Sky," <www.eurovision.tv/english/index.htm> Accessed 12 October 2004. We see here the organized production of blandness, the systematic elaboration, through a series of cultural checks and balances, of a style that is both specific and general, indigenous and international.

justified, here than in other places, in reading what might appear to be innocent gestures as signs and portents and tiny insurrections.[18] Both forms of paranoia may be at work in my reading of the lyrics to Sertab's song. But the force of that reading is made considerably stronger when we hear them sung by Erener as an odalisque in a harem. The way this piece of music was packaged and performed for the Eurovision contest certainly allowed it, in other words, to profit from paranoia; to capitalize upon certain historical and hysterical fantasies.

If Erener's song is a plea, then, it is one addressed *to* the West; and, let's not forget, in English—that is, the language *of* the West. There would seem to be a certain irony, and no little strategy, in the fact that Sertab's appropriation of the Orientalized Turk is accomplished in today's *lingua franca par excellence*, and that "Everyway That I Can" was sold on Sertab's first English-language album, along with translated versions of her previous Turkish hits (*Sertab Erener'ın İngilizce Albümü*). This would seem to be, in other words, a strategic performance, and not simply a passive process of copying or catching up.

That performance (both Sertab's in the theater at Riga, and Turkey's in the theater of Europe) may be summarized as a series of contradictory demands, simultaneously erotic and political in nature: to dominate or be dominated; to possess or be possessed; to love or be loved; to seduce or be seduced—demands that need to be made in the first place because lover and beloved (like Turkey and the West) are "separated." What "separates" them are a number of "facts" familiar to anyone with even a cursory knowledge of erotic poetry or political history: *distance*, *delay*, and *difference*.

Distance Space both separates the lover from the beloved, and mediates between them. The lover, in any case, cannot possess the beloved, but must dream of the beloved, instead, from afar: *I feel you moving on a distant course/Making the way for a distant coast*. Turkey, too, has been dreaming, for a long time, of a Europe that remains distant and elusive.

Delay The lover dreams, impatiently, of a future with the beloved; for the lover is, by definition, someone who must wait: *I thought it was over and we'd pass all that/All we've done is to pass back to frame number one/Come on, now, now ...* Turkey, too, has been waiting for a long time; it has begun to suspect it has been pursuing a beloved who will forever keep it waiting, always just a little bit longer. (Note, too, the lines of the bridge, which neatly voice Turkey's jealousy as it watches other candidates wooed by and wedded to Europe, while it is told it still must bide its time: *Tell me what you see in other girls all around/Come on closer and tell what you don't find there/Come on, now, now ...*)

---

18 Classical Western orchestras are a familiar feature at Turkish official events; recently, as part of a ceremony for the completion of a new building, an orchestra was joined by a tenor in a tuxedo, who regaled his audience with such crowd-pleasers as "It's Now Or Never," and "I Did It My Way." Predictable choices, I suppose, and yet to my ear both sounded like covert allegories of the struggle to be or not to be, simply European: passive-aggressive anthems of Westernization, Turkish style; or Orientalization, Western style—like Sertab's song.

Difference If the lover cannot be what the beloved wants, representations, reproductions, and re-enactments can be offered instead: *I wanna show you all again what it would be like*. Turkey must seduce the West by giving it a show, or by turning itself into a show (the likeness of itself); by performing for it, over and over again.[19]

This is, above all, a passive-aggressive performance: love here is not a mutual *rapprochement* but a form of domination: something to be done to someone else, even if one asks permission to do it: "*I wanna show you all again what it would be like/If you just let go and let me love you.*" This same contradictory speech act—the demand to *love* and *be loved*—structures the song from beginning to end. The desire to be possessed (*Hold me closer, oh so good/You make me feel just like I should*) competes with fantasies of control (*I know what you're thinking: uhuh good/Now the rest of the world is overruled*); self-abasement (*I'm in love with you/I'll do all you want me to*) alternates with megalomania (*Nothing in the world will stop me, no sir*). (Note that in the very last phrase alone, the will to power makes itself heard, grammatically speaking, in the mode of subservience, addressed as it is to some indeterminate "sir.") This is seduction, but seduction in the imperative.

The chorus most clearly suggests identity as something tactical, something to be performed by way of multiple roles and rhetorical ruses, *everyway that I can*: by any and all means possible—even at the risk of self-annihilation (*I'll cry, I'll die*). The subject now threatens to coerce the beloved, *I'll try to make you love me again*; now promises complete surrender, *I'll give you all my love and then* ... And then? *Make you mine again*. It may be that Westernization is really a form of domination in disguise, and that to join Europe is to conquer it. Conquer it *again*, that is. For this ode to a European future may also be an elegy to a Turkish past. In these perfect pop platitudes, if we listen carefully, we may also hear the faint echo of a plea for the resurrection of the Ottoman Empire—or at least the restoration of the power and prestige that came with it.

Oriental fantasy: watching the East watching the West watching the East

To create a new Turkish identity, Ahıska argues, something called "the West" has to be imagined. In her discussion of *Occidentalism*, Ahıska describes certain "mechanisms of *projection* that support this *fantasy*": "Projection ... operates both as a displacement of what is intolerable inside into the outside world ... as a refusal to know; and as an introjection of what is threatening in the external world so as to contain and manage it ... it describes at the same time what the subject refuses to be and desires to be."[20]

But watching Sertab's video, or her performance at Eurovision 2003, it is also clear that in order to create a new Turkish identity, something called "the East" has

---

19 Turkey here too occupies a position analogous to the "signifyin' monkey" in African-American discourse, emblem, for Henry Louis Gates, Jr in *The Signifying Monkey: A Theory of African-American Literary Criticism* (New York: Oxford University Press, 1989), of the African-American writer, simultaneously mimicking and mocking his white counterpart.

20 Ahıska, "Occidentalism," p. 366.

to be imagined. Imagined as imagined, of course, by the West. To a large extent what we have here, after all, is standard Orientalism in the Western style: a Delacroix or Ingres come to life. The only difference—and it may be a significant one—is that this time the Orientalizers are the Orientals, as it were.[21] As an *auto-Orientalist* fantasy, then, Sertab's performance is a way of projecting what the modern Turk both refuses to be, and desires to be.

And yet it is not enough to say this is an Orientalist or auto-Orientalist fantasy. It may be that, in its particular manipulation of time and space, what makes Sertab's performance "modern" is, in fact, its rejection of Orientalism and, along with it, the Orientalizer, that is, the West itself. Paradoxically, this is something achieved by embracing, by taking seriously, as it were, the very clichés that constitute Orientalism itself.[22] Because the setting here is specifically *Ottoman*, one might be tempted to read Sertab's performance as a celebration of local culture or history over and against some Western monolithic modernity, part of what Nilüfer Göle has called the "indigenization of modernity."[23] Sertab's video can, indeed, be counted part of a larger Ottoman revival that has been sweeping Turkey in recent years. One now encounters Ottoman fashion, Ottoman cuisine, and the resuscitation of Ottoman social spaces, as in the proliferation of *nargile* or water-pipe cafés for the young and the hip. Previously such manifestations of nostalgia for the pre-Republican past were taboo, smacking suspiciously of anti-modernism, anti-secularism, and anti-Kemalism.

This reading may not be entirely wrong, but even this affirmation of a local history is undoubtedly just another performance designed for the West, or for an audience (even a Turkish one) that would identify itself as Western. Like the other examples of this neo-Ottoman trend, Sertab's harem may not be so much an affirmation of some specific Turkish otherness as its exorcism, through its identification with a distant and exotic past;[24] in other words, as "the displacement of what is intolerable

---

21   Contemporary artist Gülsün Karamustafa's critique of Orientalism offers a parallel in the visual arts. In a retrospective of her work Sanne Kofod Olsen writes: "During the last few years Gülsün Karamustafa, who lives in Istanbul, has been investigating the subject of Orientalism from an 'Oriental's' point of view." See Karamustafa's "Double Action Series of Oriental Fantasies," and "fragmenting/FRAGMENTS." "Oriental Fantasies: New Works by Gülsün Karamustafa," in *Trellis of My Mind*, ed. Gülsün Karamustafa (Istanbul: n.p., 2001), p. 86.

22   Consider other groups who have fashioned a sense of cultural identity through the affirmation of the very stereotypes that marginalized them in the first place; thus the recuperation of the term "queer" by the gay community in the 1970s.

23   Göle, "Global Expectations, Local Expressions," pp. 40–42.

24   Bernard Lewis points to early efforts to resist Western influence by the revival of "indigenous" Turkish elements. This generally means by-passing Ottoman culture—equated with Oriental culture—to arrive at some authentically Turkish past. But artists do find ways to recuperate the Ottoman past: by turning it, essentially, into touristic fantasy. Lewis speaks of writers who begin to practice a "consciously evocative neo-classicism [i.e., the Ottoman style], playing on the legends and glories of a past that has become remote and exotic to the Turks themselves." Bernard Lewis, *The Emergence of Modern Turkey*, p. 440.

into the outside world." What we have here, then, is an artificial construct, an ersatz harem or McHarem, cleansed of all historical specifics, everywhere and nowhere.[25]

What kind of space is this faux-harem? Let us take a closer look. Light in this ahistorical space is diffuse; matter insubstantial: smoke, spice, rose-petals, even bodies, all act as an ether that blurs and renders indistinct. Even time here is the "mythical time" that holds sway in Orientalist conceptions of the East. Ziya Gökalp, father of Turkish sociology and linguistics, once characterized Westernization as an acceleration away from the past, proclaiming "We shall skip five hundred years and not stand still."[26] The trope of acceleration, and the motif of the time-lag is familiar by now, but Gökalp's precision here is crucial and calculated. Gökalp enjoins us, in other words, to make Turkey modern by erasing, specifically, its Ottoman past. Hasan Bülent Kahraman reminds us that from the beginning of the modern Turkish state a "memory lapse ... problematized the issue of culture and made it the playground of political struggles."[27] The harem in "Everyway That I Can" is both absolutely static, and a state-of-the-art technological artifact, an MTV harem.

Like all Orientalist spaces, the harem is super-saturated with desire. Ahıska argues that reigning conceptions of modernity all depend on the gendering of space, time, and territory. The West has tended to represent itself as temporality itself, always moving forward: a specifically masculine force. The East, on the other hand, has for long been imagined as a static, spatial, and feminine entity. In fact, this gendered scheme is considerably more flexible than that. The East, from the Western perspective, is sometimes cast in the passive, feminine role, and at other times is made to play the part of the aggressive, predatory male. Mazower, reviewing the history of descriptions of the Balkans as a critical meeting ground between East and West, finds evidence of both gendered models. On the one hand, the "disconcerting inter-penetration of Europe and Asia, West and East, finds its way into most descriptions of the Balkans ... Europe is seen as a civilizing force, a missile embedding itself in the passive matter of the Orient." On the other hand, "Sir John Marriot begins his sober history of the Eastern Question with the stark assertion that 'the primary and most essential factor in the problem is the presence, embedded in the living flesh of Europe, of an alien substance. That substance is the Ottoman Turk.'"[28]

A static, spatial, and purely feminine space: such is the harem as the West liked to imagine it. So privileged is that space, so frequented in the Western imagination,

---

25 Some time beginning in the 1980s, Hasan Bülent Kahraman asserts, Turkey "decided that its admission to Europe was going to be a function of its own authenticity. From that moment on, 'a culture of rupture' was ... replaced by 'a culture of articulation.' With the help of globalization, Turkey represented the importance of the local. This recognition then led it to rediscover its past, recapture its memory and to make peace with itself. Such an evolution could be considered as an extension of the process of globalization. Globalization is, as Malcolm Waters puts it, the 'universalization of the local, and the localization of the universal.'" This is an apt description of what happens in Sertab's harem. "A Journey of Rupture and Conflict: The Culture in Purgatory," p. 9 <www.tusiad.org.tr> Accessed 3 March 2004.

26 Ahıska, "Occidentalism," 367.

27 Kahraman, "A Journey of Rupture and Conflict," p. 1.

28 Mazower, *The Balkans*, pp. 9–10, 13.

that it stands as the very symbol or synecdoche of the East itself. It is a space, we have seen, super-saturated with desire; but, from the perspective of the East, a space, also, in which desire—*for* the other, to *be* the other—is safely contained or internalized. Sertab's harem thus allows, in Ahıska's terms, the "introjection of what is threatening in the external world so as to contain and manage it." For the harem is the most purely internal of spaces—the very notion of containment itself— and here, in Sertab's video, there is no outside: only interior space within which desire is enacted or performed. Even movement here is static: hypnotic, repetitious, undulatory. Desire itself becomes a form of paralysis: an eternal paroxysm of passion without cause or consequence.

Desire for whom? Enacted for what audience? On the most obvious level this video allows us to be voyeurs and eavesdroppers in the forbidden space of the harem. But within that space desire is represented as something both autonomous or masturbatory, and something performed *for* an audience. Sertab's harem girls are dancing both for themselves and for us. Hence the homoerotic structure of desire in this video, so typical of Orientalist literature and painting, which allows both conditions to be fulfilled simultaneously. In this way, desire for the other is safely converted into desire for the self. And thus, once again, Orientalism is reclaimed and reproduced as auto-Orientalism.

Chapter 14

Idol thoughts: Nationalism in the pan-Arab vocal competition *Superstar*

Katherine Meizel

In August 2003, a riot in the Middle East made international headlines. This conflict was not connected to the American occupation of Iraq, nor to mounting Israeli-Palestinian tensions, but instead arose at a Beirut television studio where a singing competition was taking place. The Future Television station was stormed by 150 fans just after 21-year-old Lebanese singer Melhem Zein was eliminated from *SuperStar* during the show's penultimate broadcast. Spectators inside threw chairs and shouted "With our blood and souls, we sacrifice for you, Melhem."[1] Zein, the Lebanese contestant, had received fewer audience votes than the other two finalists, Syrian singer Ruweida Attiyeh and the eventual winner, Diana Karazon of Jordan. The two women, still on the stage, were reportedly overcome by the incident, fainted, and had to be rushed to the hospital.[2] The riot over *SuperStar* came at the end of several months of competition, after 11,000 initial applicants had been reduced to 12 finalists, and at last to just Zein, Attiyeh, and Karazon. In addition to the nations represented by these three, other finalists came from Algeria, Egypt, the West Bank and Gaza,[3] and the United Arab Emirates.

SuperStar debuted in 2003 as an extension of the global reality television franchise known as *Idols*, introduced two years earlier in the United Kingdom with *Pop Idol*. The proliferation of *Idols* shows has grown to include over 30 versions worldwide, such as *American Idol, Deutschland sucht den Superstar* (in Germany), *South African Idol, Australian Idol* and *Malaysian Idol*. The format remains essentially the same in each incarnation, with young singers competing for a recording contract and potential stardom. Contestants are critiqued by a panel of expert judges, and a winner is selected through audience voting.

This ever-increasing array of *Idols* programs has created a multinational set of studio stages wherein the politics of national, regional, ethnic, and even religious identity are continuously being performed. In this sense the *Idols* series invites comparison to the Eurovision Song Contest (ESC). Many of the nations hosting

---

1 "Bi-ruh bi-dam nafdīki ya Melhem." This chant in Arabic is based on a widely used political slogan; its opening words "Bi-ruh bi-dam" rhyme handily with the singer's name, "Melhem" (Amy Cyr, personal communication, 12 November 2005).

2 "Mob Storms Lebanese TV Studio," *Aljazeera.net* (12 August 2003) <http://english. aljazeera.net/NR/exeres/701237A0-9FD7-4A3E-9DC7149F1050BCDD.htm> Accessed 6 March 2004.

3 These territories are frequently referred to together by the United Nations as the Occupied Palestinian Territory, though this language is controversial.

variants of the *Idols* series are recent converts to democratic government, having made the change in the years immediately following the fall of the Berlin Wall. Most also belong to the European Broadcasting Union and participate in Eurovision as well.[4] Some *Idols* programs have served as springboards for winners to represent their nations in the ESC: Alicja Janosz, the Polish delegate in *World Idol*, sang "I'm Still Alive" for Poland in the 2004 ESC, and the 2003 winner of France's *A la recherche de la nouvelle star*, Jonatan Cerrada, came 15th in the 2004 ESC.

SuperStar occupies a unique position within the *Idols* franchise, with three key distinctions setting it apart from other versions. First, while most shows in the series maintain a single-nation focus, *SuperStar* is a transnational competition comprising contestants and an audience from the 22 countries of the Arab League (the second season, in 2004, extended its audition range to include Arabic-speaking communities in France). Like Eurovision, *Superstar*'s multinational configuration has provoked expressions of intense nationalistic feeling among contestants and their compatriot supporters. A second distinguishing factor is that *SuperStar* has been situated within the *Idols* framework as a "Pan-Arab" competition.[5] Supporters and detractors alike have found political significance in the show's implications of Arab unity. A third unique element is that its "Pan-Arab" design distinguishes *SuperStar* within the otherwise largely Euro/American-centric *Idols* enterprise.

This chapter explores *SuperStar*'s participation in the dialectic between local and pan-Arab nationalisms as well as the implications of its situation in the global *Idols* franchise. Among viewers and participants, *SuperStar* inspires sentiments both of national pride and of transnational Arab unity. In the broader arena of *World Idol*, these nationalisms are set in opposition to external views approaching the "Arab world" as a single conflated cultural entity. Furthermore, this chapter considers the *Idols* franchise as illustrative of the ways in which the transnational media industry figures in the politics of democracy promotion.

Local and pan-Arab nationalism in *SuperStar*

Toward the end of the first season of *SuperStar*, full-scale campaigns in Jordan and Syria urged viewers to vote for their national representative. These multimedia campaigns often involved distinctly commercial interests—Jordan's competitive mobile phone services MobileCom and Fastlink ran daily press advertisements devoted to Diana Karazon, and sent text and voice messages to their customers promoting the singer, while Ruweida Attiyeh was backed in her home country by SyriaTel. A program that aired on state-run Jordanian television was entirely dedicated to the endorsement of Karazon, and a similar program appeared in Syria

---

4   Eleven *Idols* shows are located in countries not affiliated with the EBU; these are all outside of Europe, with the exception of the Czech Republic.

5   In the 2003 program *World Idol*, discussed below, the caption "Pan Arab Nations" appears on the screen above Karazon's name. Additionally, FremantleMedia's website lists a broadcast region called the "Pan-Arabic Region" (www.fremantlemedia.com).

supporting Attiyeh.[6] These campaigns met with great success: according to the Arab Advisors Group, 80 per cent of the total votes placed just before the penultimate episode came from the finalists' home countries. An overwhelming number of votes from these nations were in favor of their respective compatriots: 84 per cent of the Jordanian votes supported Karazon and 97 per cent of the Syrian votes supported Attiyeh.[7]

A sense of patriotic obligation motivated many fans; Jordanians told journalists "Voting for Diana is a national duty," and "she represents what is beautiful in our country. We must stand beside her."[8] Nationality seemed even more important to many voters than contestants' talent; one fan in Syria admitted to voting for Attiyeh "first because she is Syrian, and second because she has a nice voice."[9] Thousands of fans watched the last broadcast around enormous screens in Syrian and Jordanian cities, with the largest single gathering, in Amman, reportedly numbering over 20,000 viewers.[10] In the final selection, 4.8 million votes were cast in total through the Internet, mobile telephone calls, and text messaging. Of these votes, 52 per cent were for Karazon, a majority that won her the title of "SuperStar El Arab." Upon her victory she was congratulated over the phone by Jordan's King Abdullah and Queen Rania, as well by Lebanon's then-prime minister Rafiq Al Hariri— who, until his assassination in February 2005, was also the owner of Future Television.[11] Karazon, a Jordanian of Palestinian origin, dedicated her victory to "the people of Lebanon, Jordanians, on top of them his majesty King Abdullah, and the children of Palestine."[12]

The second season in 2004 saw comparable tactics exercised for its final two contestants, Libyan medical student Ayman al-Aathar and Palestinian musician Ammar Hassan. Al-Aathar and Hassan received verbal support from their respective political leaders: Moammar Gadhafi, who met with both finalists during their visit to Libya, and Yasser Arafat. The Palestinian Ministry of Culture in Gaza advertised a public viewing of the show's finale, citing "our deep belief that the creative art can participate in the life of the people and its struggle for freedom and independence."[13]

---

6   Bassem Mroue, "Contestants in Arab Version of 'Idol' Stir Nationalist Pride," *StarTelegram.com* (19 August 2003) <www.dfw.com/mld/dfw/news/world/6566533.htm> Accessed 7 February 2004.

7   "*Miami Vice* in Dubai, *Baywatch* in Egypt!" *AME Info* (16 November 2003) <www. ameinfo.com/news/Detailed/31215.html> Accessed 7 February 2004.

8   "Pan-Arab Song Contest Fuels Passions in Jordan," *Jordan Times* (17 August 2003) <www.aljazeerah.info/News%20archives/2003%20News%20archives/Auust/17n/PanArab% 20song%20contest%20fuels%20passions%20in%20Jordan.htm> Accessed 7 February 2004.

9   Mroue, "Contestants in Arab Version of 'Idol.'"

10   "Arab SuperStar Diana Karazone Celebrates the Release of Her First Album," *Radio New Power* (1 October 2003) <http://radionewpower.com/Entertainment/Archived/October_ 2003/SUPERSTR2.asp> Accessed 7 February 2004.

11   "Jordanian Wins Arab 'Idol,'" *BBC News World Edition* (19 August 2003) <http:// news.bbc.co.uk/2/hi/entertainment/3162169.stm> Accessed 7 February 2004.

12   Mroue, "Contestants in Arab Version of 'Idol.'"

13   Steven Erlanger, "Palestinian Carries Tune and His People's Dreams," *The New York Times* (22 August 2004).

The Palestinian mobile phone company Jawwal discounted text messaging by up to 20 per cent from May through August, urging its customers to vote for Hassan.[14] However, the intense promotion of Hassan caused some controversy in August, as the show's climax coincided with the peak of a hunger strike carried out by thousands of Palestinian prisoners to protest conditions in Israeli detention centers and prisons. Hamas members criticized the Ministry of Culture and Jawwal for allocating funds in support of *SuperStar* and Hassan instead of supporting the prisoners and other more overtly political causes.[15] But some of Hassan's fans recognized his political potential, explaining, "He is our hero, and we want him to win in order to prove to the whole world that the Palestinians are not violent and are not terrorists."[16] Hassan, a West Bank native who had been living in the United Arab Emirates for several years, expressed similar sentiments to a *New York Times* reporter: "I want to reflect a human image of the Palestinian people."[17]

In spite of the nationalist rivalries permeating *SuperStar*, some critics have sensed a spirit of unity related to the "Pan-Arab" scope of the show. A Lebanese journalist declared that *SuperStar* had been "the most successful initiative … at granting the entire Arab world the opportunity to reach out and unite as one single family."[18] In the second season, pan-Arab support for the Palestinian cause came into play as the winning Libyan singer and the Palestinian runner-up stood onstage together, in a gesture of solidarity, with a Palestinian flag draped over their shoulders. The "Pan-Arab" concept of *SuperStar* came from Future Television itself, proposed in contract negotiations with FremantleMedia.[19] Isabelle Garcia, the Middle East manager of FremantleMedia (co-owner and distributor of the *Idols* format), emphasizes the idea that "the music is Arab, the contestants are Arab, the judges are Arab, the hosts are Arab."[20] The chair of Future Television's board of directors, Nadim Munla, told Beirut's *Daily Star* that *SuperStar* "represented the Arab who was looking to the past and hoping for a better future."[21]

Munla's statement epitomizes an important ideological resource of nationalism, the use of what Benedict Anderson has called "spectacles of the past and future" to

---

14 "SMS Sent by Jawwal," *Jawwal, The Network of Palestine* (22 August 2004) <www.myjawwal.com/press/sms_sent.asp> Accessed 22 August 2004.

15 Khaled Abu Toameh, "PA Pins Hopes on its Own 'SuperStar' Contestant," *Jerusalem Post* Online Edition (18 August 2004) <www.jpost.com/servlet/Satellite?pagename=JPost/JPArticle/ShowFull&cd=1092712292218> Accessed 22 August 2004.

16 Saud Abu Ramadan, "Gazans Support Singer Competing in Beirut" *The Washington Times* (17 August 2004) <http://washingtontimes.com/upi-breaking/20040817120915-3790r.htm> Accessed 22 August 2004.

17 Erlanger, "Palestinian Carries Tune."

18 Mohamed Ajami, "Quest for Arab SuperStar Finally Over as Jordanian Wins," Special to the *Daily Star*, *Lebanonwire* (20 August 2003) <www.lebanonwire.com/0308/03082010DS.asp> Accessed 7 February 2004.

19 Ibid.

20 "*Miami Vice* in Dubai, *Baywatch* in Egypt!"

21 Ajami, "Quest for Arab SuperStar."

naturalize officially sanctioned constructions of the nation.[22] *SuperStar* broadcasts and subsequent recordings reflect this idea, as well. Guests scheduled on the show have included legendary names such as Sabah Fakhri, a Syrian singer of great international renown. Performances of older, well-known songs associated with pan-Arab superstars such as Fairouz and Umm Kulthum have been juxtaposed with contemporary pop. This variety, along with the production of new music for the winners' debut albums, allow the show to simultaneously "look to the past" and to the future.

SuperStar has also contributed to political discourse within and about the "Arab world." Premiering shortly before the United States initiated military action in Iraq, the show was suspended for a month in deference to news coverage. But this postponement was not enough for some; the Islamic Action Front, the Jordanian political branch of the Muslim Brotherhood Movement, issued a statement after *SuperStar*'s first season condemning the show as a distraction from the situation in Iraq.[23] Moammar Gadhafi also expressed concern that the series might divert public attention from the more important Iraqi and Palestinian issues.[24]

Discourse surrounding *SuperStar* has posited political significance in the voting procedure as well. American writers in particular have even praised *SuperStar* as a step toward democratization in the Middle East, though the process is far from truly democratic—especially in that a single person may submit multiple votes. But American journalists are not alone in their conjecture. After the end of *SuperStar*'s first season, Beirut *Daily Star* editor Rami Khouri was quoted in the *New York Times*: "I do not recall in my happy adult life a national vote that resulted in a 52 to 48 percent victory. ... Most of the 'referenda' or 'elections' that take place in our region usually result in fantastic pre-fixed victories ... so a 52 to 48 percent outcome—even for just a song contest—is a breath of fresh air."[25]

SuperStar vs. the world

Winners of the first 11 versions in the *Idols* franchise met in London between Christmas 2003 and New Year's Day 2004 to contend for the title of "World Idol." Participants included representatives of Australia, Belgium, Canada, Germany, the Netherlands, Norway, the "Pan Arab Nations," Poland, South Africa, the United Kingdom and the United States. This event staged an ostensibly "global"

---

22 Benedict Anderson, "Western Nationalism and Eastern Nationalism: Is There a Difference that Matters?" *New Left Review* 9 (May–June 2001) <www.newleftreview.net/NLR24302.shtml> Accessed 5 March 2004.

23 Mroue, "Contestants in Arab Version of 'Idol.'"

24 "In Pictures: Arab Pop Idol Finale," *BBC News World Edition* (23 August 2004) <http://news.bbc.co.uk/2/hi/in_pictures/3590136.stm> Accessed 27 August 2004.

25 Thomas L. Friedman, "52 to 48," *The New York Times* Online Edition (3 September 2003) <www.nytimes.com/2003/09/03/opinion/03FRIE.html?ex=1078808400&e=250bd930e0c47778&ei=5070> Accessed 6 March 2004. It is important to note the context in which the comment was made—to an American reporter, by the editor of an English-language Lebanese newspaper.

competition in which *Idols* was confirmed as an international phenomenon. During *World Idol*, it became apparent that *SuperStar* and the other ten participating shows were not as similar as their uniform design would suggest. Tensions arose among the judges, one from each *Idols* series, particularly regarding the appropriateness of certain musical genres and performance styles to the competition. The performance of Diana Karazon, representing *SuperStar*, also elicited some discomfort among the judging panel, as Karazon was placed in a unique circumstance among her colleagues in *World Idol*. The other ten contestants all sang popular songs in English, mostly covers of songs associated with performers recognizable to the largely North American and European Idols audience: Elton John ("Sorry Seems to Be the Hardest Word"), Aretha Franklin (Carole King's "Like a Natural Woman"), U2 ("Beautiful Day"), and Aerosmith ("I Don't Want to Miss a Thing"). Karazon's selection, "Insāni ma binsāk" (Forget me, I won't forget you), was a new song, not a cover version, from her debut album of September 2003. This recording was entirely in Arabic, and while Karazon is able to sing in English, she preferred to sing in Arabic at *World Idol*.[26] In the broadcast of *World Idol* edited for American audiences, Karazon was announced by the British hosts Anthony McPartlin and Declan Donnelly as "the only person not to sing a *Western* song." They asked the television audience, "Can she secure the world's vote?"[27]

There was much in the presentation of Karazon's performance that may be interpreted as implicitly or explicitly political choices. Karazon's stylized dress suggested visually that she would be contributing something different—not European and not American—to the competition. As the representative of a large group of nations, she was identified throughout the *World Idol* program as the "Pan-Arab" contestant, but when the camera turned to Karazon's cheering fans they were specifically holding Jordanian flags. Karazon also flashed the two-fingered "V" sign as she came onstage with the other contestants—in parts of the Middle East, this "victory" gesture has been strongly associated with Yasser Arafat and Palestinian causes. *SuperStar*'s delegated judge in *World Idol*, Elias Rahbani, was also given the captioned designation "Pan-Arab."[28] We have already seen this term used in the sense of transnational Arab unity, but in the context of *World Idol* it implies both a cultural and political unity among the participating nations and the show's wider audience. The phrase does not take into account the complex of nationalisms that so famously characterized *SuperStar* in its first season.

The label may also facilitate the evasion of more inflammatory politics. It is noteworthy that official *Idols* press coverage in English never mentions the Arab League by name, though McPartlin and Donnelly did refer during the *World Idol* broadcast to the "22 nations" involved in *SuperStar*. The judges' comments, as offered in the broadcast edited for the American audience, simultaneously emphasized

---

26 "Music: Diana Karazon," *Where@Lebanon.com* (18 January 2004) <www.lebanon. com/where/entertainment/musicnews230.htm> Accessed 27 February 2004.

27 *World Idol*, broadcast on the Fox Network (25 December 2003).

28 Rahbani, a renowned Lebanese composer, is the youngest brother of Assy and Mansour Rahbani, with whom he sometimes worked during their famous association with celebrated Lebanese singer Fairouz.

difference and universality. *American Idol* judge Simon Cowell maintained that he had no idea whether Karazon's performance was "any good." Treating the performance as if it *were* something political, Belgian judge Nina De Man assessed it as "inspiring" despite the language issue, and told Karazon, "I'm sure people all over the world will ... feel the strength in your voice." However, De Man believed that the singer's decision to perform in Arabic would prevent her from acquiring the title of "World Idol." Australian judge Ian Dickson invoked the metaphor of music as a universal language, asserting that "the true beauty of music is that it translates language barriers." He thanked Karazon for representing "a huge part of the world," and declared that he was "very proud to be part of a program that can embrace a culture like [Karazon's]."[29] Karazon's performance was thus addressed in terms that reinforced both a sense of cultural distance and a sense of multicultural inclusiveness, at once exoticizing and superficially assimilating.

The international audience vote, weighted in a manner appropriated from the Eurovision Song Contest, resulted in the victory of Norwegian singer Kurt Nilsen as "World Idol." Karazon placed near the bottom in the results from most of the 11 national/regional counts. Voting nations were not permitted to vote for their own representative, and each contestant was automatically awarded the maximum of 12 points from his or her own contingency. All other contestants were given between one and ten points (ten being the highest). Aside from the "Pan Arab" vote, Karazon received her highest rating from the United States, which placed her fourth overall in its results. Her relatively high placement in the American vote is striking—this could perhaps be due to the impact of diasporic Arab communities in the United States voting for their home country or region. A similar dynamic has been frequently noted in relation to the ESC, especially when Germany awards its highest score to the Turkish entry.

Globalization and geopolitics

The intense audience response to *SuperStar* reflects not only the dynamic network of nationalisms detailed above, but also the underlying processes of globalization and consolidation in the media industry, and of the most recent worldwide wave of democratization.[30] Together, these elements demonstrate the continuing relevance of Arjun Appadurai's concept of global landscapes as introduced in his influential *Modernity at Large*.[31] For Appadurai, the globalized economy works through the interconnected, yet also disjunctive, dimensions he calls ethnoscapes (constructed by people always in motion), technoscapes (technology distribution), and financescapes (capital distribution).

---

29 *World Idol* (25 December 2003).

30 The idea that democratization has historically occurred in "waves" was introduced in Samuel P. Huntington's 1991 book, *The Third Wave: Democratization in the Late Twentieth Century* (Norman: University of Oklahoma Press, 1991).

31 Arjun Appadurai, *Modernity at Large: Cultural Dimensions of Globalization* (Minneapolis: University of Minnesota Press, 1996).

As we have seen, the shifting and overlapping ethnoscapes involved in *SuperStar* are shaped through national and transnational identity politics. The distribution of technology throughout the Arab League nations is another crucial consideration in *SuperStar*, since voting depends on variable access to the Internet and to mobile phones. In the first season, Internet votes accounted for most of those placed in Kuwait and Saudi Arabia.[32] Financial capability is also a factor; as noted above: mobile phone services offered discounts on voting calls and messages related to particular *SuperStar* singers, and pricing competition among rival companies in separate countries may even contribute to the final outcomes of the contest. A data services manager at the Jordanian mobile-phone service Fastlink suggests that the low voting costs in Jordan may have played a role in Karazon's *SuperStar* victory.[33]

It is also important to note that the success of *SuperStar* is a testament to the power potentially wielded by a small group of corporate players in the transnational media industry operating at both localized and global levels. The *Idols* format came from 19 Entertainment, headed by Simon Fuller (also associated with the cross-media successes of the Spice Girls and S Club 7) and is owned jointly by 19 and FremantleMedia.[34] Fuller created *Idols* with BMG executive Simon Cowell, who has appeared as a judge on both the British and American versions of the show. Until its recent merger with Sony, BMG (the music branch of Bertelsmann AG) was one of the "Big Five" in the recording industry oligopoly. Bertelsmann also owns 90 per cent of the broadcasting company known as the RTL Group, of which FremantleMedia is a division. Through their originally joint ownership of AOL Europe, Bertelsmann is also connected to Time Warner, whose recording division has been associated (along with the Music Master International label, in addition to BMG) with *SuperStar*'s winners. In Appadurai's analysis, production may be fetishized in terms of locality, masking the global nature of the productive process.[35] The competitive nationalisms supported through *SuperStar* are exemplary of this situation, and they seem to occupy public attention to such an extent that there is relatively little interest in resisting the intrusion of foreign commercial franchises.

Closely tied to these mediascapes are the more plainly political ideoscapes, images and narratives that Appadurai links to Enlightenment concepts such as "freedom," "representation," and, significantly, "the master term *democracy*."[36] The relationship between democracy and the *Idols* enterprise reflects two key ideas: the mythology of the American Dream[37] and the concept of suffrage. The new accessibility of fame

---

32 "Arabic SuperStar's Voting Grosses Over US \$4 Million in Voting Revenues Alone," *Arab Advisors Group* (24 August 2003) <www.arabadvisors.com/Pressers/presser240803. htm> Accessed 7 February 2004.

33 "Entertainment: Millions Vote For Middle East Pop Idol," <www.jmtsfastlink.com/ on_news_ details.asp?news_type=3&news_id=146> Available at <www.160characters.org/ news.php?action=view&nid=92> (26 August 2003), Accessed 13 March 2004.

34 In early 2005, 19 Entertainment was acquired by Robert FX Sillerman's New-York-based company CKX.

35 Appadurai, *Modernity at Large*, pp. 41–2.

36 Ibid., p. 37, emphasis in original.

37 For an excellent discussion of the American Dream and capitalism in Britain's *Pop Idol*, see Su Holmes, "'Reality Goes Pop!' Reality TV, Popular Music, and Narratives of

presented in reality television reinforces the Dream that someone ordinary may be recognized as extraordinary. This idea has long been an incentive for population movement to (and within) the United States, but it is now offered "on location" wherever the shows are filmed. The rise of the *Idols* franchise, however, indicates that America is no longer a geographical requirement for living the Dream, which is dislocated, de-territorialized and reconfigured in the fluid context of globalization.

The significance of the voting process in the *Idols* design cannot be overemphasized. The interactive audience is offered a compelling sense of agency, both in the narrative of the televised program and in the selection of the end product. It is the zenith of consumer choice packaged in the familiar ritual of the democratic process and its hallmark component, the election. John Hartley suggests that "citizenship is profoundly *mediated* in the modern/postmodern period,"[38] and coins the term "democratainment" to refer to television programs that convey concepts of citizenship to their audience. Hartley presents this idea in relation to issues of globalization, and similar concepts make their way into *Idols* discourse. David Lyle of FremantleMedia North America even implies that the *Idols* enterprise contributes directly to the worldwide spread of democracy:

> We did a pan-Arabic version ... and as that got to the sort of pressure point, there was a small riot in which some members of the audience ... did resort to bringing out blades. You've got to realize that for many countries ... this was the first time the public ever had to cope with something as unusual as voting, so it was a very novel moment for them—the idea of casting a vote, and probably even more novel, that the votes actually were counted correctly and the right person won.[39]

It is not coincidental that the *Idols* shows have flourished during a time when the promotion of democracy is a central international concern. But *Idols* highlights the concept of voting in a manner that essentially reduces the totality of democracy—as a political, economic, and social system—to its hallmark ritual, the election.[40] Under these conditions, the impression of agency is paramount. Appadurai asserts that in global cultural landscapes "the consumer is consistently helped to believe that he or she is an actor, where in fact he or she is at best a chooser."[41] However, the socio-political complexities surrounding *SuperStar* suggest that, among this interactive *Idols* audience, consumer choice and political agency might not always be mutually exclusive. The choices made by *SuperStar*'s audience generate exquisitely political meanings inseparable from the national and transnational politics at the forefront of public attention.

Stardom in *Pop Idol*," *Television & News Media* 5/2 (2004), pp. 147–72.

38   John Hartley, "Democratainment," in *The Television Studies Reader*, ed. Robert C. Allen and Annette Hill (London: Routledge, 2004), p. 526, emphasis in original.

39   Brooke Gladstone, "Idol Worship," interview with David Lyle, *On the Media*, WNYC (17 October 2003) <www.onthemedia.org/transcripts/transcripts_101703_idol.html> Accessed 27 February 2004.

40   See William I. Robinson, "Globalization, The World System, and 'Democracy Promotion' in U.S. Foreign Policy," *Theory and Society* 25/5 (1996): 623–4.

41   Appadurai, *Modernity at Large*, p. 42.

Conclusion

In 2004–05, a second *World Idol* failed to materialize. Perhaps as a consolation prize, on 19 May 2005, *American Idol* aired an hour-long special entitled *American Idol Presents: The World's Worst Auditions*. This included clips of auditions from several *Idols* shows, including *SuperStar*. Though the title implied an external American perspective, it was a case of equal-opportunity ridicule, a montage of insults regarding musicality, dancing, and appearance. Curiously, the theme of this broadcast celebrated (in the negative) the global resemblance of all *Idols* contestants: "It is estimated that over a million people have auditioned to be their country's idol … There's one thing they have in common," the narrator explains over an off-key rendition of "Rhinestone Cowboy," "—they suck, big time."[42] Stressing the universal ordinariness of these rejected contestants, the program stood somewhat in opposition to the original *World Idol*, which had thrown cultural and linguistic differences into stark relief. Here, those who sang in Arabic were judged to be no worse (and no better) than those who sang in English, Polish, or Danish. Humiliation in reality television plays an equalizing role; not only is it possible for anyone to be a star, but anyone can also be an international laughing-stock. It is this celebration of failure that produced the astonishing career of *American Idol* reject William Hung, which has spanned the United States and several Asian countries. Such failure is part and parcel with the American Dream. With its internal mechanisms exposed on camera, the vulnerability of the Dream also becomes startlingly apparent.

Since I originally wrote this essay in 2004, the world around *SuperStar* has been profoundly shaken more than once. But the show, it seems, must go on. Though first-season *SuperStar* runner-up Ruweida Attiyeh cancelled her North American tour after the assassination of Rafiq al-Hariri, and the regular broadcast season of the show was delayed, *SuperStar* did not fade from view in the wake of the tragedy. Following the former Prime Minister's death, Future Television included *SuperStar* participants from previous seasons in its round-the-clock coverage of the situation, featuring songs performed in tribute to Hariri.[43] Though there was further interruption after the assassination of Lebanese member of Parliament and publisher Gebran Tueni,[44] the season was completed, ending with the victory of Saudi Arabian contestant Ibrahim Al Hakami. And in spite of the devastating conflict with Israel in the summer of 2006, which left Beirut deeply scarred, Season 4 began at last at the end of January 2007. The casting field for the show has expanded greatly in the past two seasons, and now includes Arab Americans and Arab Canadians (for Season 4, auditions were added in Los Angeles, Detroit, and Montreal). As the Arab world's internal political frictions continue to be played out on *SuperStar*'s stage, the participation of North

---

42 *American Idol Presents: The World's Worst Auditions*, broadcast on the Fox Network (19 May 2005).

43 Marwan M. Kraidy, "Reality Television and Politics in the Arab World: Preliminary Observations," *Transnational Broadcasting Studies* 15 (January–June 2006) <www.tbsjournal. com/Archives/Fall05/Kraidy.html> Accessed 17 January 2007.

44 Ali Jaafar, "Mideast," in "The Whole World Goes Pop: A Look at 'Idol's' Performance Internationally," *Variety* (7 May 2006) <www.variety.com/article/VR1117942662.html?categ oryid=14&cs=1> Accessed 16 March 2007.

American contestants again underscores the commitment of the show to a Pan-Arab structure. *SuperStar* provides an illuminating glimpse of the intricate dialectic between local and extended nationalisms in the context of global popular culture. The ever-expanding presence of the *Idols* franchise worldwide offers an increasingly fertile field for the study of these interactions and their attending ramifications.

Chapter 15

"Changing Japan, unchanging Japan": Shifting visions of the Red and White Song Contest

Shelley D. Brunt

Dazzling colored lights pan across the stage and illuminate a group of pretty teenage girls clad in sequined miniskirts and feather boas. The driving beat of a pre-recorded backing track begins and the girls perform a series of coordinated dance moves while enthusiastically singing their upbeat pop song. Afterward, the cameras focus on a handsome man dressed in a stylish suit as he enters the stage, takes his turn and gently croons an emotional ballad. Later in the evening, wailing distorted guitars and gravelly vocals herald the start of a rock band's song performance and the in-house audience of thousands begins to cheer…

These scenes could easily be from the Eurovision Song Contest, but they instead typify Japan's similarly prestigious and long-running Red and White Song Contest (*Kōhaku Utagassen*). The Red and White (*Kōhaku*), as it is commonly known, is a professional song contest which features Japan's most successful popular music stars. The concert takes place annually on New Year's Eve in front of a select live audience inside a Tōkyō concert hall, and it is broadcast to an international audience of millions. With its custom-built stage designs, exquisite costumes, vivid light displays, falling paper snow and billowing clouds of dry ice, the extravagance and grand scale of this song contest arguably surpasses Eurovision's most memorable productions. Even though the contests have similar formats, the premise of the Red and White varies from its European counterpart. It is a collaborative, team-based contest: women are grouped together in the Red Team and men in the White Team, and singers alternate performances throughout the evening.[1] Each team has an emcee who encourages spirited rivalry, provides between-song banter and introduces the singers. Performances are judged individually, but only one team (not a song or a singer) can win, making this contest somewhat a "battle of the sexes." Winners are determined by voting members of the Japanese public, the in-house audience and a panel of celebrity judges.

I gratefully acknowledge and thank Dr Kimi Coaldrake from The University of Adelaide for her helpful comments on earlier versions of this chapter. All translations are my own unless otherwise acknowledged.

1   Some bands, however, have both female and male members. In these instances, which are quite common, the sex of the lead singer usually determines to which team the band is affiliated.

The Red and White is designed to appeal to all audience demographics. Singers range in age from pre-teen to elderly, and the large number of acts—in 2006 there were 54 in total—means that a wide variety of genres can be represented, such as electronic-based J-pop and the traditional ballad *enka*.[2] The program also includes incidental segments throughout the evening to provide contrast with the song performances. In some segments, celebrity guests relay simple messages of goodwill to the performers, while other more lavish segments may, for example, honor Japan's sporting heroes of the year. Segments also showcase the singers' talents and their ability to work as a team by performing, for instance, complicated dance routines or hand-eye coordination tricks.

Overall, the Red and White is pitched as an honest and clean-cut program with variety for the whole family. Much of its image of respectability lies in the fact that it was created by Japan's morally upright national broadcaster NHK (Nippon Hōsō Kyōkai), established in 1926. NHK's dedication to the Japanese people was clear even during its early years under state governance: it must "maximize the listener's benefit and the public good."[3] This aim was expanded in 1950 when NHK was re-established as a public broadcaster by the postwar occupying Allied forces. A significant broadcast law—still in effect in 2007—marked "a decisive break with the pre-war system of state-controlled broadcasting"[4] and provided clear guidelines for the broadcaster's structure, function and related activities: it "must operate in a manner befitting its public role, must not pursue profit, and must remain independent of national institutions."[5] Today, the "station for the people" is financially independent and generates revenue from fees paid by households. Most importantly, NHK adjusts its program content to suit the tastes of the Japanese public and conducts nationwide surveys to determine which singers audiences would like to see in the New Year's Eve program.

The Red and White has its critics, but in general it is a beloved event that is, like Eurovision, highly anticipated by legions of dedicated fans. In the months preceding the broadcast, the contest becomes a frequent and passionate topic of conversation. The media, meanwhile, feverishly reports the first whisperings of who will perform and, post-broadcast, critically dissects audience ratings. In 2005, Eurovision's milestone 50th program generated unprecedented interest with fans and media pondering the contest's modest origins and subsequent development. The 50th Red

---

2   For a summary of popular genres in Japan, see Keith Cahoon, "Popular Music in Japan," in *Japan: An Illustrated Encyclopedia*, ed. Alan Campbell and David S. Noble (Tōkyō: Kodansha, 1993), pp. 1286–7. For a more substantial overview see Linda Fujie, "Popular Music," in *Handbook of Japanese Popular Culture*, ed. R.G. Powers and H. Kato (New York: Greenwood Press, 1989), pp. 197–220. For an excellent examination of the *enka* genre and its cultural context, see Christine R. Yano, *Tears of Longing: Nostalgia and the Nation in Japanese Popular Song* (Cambridge, MA: Harvard University Asia Center, 2002).

3   Gregory J. Kasza, *The State and the Mass Media in Japan 1918–1945* (Berkeley: University of California Press, 1988), p. 81.

4   *Broadcasting in Japan: The Twentieth Century Journey from Radio to Multimedia* (Tōkyō: Nippon Hōsō Kyōkai Broadcasting Culture Research Institute, 2002), p. 6.

5   Katsuji Ebisawa, "NHK Annual Report 2000," Nippon Hōsō Kyōkai (2000), <www.nhk.or.jp/pr/keiei/nhk2000/main_en.html> Accessed 22 April 2002.

and White, held in 1999, aroused comparable levels of expectancy and reflection. This chapter examines the program's historical shaping from a humble national radio show to the extravagant, internationally televised gala event of the 50th Red and White. Most notably, it explores how and why the program has integrated international and intercultural dimensions over time while retaining elements that remain distinctly "Japanese." In all, it traces the shifting visions of the Red and White, a contest that is changing and unchanging like Japan itself.[6]

Early years

The Red and White was modeled on an earlier song contest created in 1945 when postwar Japan was still under Allied Occupation. Designed to spiritually uplift the "defeated and poverty stricken nation,"[7] this live-to-air show boasted a "battle of the sexes" theme, used an in-house orchestra and was broadcast on New Year's Eve. It was called the Red and White Music Battle (*Kōhaku ongaku gassen*), a contentious title at the time considering Occupation authorities had prohibited the use of the word "battle" (*gassen*) because it was "reminiscent of war."[8] Its name was modified accordingly, but the program was nevertheless discontinued.

A few years later, a new incarnation—the Red and White—was broadcast in early January 1951. It was a smaller scale version of today's Red and White, and featured only 14 singers performing in front of a limited number of radio studio guests. The audience response was reportedly overwhelming: "from the moment the first artist ... began to sing, the excitement in the studio spread to the whole country, and NHK's phone lines were buzzing with comments and inquiries."[9] Some listeners wrote letters of encouragement to the performers while others traveled to the NHK Tōkyō studios to express their delight in person.[10] Early editions of the Red and White clearly resonated with Japanese audiences during a time of great cultural, economic and cultural uncertainty. Japan's release from Occupation in 1952 caused the people "to feel a greater ease with native traditions and a need to peel back the

---

6   Japan has a rich culture with many features derived from nearby Asian countries. Other customs deemed "uniquely Japanese" developed during Japan's self-imposed isolation from trade, which culminated in the Tokugawa period (1600–1867). During the Meiji era (1868–1912), however, Japan began to embrace and integrate Western (in particular European and American) ideologies in a bid for modernization. Contemporary Japan is, as Fujie notes, "an intense, fascinating and sometimes confusing combination of old and new, of Eastern and Western and things beyond categorization." Linda Fujie, "East Asia/Japan," in *Worlds of Music*, ed. Jeff Todd Titon, 3rd ed. (New York: Shirmer Books, 1996), p. 369.

7   Mark Schilling, *The Encyclopedia of Japanese Pop Culture* (New York: Weatherhill, 1997), p. 94.

8   *Broadcasting in Japan*, p. 90.

9   "A Celebration of Popular Song," in *50 Years of NHK Television: A Window on Japan and the World* (April 2003), p. 54 <www.nhk.or.jp/digitalmuseum/nhk50years_en/categories/p54/index.html> Accessed 19 March 2007.

10   Tadayuki Takahashi, *50 kai: eikō to kandō no zen kiroku shu o hakkou*, special edition for Nippon Hōsō Kyōkai uiikurii sutera (Tōkyō: Nippon Hōsō Kyōkai Sēbisu Sentā, 2000), p. 171.

artificial layer of American-imposed ideologies."[11] The program's appeal lay with its light-hearted songs and refreshing "women vs. men" premise, and it heralded a new beginning for Japan, unmarred by wartime anxiety.

In 1953 the show moved out of the studio and in front of a large audience in the Japan Theatre (Nihon Gekkijō). This program, the 4th Red and White, was the first to be televised, thus a greater importance was placed on the visual aspects of the contest.[12] Singers wore ceremonial ball gowns and exquisite *kimono*; despite the limited sense of color for home audiences (due to the black-and-white broadcast), red and white colors featured prominently in the staging. These were the colors of Japan, seen in the country's then-unofficial flag, the *hinomaru* (a red disc surrounded by a white border),[13] but the colors were also associated with gender: crimson red (*kō* in *kōhaku*) was the color of female beauty, of women's lips and a *geisha*'s *kimono* lining, while white (*haku* in *kōhaku*) was a marker of masculinity and virility.[14] The Red and White played on these established cultural meanings and represented the two halves of Japan (red/women and white/men).

The 4th Red and White (1953) was also the first to be broadcast on New Year's Eve. This "grand last day" (*ōmisoka*) of the year is traditionally when Japanese people return to their hometowns and reunite with family in readiness for the culturally significant New Year period so closely connected with Shintō and Buddhist faiths. The lead-up to New Year is a time to attend "forget-the-year" (*bōnenkai*) parties, to clean and spiritually purify the home (*susuharai*) to remove all traces of the past year, and to exchange year-end gifts (*seibo*) to settle outstanding debts. During the 1950s, watching the Red and White—with its summary of the past year's hit songs and singers—on New Year's Eve became firmly integrated into these customs. The program also presented special segments to reinforce its connection with year-end. Photographs from the 9th Red and White (1958), for example, depict members of both teams uniting at the close of the contest, minutes before midnight, to perform "Hotaru no hikari" (The light of the fireflies), Japan's version of "Auld Lange Syne."[15] This quickly became the customary way to wind up the program, to "sing out" the old year and allow audiences time to leave their homes and walk to the nearest temple to pray and hear the bell tolling to "ring out" the old year (*joya no*

---

11 Alan M. Tansman, "Mournful Tears and Sake: The Postwar Myth of Misora Hibari," in *Contemporary Japan and Popular Culture*, ed. John Whittier Treat (Surrey: Curzon, 1996), p. 108.

12 In all likelihood, only a small audience witnessed the broadcast because few Japanese owned or had access to a television set at this time.

13 Even today, this evocative combination permeates all aspects of Japanese life, from the celebratory dish of white rice and red beans served at weddings to the alternating stripes of color on awnings at festivals and the red and white colors of prized carp. Tom Gill, "Transformational Magic: Some Japanese Super-heroes and Monsters," in *The Worlds of Japanese Popular Culture: Gender, Shifting Boundaries and Global Cultures*, ed. D.P. Martinez (Cambridge: Cambridge University Press, 1998), p. 51.

14 Ibid., p. 42.

15 See photographs in Takahashi, *50 kai*, p. 163. It is unclear when "Hotaru no hikari" was first performed in the Red and White, but this photograph indicates it may have been as early as 1958.

kane). The 15th Red and White (1964)—the first to be transmitted in color—featured several live crossovers to various Japanese regions where activities associated with the New Year, such as preparing special food (*osechi-ryōri*), were displayed on a large projection screen inside the Red and White venue. These images highlighted the regional variations in year-end customs and brought Japan's out-of-the-way places into the homes of viewers, creating a sense of the "internal exotic."[16] Most significantly, however, these images presented simultaneous shared experiences and depicted the nation, in accordance with Japanese social classifications, as a united "in-group" (*uchi*), the "center of participatory belonging, the center from which one can create relationships with the outside world."[17]

The Red and White upheld its domestic focus through its voting procedures as well. Each year the official judging panel comprised Japanese people from all walks of life: some were NHK employees, others were from the entertainment industry (*geinōkai*) and many were members of the in-house Tōkyō audience. The panel was not required to evaluate a singer's vocal abilities but to compare each team's collective merits—a task that did not require musical training. It was, after all, a friendly contest, not judged by music professionals but by laypersons. Indeed, by the 14th Red and White (1963), representatives from various Japanese regions began casting votes in addition to the judging panel. These representatives provided a voice for regional Japan, not just Tōkyōites, and collectively symbolized votes from the nation. The Red and White was created as a program "for the people," and now the people played a significant role in deciding the contest's outcome.

The public was clearly appreciative, and the Red and White consistently captured higher ratings than any other program during the year, making it "not just an annual NHK program, but the biggest event in the entire music industry—and a national event."[18] In 1962 an astonishing 80.4 per cent of Kantō audiences viewed the program,[19] and 81.4 per cent tuned in the following year.[20] Its status as an event for the nation was reinforced by the wider range of Japanese guests on the program, many from outside the music industry. Yoshinori Sakai, the final torchbearer for the 1964 Tōkyō Olympic Games, for example, participated in the ceremonial proceedings for the 15th Red and White (1964).[21] Yoshinori was born in Hiroshima on the day the city was destroyed by the atomic bomb and, as such, he was a symbol of hope and

---

16 See Marilyn Ivy, *Discourses of the Vanishing: Modernity, Phantasm, Japan* (Chicago: University of Chicago Press, 1995).

17 Dorinne K. Kondo, *Crafting Selves: Power, Gender, and Discourses of Identity in a Japanese Workplace* (Chicago: University of Chicago Press, 1990), p. 142. See also Yoshio Sugimoto, *An Introduction to Japanese Society*, 2nd ed. (Cambridge: Cambridge University Press, 2003), pp. 28–30.

18 *50 Years of NHK Television*, p. 54.

19 Kantō is a densely populated region which encompasses several prefectures and large cities, including Tōkyō and Yokohama.

20 The 14th Red and White (1963) was Japan's most watched program that year and also achieved the highest ratings of all time for any program in Japan between 1962 (when television audience ratings were first measured in Japan) and 2001. *Broadcasting in Japan*, pp. 162–3.

21 Takahashi, *50 kai*, p. 134.

survival. His involvement in the Red and White indicated that it was not simply a song contest but a cultural review of the nation's year and an occasion to reflect on Japan's successful postwar reconstruction.

New directions

Japan's musical scene was rapidly changing during the late 1950s and early 1960s, and the Red and White accommodated these shifts by keeping abreast of emerging musical trends. Japanese-language cover songs of Western hits were extremely popular, and Japanese songwriters also began producing original songs that were influenced by Western pop structure and instrumentation. One of the biggest hits of 1961 was Kyū Sakamoto's Western-styled "Ue o muite arukō" (I look up when I walk); it was released only weeks before the 12th Red and White (1961), but producers still secured the singer and his song for the program.[22] Internationally-produced music was especially popular in Japan, further heightened by successful tours by The Ventures in 1965 and The Beatles in 1966.[23] In keeping with its domestic focus the Red and White only featured Japanese singers, but in 1970 the program's direction began to shift in a bid to represent Japan's popular music scene more accurately. That year, for the 21st Red and White, a non-Japanese singer performed for the first time. Although Italian-born singer Rosanna's presence was somewhat played down—she appeared with Japanese singer Hide as a duo—it was the earliest indicator of the contest's imminent move toward internationalization. In addition, new satellite technologies enabled the NHK to extend its broadcast reach outside Japan to Brazil, home to Japanese expatriate communities. In a sense, this served to symbolically reconnect the Japanese diaspora with its homeland via the Red and White, a much-loved national institution.

Around this time, the Red and White began to incorporate segments which indicated the program was considering its place and Japan's place in the international arena. The 26th Red and White (1975), for example, featured live images of New Year's Eve celebrations from other countries. This provided points of comparison for Japan's New Year customs and confirmed the concept of Japan as an "in-group" (*uchi*) by clearly marking the "outsiders" (*soto*) beyond this realm.[24] The program also

---

22   Sakamoto became the first (and perhaps only) Japanese singer to achieve significant commercial success on an international scale when this song was released in the US under the title "Sukiyaki." In Europe, the song was translated into local languages, except in the Netherlands and England where it was called "Unforgettable Geisha" and "Sukiyaki," respectively. Schilling, *Encyclopedia*, pp. 215–16.

23   These bands were highly influential and, as a result, new local genres such as the "electric guitar boom" (*ereki būmu*) and the "group sounds" movement emerged. See Tōru Mitsui, "Twentieth Century Popular Music in Japan," in *The Garland Encyclopedia of World Music*, ed. Robert C. Provine, Yoshihiko Tokumaru and J. Lawrence Witzleben (New York: Routledge, 2002), vol. 1, no. 7, pp. 743–7.

24   In his study of Japanese daytime programs, Painter notes that a common ideological strategy used by television producers to represent Japanese unity is to present *soto* segments that focus on the "alien nature of other ways of life." Andrew A. Painter, "Japanese Daytime

reinforced a sense of connectedness and national unity though communal singing. From the 33rd Red and White (1982), lyrics for all songs were reproduced onscreen to encourage viewers to sing along. This strengthened a sense of unisonance for the nation, which had originated with singing "Hotaru no hikari" at the end of the program; now all songs could be used for the "experience of simultaneity" whereby "people wholly unknown to each other [could] utter the same verses to the same melody" at precisely the same moment.[25] The Red and White also brought together singers and celebrity guests from the Japanese entertainment world, depicting them as "intimate, friendly and on the best of terms."[26] This congenial and harmonious atmosphere extended beyond the venue, via television, into the homes of audiences.[27] The Red and White was keeping the nation together, close at hand, while it also broadened its scope.

By the mid-1980s, the contest was undergoing dramatic change. The 38th Red and White (1987) featured a variety of non-domestic genres such as stage-musical songs, classical opera and French *chanson*.[28] The following year, more performers than usual added Japanese lyrics to Western songs—the jazz vocal group Time Five (Taimu fuaibu), for example, sang "Hoshi ni negai o," a version of the Walt Disney film song "When You Wish Upon a Star." In addition, several performers who customarily sang in Japanese began to use other languages. The soloist Yōichi Sugawara sang entirely in Spanish, Yūzō Kayama sang in English, and Shinobu Satō began his song in German and later switched to Japanese. Was the Red and White still accurately reflecting Japan's musical landscape, or was it destined to become another international song contest?

Poor ratings in the latter half of the 1980s indicated the program was falling out of favor with Japanese audiences. NHK speculated that "the kinds of music that were popular had diversified, and people's tastes had changed. On the one hand, young people found the kind of songs performed on [the Red and White] old-fashioned and boring, while their elders, on the other, found the music favored by younger people unfamiliar and hard to appreciate. There was also a dearth of major hit songs."[29] Red and White viewers were also lured away by other exciting television programs such as the *samurai* period dramas offered by rival networks.[30] The program's waning popularity provoked rumors that NHK would terminate the program.[31] These were, however, rapidly dispelled for "even though the ratings for [the Red and White] were

Television, Popular Culture and Ideology," in *Contemporary Japan and Popular Culture*, ed. John Whittier Treat (Surrey: Curzon, 1996), pp. 202–203.

25   Benedict Anderson, *Imagined Communities: Reflections on the Origin and Spread of Nationalism*, 2nd ed. (London: Verso, 1991), p. 145.

26   Painter, "Japanese Daytime Television," pp. 199–200.

27   Ibid., pp. 197–234.

28   Takahashi, *50 kai*, p. 68.

29   *Broadcasting in Japan*, p. 164.

30   Hiroshi Ogawa, "The Rise and Fall of the Red-and-White Show," *Pacific Friend* 18/8 (1990): 33.

31   Schilling, *Encyclopedia*, p. 97.

low by comparison to previous years, they were still the highest for any program shown that year."[32]

In an attempt to recover its lost audience, the first half of the 40th Red and White (1989) included past song performers and guests who reminisced about the contest's historical development. The second half, by contrast, featured the current performers of the day, including foreigners such as Korean singers Patty Kim and Kim Yonja, and the Hong Kong performer Alan Tam. Another guest was the British-born Australian singer/actor Olivia Newton-John in an interview via satellite from Australia; she cheered in Japanese "Aka-gumi ganbatte!" ("Good luck, Red Team!"), a clearly scripted statement designed to demonstrate that the contest and its conventions were meaningful to non-Japanese audiences. But audiences were not receptive to the program's increasing international content, and the program had its lowest ratings.[33] Sadly, "viewers, whatever their age, probably knew only half of the performers and just a few of the tunes."[34] The program's failure to resonate with audiences also put into question its validity in the lives of Japanese people; some critics labeled the "battle of the sexes" premise "anachronistic."[35] Instead of a fresh start after its 40th anniversary, the Red and White faced an uncertain future.

The program continued to embrace international elements into the early 1990s. This direction was clearly articulated at the 41st Red and White (1990) though the first official theme: *Nijūisseiki ni tsutaeru nihon no uta: sekai no uta* (Passing on Japan's songs to the twenty-first century: World songs). Strangely, the program did not focus on "Japan's songs" but rather appropriations of foreign songs. Shinobu Satō performed "Tonight" from *West Side Story*, the vocal trio Eve sang John Lennon's "Imagine," and the teenage idol Rie Miyazawa sang "Game," a Japanese-language adaptation of the 1990 re-mix of David Bowie's 1975 song "Fame." In fact, many singers in the 41st Red and White were foreigners. The American singer/songwriter Paul Simon, for example, performed (via video link from New York) "Bridge Over Troubled Water," which was billed as "Asu ni kakeru hashi" (a literal translation of the English) and included Japanese-language subtitles onscreen. The Red and White Contest had clearly embraced internationalization.

The most striking performance that year was "I Drove All Night" by the flamboyant American vocalist Cyndi Lauper. Her act began with three men carrying a palanquin-style box from which Lauper emerged, dressed in a red *kimono* and a long red wig. In a rapid transformation, she abruptly ripped the formal *kimono* from her body and revealed another outfit underneath: a risqué red halter-top, hotpants with hanging tassels, red stockings and heeled ankle-boots. Throughout the song, Lauper danced wildly; at the end she fell to her knees with one arm flailing and proceeded to head bang, accompanied by a cacophony of feedback noise. Lauper

---

32　*Broadcasting in Japan*, p. 164.

33　That year's contest was watched by 47 per cent of viewers (in the Kantō region), a significant fall in ratings when compared with the 1984 contest, which captured 78.1 per cent. "Kōhaku Utagassen Ratings Data Table 1962–2004," Video Research Limited (January 2007), <www.videor.co.jp/data/ratedata/program/01kouhaku.htm> Accessed 19 March 2007.

34　Ogawa, "The Rise and Fall of the Red-and-White Show," p. 33.

35　Ibid., p. 33.

clearly had little knowledge of the program's customs and etiquette. Her red-themed outfit and wig may have been a conscious demonstration of her association with the Red Team, but her extremely chaotic bodily gestures, carefree dancing and music were conspicuously out-of-place on the Red and White stage. Immediately after her performance, moreover, she naïvely asked her translator "Did we win?" even though the program was yet to reach the halfway point and the vote tallying had not taken place. Lauper then haphazardly exited the stage in the direction of the White (men's) Team area, oblivious to protocol requiring her to return to the Red (women's) Team. Lauper's performance and behavior made clear that the Red and White did not hold the same prestige for performers outside of Japan. After several years of incorporating international elements and foreign performers, it was time for NHK to re-evaluate the direction of the Red and White.

Approaching the 50th Red and White

Through the 1990s the contest demonstrated further efforts to balance tradition with innovation and its national focus with an international scope. The 42nd Red and White (1991) also included foreign singers, but they were considerably less provocative than Lauper. The American singer Andy Williams performed the inoffensive "Moon River," British soloist Sarah Brightman sang Andrew Lloyd Webber's "The Phantom of the Opera," and there was also a young Filipino vocal quartet and a Latvian singer. In a remarkable shift of focus for the program, however, several famous Japanese singers used their performances to highlight domestic issues and other events that had affected the nation. Members of both teams gathered together onstage to collectively sing "Smile Again," a song composed by Red and White singer Masashi Sada to honor the survivors of the horrific Unzen–Fugendake volcano that had erupted that year. On a lighter note, the comedic duo Tunnels (Tonneruzu) revealed a bold message painted on their backs, asking viewers to support NHK by paying the television subscription fee. This reference to a local disaster, and the cheeky in-joke that only Japanese audiences would understand, could be viewed as an attempt to keep the contest directed toward Japan.

The following year, NHK producers significantly reduced the number of foreign artists for the 43rd Red and White (1992). In their place were Japanese music stars from the past 40 years performing a wide variety of contemporary genres such as folk, rock, and *enka*. It was a nostalgic program, with established singers Kazuo Funaki and Michiyo Azusa performing their signature songs from the 1960s and singer/songwriter Kōsetsu Minami performing "Kanda gawa" (Kanda river),[36] a 1973 song that was representative of the folk music boom of that decade. Most notably, the official theme for the contest was *Terebi 40nen: nihon soshite kazoku* (40 years of television: Japan and family)[37]—a welcome return to the program's long-established, but recently overlooked, domestic focus. In effect, the Red and White was paying homage to Japan's musical history and its "family" of Japanese

---

36 Ibid., p. 44.
37 Ibid.

song performers, many of whom had appeared in the program year after year for decades.

The theme for the 44th Red and White (1993), *Kawaru nippon, kawaranu nippon* (Changing Japan, unchanging Japan),[38] confirmed the program's new direction. Japan was portrayed as a nation that maintained pride in its traditions while simultaneously embracing new ideas and changing with the times. One Japanese rock song included traditional scales from Okinawa, thus demonstrating how "unchanging" musical elements could combine with the modern genres of "changing Japan."[39] Domestic genres such as *enka* were performed alongside Latin *salsa*. A few foreign singers appeared on the program, but not as key performers. In these ways the contest was presented as neither insular nor transnational, but selectively incorporating international dimensions.

The contest maintained its domestic focus for the 45th Red and White (1994), where an overview of postwar Japanese music was presented under the theme *Sengo 50nen: meikyoku wa sedai o koete* (50 years postwar: Famous musical works spanning generations).[40] The following year, however, a number of devastating and demoralizing events occurred in Japan. The Great Hanshin–Awaji Earthquake struck Kobe, the religious cult Aum Shinrikyō conducted a sarin gas attack in downtown Tōkyō, and the failing economy reached a new low when several prominent financial organizations declared bankruptcy. As a cultural review of the nation's year, the 46th Red and White (1995) acknowledged these events and Japan's anguish by adopting the theme *Nippon arata naru tabidachi* (Japan: A new start).[41] In a sense, this contest served a similar function to the 1945 Red and White prototype—to boost the nation's morale—and it was very well received with ratings far surpassing other New Year's Eve television programs that year.[42]

The 47th Red and White (1996) projected a sense of pride in Japan's musical heritage, as articulated in the program theme *Uta no aru kuni: nippon* (The country with songs: Japan).[43] Although older singers and genres were presented, the program also featured the very latest stars and their hits. Most were performers from the "Komuro Family"—singers and musicians who worked with the J-pop talent scout, producer, songwriter, and performer Tetsuya Komuro. There were also unusual collaborations between Red and White performers which spanned genres: Shin'ichi Mori, an *enka* singer usually known for his pensive ballads, was accompanied onstage by guitarist Hatake from the pop/rock band Sharan Q, for example. Such close associations were not only staged to celebrate Japanese artists and their music, but also designed to express comradeship between team members, reinforcing the image of Japan's entertainment world as an interconnected and friendly community and the nation as a united "in-group" (*uchi*). This domestic focus continued with the 49th Red and White (1998) under the theme *Nippon niwa uta ga aru: yume, kibō,*

---

38 Takahashi, *50 kai*, p. 40.
39 Ibid.
40 Ibid., p. 36.
41 Ibid., p. 32.
42 Schilling, *Encyclopedia*, p. 98.
43 Takahashi, *50 kai*, p. 28.

soshite mirai e (There are songs in Japan: Dreams, hopes and looking to the future).[44] This contest struck a chord with audiences and it achieved the highest ratings in 12 years.

It was the 50th Red and White, however, that became an important opportunity to examine Japan's musical past and future on the eve of the new millennium. This concept was clearly articulated though two themes, namely the major theme *Utaoo mirai e: jidai to sedai o koete* (Looking to the future through song: Spanning eras and generations) and the minor theme *Nijūisseiki ni tsutaetai uta* (Songs we would like to pass on for the twenty-first century). As indicated by the major theme, the contest presented songs that spanned eras and generations and, most interestingly, only Japanese singers, guests, and songs were featured.[45] Yūzō Kayama's 1965 song "Kimi to itsumademo" (You, forevermore) was representative of the tender ballads of the 1960s, Godiego's 1979 song "Byūtifuru nēmu" (Beautiful name) was typical of the cheerful songs of that decade, and Seiko Matsuda's 1983 song "Sweet Memories" was characteristic of the idol pop of the 1980s. By appearing onstage and singing their time-honored songs, these performers enhanced the sense of nostalgia, which was further heightened by the fact that some singers and groups, such as Godiego, had long disbanded but reformed especially for the 50th Red and White. In addition, selected songs from times gone by were covered by current artists. The vocal duo Saori Yuki and Sachiko Yasuda, known for singing children's songs with classical Western melodies and Japanese lyrics (*doyo*), performed the 1914 pre-war classic "Furusato" (Hometown). This song, which reminisces about a childhood home, was one of many compulsory primary school songs taught throughout Japan in the early 20th century, and like "Hotaru no hikari"—the song that concluded the program—is still well known.[46]

The most memorable cover at the 50th Red and White (1999) was the performance of Hibari Misora's signature song "Kawa no nagare no yō ni" (Like the river's flow) by *enka* singer Yoshimi Tendō. Misora was a unique figure in Japan's entertainment world. A highly acclaimed postwar celebrity, Misora had charisma, sincerity, and the ability to embody the "Japanese spirit of perseverance through adversity" which made her a singer for the people and "reminded them of what was 'authentically' Japanese" in a time of Occupation and defeat.[47] Misora later became one of Japan's first television stars and greatly contributed to the success and development of the Red and White during its formative years. "Kawa no nagare no yō ni" was, moreover, Misora's final recorded song before her death in 1989, and it was released in a tumultuous year that also marked the Emperor's death and the shift from the Shōwa era (1926–1989) to the Heisei era (1989–). The song, with its contemplative

---

44 Ibid., pp. 20, 24.

45 Two songs that year were performed in Japanese by Japanese singers but had originated from international performers: Hiromi Gō's "Goldfinger '99," a version of Puerto Rican singer Ricky Martin's song "Livin' la vida loca," and Hideki Saijō's "Bairamos" (Let's dance), a version of Spanish singer Enrique Iglesias's song of the same name.

46 "Hotaru no hikari" was taught in compulsory education courses since 1881, when it was created for the first volume of *The Primary School Music Textbook*. Ichiro Nakano, trans., *101 Favorite Songs Taught in Japanese Schools* (Tōkyō: The Japan Times, 1983), p. 246.

47 Tansman, "Mournful Tears and Sake," p. 108.

lyrics comparing the cycle of life and the passing of eras to the gentle current of a river, eloquently captured this time of transition in Japanese history. It immediately found resonance with audiences and, years later, was declared the best Japanese song of the 20th century in a 1997 NHK poll in which vast numbers of songs spanning all genres were publicly nominated.[48] "Kawa no nagare no yō ni" was, as such, highly appropriate for the 50th Red and White. It was also a timely inclusion as 1999 marked the ten-year anniversary of Misora's death and, as one magazine noted that year, she was the "face of the Red and White's 50-year history."[49] Indeed, the covering singer Yoshimi Tendō paid tribute to her by adopting distinctive aspects of Misora's vocal style and wearing a similar costume to that worn during Misora's last live performance. Tendō symbolically passed on this timeless song and its many associations to the twenty-first century and future generations.

Considering its constantly shifting balance of "changing and unchanging" elements, the Red and White Song Contest presents a richly nuanced mirror to the transformations that Japan has gone through as a nation and a culture in the postwar period. Tradition must be balanced with innovation, and a focus on enduring domestic values with an openness to contemporary global influences. With remarkable longevity, the Red and White contest has remained a permanent fixture on the Japanese calendar at a special time when the nation comes together. Through decades of shifting visions, it has retained its fundamental function as a surveyor and time capsule of the nation's popular songs and, with each year, continues to play an important role in upholding Japan's musical heritage.

---

48   "New Realms of Creativity: A New Mix of Entertainment and Culture," *50 Years of NHK Television: A Window on Japan and the World* 11/59 (April 2003), <www.nhk.or.jp/ digitalmuseum/nhk50years_en/categories/p59/index.html> Accessed 19 March 2007.

49   "TV gaido zōkan: uta no hon bestu hitto '99," (Tōkyō: Tōkyō News Tsūshinsha, 1999), p. 16.

Index

Song Titles